WEST VANCOUVER MEMORIAL LIBRARY

DAMAGE NOTE

03/08
22.99

About the Author

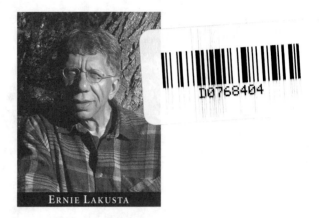

ERNIE LAKUSTA

Ernie Lakusta was born in Hardisty, Alberta, in 1944, but was raised in Calgary. He attended the University of Calgary, where he received both B.Ed. and M.Sc. degrees before becoming a high school biology teacher and science department head in Calgary. An avid hiker and scrambler, Ernie's passion for the outdoors has led him to explore, photograph, and write about many of the areas James Hector mapped for the Palliser Expedition. Ernie lives in Calgary with his wife of thirty-eight years, Jean, who shares his love of the outdoors.

Withdrawn from Collection

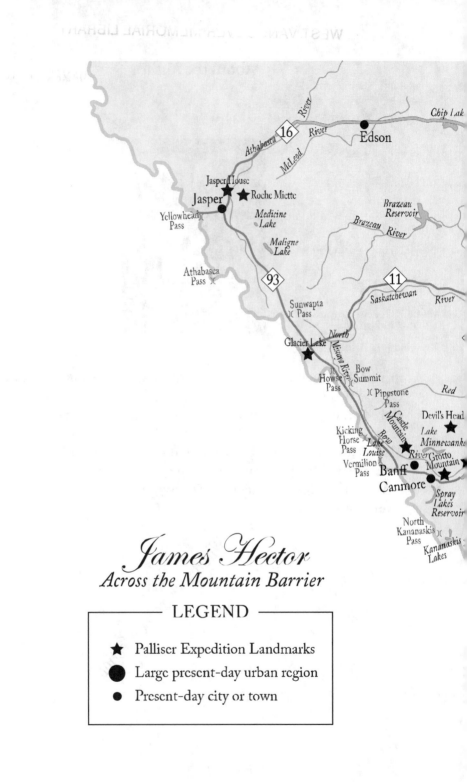

James Hector
Across the Mountain Barrier

---- LEGEND ----

★ Palliser Expedition Landmarks

⬤ Large present-day urban region

● Present-day city or town

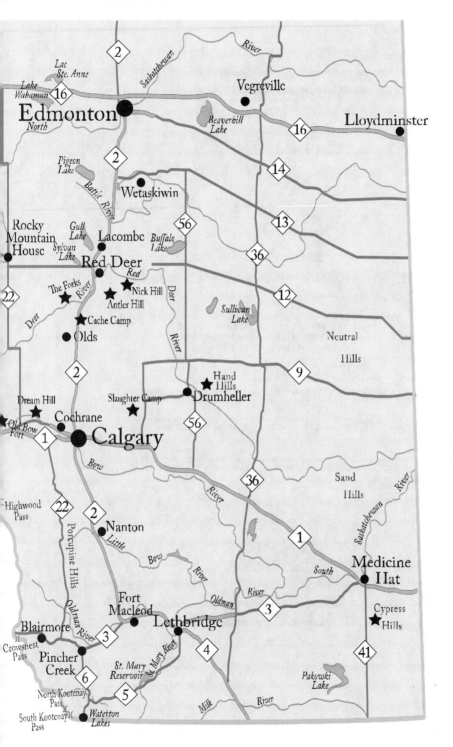

EXPLORATION.—BRITISH NORTH AMERICA

THE
JOURNALS, DETAILED REPORTS, AND OBSERVATIONS

RELATIVE TO

THE EXPLORATION,

BY CAPTAIN PALLISER,

OF

THAT PORTION OF BRITISH NORTH AMERICA,

WHICH,

IN LATITUDE, LIES BETWEEN THE BRITISH BOUNDARY LINE AND THE
HEIGHT OF LAND OR WATERSHED OF THE NORTHERN
OR FROZEN OCEAN RESPECTIVELY,

AND

IN LONGITUDE, BETWEEN THE WESTERN SHORE OF LAKE SUPERIOR AND
THE PACIFIC OCEAN

During the Years 1857, 1858, 1859, and 1860.

Presented to both Houses of Parliament by Command of Her Majesty,
19th May 1863.

LONDON:
PRINTED BY GEORGE EDWARD EYRE AND WILLIAM SPOTTISWOODE,
PRINTERS TO THE QUEEN'S MOST EXCELLENT MAJESTY.
FOR HER MAJESTY'S STATIONERY OFFICE.

1863.

THE INTREPID EXPLORER

James Hector's Explorations
in the Canadian Rockies

Ernie Lakusta

FIFTH
HOUSE

Copyright © 2007 Ernie Lakusta

All rights reserved. No part of this publication may be reproduced, stored in a retrieval system, or trans-mitted, in any form or by any means, electronic, mechanical, recording, or otherwise, without the prior written permission of the publisher, except in the case of a reviewer, who may quote brief passages in a review to print in a magazine or newspaper, or broadcast on radio or television. In the case of photo-copying or other reprographic copying, users must obtain a license from Access Copyright.

Cover and interior design by John Luckhurst
Cover image courtesy Library and Archives Canada, *The Rocky Mountains From Near the Bow of the Askow River*, Henry James Warre (1845); James Donald Hector, *James Hector, CA 1850s*
Edited by Alex Frazer-Harrison
Copyedited by Geri Rowlatt
Proofread by Ann Sullivan
Scans by ABL Imaging

The type in this book is set in Minion.

The publisher gratefully acknowledges the support of The Canada Council for the Arts and the Department of Canadian Heritage.

 Canada Council **Conseil des Arts**
for the Arts **du Canada**

We acknowledge the financial support of the Government of Canada through the Book Publishing Industry Development Program (BPIDP) for our publishing activities.

Printed in Canada

07 08 09 10 11 / 5 4 3 2 1

First published in the United States in 2007 by
Fitzhenry & Whiteside
311 Washington Street
Brighton, MA 02135

Library and Archives Canada Cataloguing in Publication

Lakusta, Ernie
    The intrepid explorer : James Hector's explorations in the
Canadian Rockies / Ernie Lakusta.

Includes bibliographical references and index.
ISBN 978-1-894856-82-9

    1. Hector, James, Sir, 1834-1907. 2. British North American
Exploring Expedition (1857-1860) 3. Rocky Mountains, Canadian
(B.C. and Alta.)—Discovery and exploration. 4. Explorers—Canada—
Biography. 5. Explorers—Great Britain—Biography. I. Title.

FC3213.H34L35 2007   917.1104'2   C2006-906078-9

FIFTH HOUSE LTD.   FITZHENRY & WHITESIDE
A Fitzhenry & Whiteside Company   311 Washington Street
1511-1800 4 St. SW   Brighton, MA 02135
Calgary, Alberta, Canada
T2S 2S5

1-800-387-9776
www.fitzhenry.ca

CONTENTS

JAMES HECTOR, CA.1850S
(COURTESY OF JAMES DONALD HECTOR,
HIS GREAT-GRANDSON)

SIR JAMES HECTOR (1834–1907)

During the second week of February 1858, while we were experiencing a most unusual period of warm weather, I heard that Dr. Hector had passed through Edmonton on his way to Rocky Mountain House, and had left word with the factor that he wished to see me on his return and that he wanted me to go with him. ...

Around the first of March Dr. Hector returned to Edmonton, and I had an opportunity to meet him. He was a man about my own age. I had expected to see a scholarly type, but his athletic appearance and brisk step impressed me very favourably. His handshake was firm and had a hint of strength that captured my interest immediately. He had an affable, easy manner of conversation with any person he was speaking to. A thoroughly pleasing personality that had nothing of that assumed superiority or condescending mannerism that I was beginning to associate with all Englishmen of my narrow acquaintance. I liked the man at once and nothing in my experience on the expedition or elsewhere ever changed this good opinion. ...

I was to learn later that Dr. Hector alone of all the men of my experience asked no quarter from any man among us, drivers or guides. He could walk, ride, or tramp on snowshoes with the best of our men, and never fell back on his position to soften his share of hardships, but in fact glorified in his physical ability after a hard day's run to share in the work of preparing camp for the night, building shelters from the wind, cutting spruce boughs, or even helping get up wood for an all-night fire. He was admired and talked about by every man that travelled with him, and his fame as traveller was a wonder and a byword among many a teepee that never saw the man.

—Peter Erasmus, special assistant and interpreter for the Palliser Expedition, describing James Hector in *Buffalo Days and Nights*

PREFACE

James Hector was a remarkable young man, the youngest member of the Palliser Expedition, a British government-sponsored mission that explored vast areas of western Canada between 1857 and 1860. A medical doctor by training, Hector's exploits as an explorer, geologist, surveyor, and naturalist contributed to the success of this expedition. Four Parliamentary Papers published in 1859, 1860, 1863, and 1865—cited as *Reports, Papers, Further Papers, Maps*—and the scholarly work of Irene Spry, *The Papers of the Palliser Expedition*, form the basis of his remarkable story. In order to avoid copious endnotes, all citations, unless otherwise noted, are from these sources and are not footnoted.

My aim is not only to provide an accurate, clear, and vivid account of Hector's explorations as a member of this storied expedition, but also to reveal something of the character of this extraordinary young man. I have endeavoured to recount his story of triumph, failure, hardship, strength, and courage in his own words or in the words of his colleagues from daily records kept during their travels. Where events required, even demanded, a more thorough accounting, this narrative has been enhanced with accounts and even conversations he had with those who worked with him or met him later in life. In this respect, the memoirs of his loyal assistant, Peter Erasmus, and recollections by Mary Schäffer Warren, who met Hector during his final visit to Canada in 1903, proved invaluable. Only as a last resort, and at considerable risk, have I dared to impose my own interpretations or thoughts on the events surrounding this story.

For the sake of authenticity, the spelling, punctuation, and diction found in the original sources have been retained. Since all units of measure in these documents were in imperial units, those measures have also been retained. Unless otherwise noted, all sketches featured in this book are by Hector himself. I am indebted to Sean Doyle for his own wonderful sketches depicting major events in this story.

This is James Hector's story of the brief time he spent wandering in the Canadian Rockies. From this work emerges an insight not only into the characters of Hector and his colleagues but also the character and social fabric of the people of Canada's First Nations.

—*Ernie Lakusta, Calgary, Alberta, 2006*

PROLOGUE

A REGULAR RIP VAN WINKLE

THE LETTER

THE SILVER-HAIRED, AGING PROFESSOR WAS DEEP IN THOUGHT, reviewing yet another paper on the geology of the New Zealand province of Otago. It was at times like this, mulling over endless calculations and preoccupied with notations, that he became oblivious to his surroundings, half a world away from where he was born and across a vast ocean of both distance and time from the site of his greatest achievement. At times like this, nothing could disturb his concentration and he didn't hear the quiet knock on his office door. The knock became louder until, finally, the old man was jolted out of his trance and brought back to reality.

His assistant rather reluctantly poked his head through the door and apologetically informed the professor that his weekly correspondence had arrived. A pleasant thank you quickly reassured the assistant that his transgression had been forgiven.

For the aging Chancellor of the University of New Zealand, a cursory glance at the mail revealed nothing out of the ordinary, just more requests from academics to review their papers, politicians inquiring about university funding, and appeals requesting the esteemed geologist as a guest lecturer. The demands on his time seemed endless and his cluttered desktop was testament to that fact.

As he thumbed through his correspondence, a discoloured and tattered envelope caught his attention. Its ragged appearance suggested a long and tortuous journey. It was addressed to "Sir James Hector, Director of Geol. Survey, Wellington, New Zealand," in shaky handwriting he did not recognize. The stamp informed him that it had originated from the Dominion of Canada and this piqued his curiosity.

As he scratched and twisted the whiskers of his silvery beard around his fingers, he wondered as to the letter's originator, but even though his mind was as sharp as ever, belying his sixty-six years, he couldn't think of who it could be. Many names came to mind, but none reminded him of a colleague, acquaintance, or friend presently residing in Canada. He tore open the envelope and perused its contents.

Victoria, Pakaw P.O.[1]
Alberta, N.W.T.
June 27th 1900

Dear Sir

In the first place I must apologise for presuming to write to you, but I have so often thought of you I cannot resist from troubling you with these few lines which will show you that it was with a proud heart that I came across your name mentioned in great distinction in connection with the Geol. Survey in New Zealand. Many changes have taken place since we parted. The iron horse climbs the R. mountains on to the Pacific through the Kicking horse pass. The cars pass within 10 yards from the spot where the Blonde horse kicked you—little did we think then, when I was so much afraid you were killed, that I would at a future day ride on a different horse from the sorrel through the same grounds. Wonders never cease! You and I are the only two living of the party that explored the Kicking horse pass. Sutherland, Brown and our great Nimrod are dead. The Buffalo are [a] thing of the past – the last living and dead one I saw killed was in '82 near the Cypress Mountain. The country is getting settled up very fast, all from Fort a la Corne away beyond Edmonton is so settled up that there is no need of camping out of doors in the open air. There is a town on each side [of] the River at Edmonton. Another on the Bow R. about 20 miles

PETER ERASMUS, CA. LATE 1890S
(GLENBOW ARCHIVES, NA-3148-1)

below the Ghost River, and all along the forst [*sic*] hills from the Red Deer river to Montana there are ranchers some with thousands of cattle and horses. There is also another town where we camped at the foot of the Cypress Mountains where the hunters killed the Red Deer if you remember.

Oh I wish I could fly and go to you for an hour or two then I could tell you all what has happened, and what is going on. A year ago I saw Nimrod at Morley Mission on the Bow. R. across the Ghost R. at the foot of the Mountains. We had a long talk about you and our wanderings through the Mountains. He was then still able to kill moose, but poor old fellow died that winter. There are gold mines all through the country we travelled through, on the Tobacco Plains and the Koteny [*sic*] Lake as well. All the old that you knew are gone the way of all flesh. Mr. Moberly left the H.B.C. and is living at a place called Prince Albert below Carlton near the junction of the rivers where there is a large settlement and a big town. When I think of the past there is one thing I am ashamed of and which I cannot forgive myself, that is, when I left you at the foot of the Mountains. If I had not been induced by some fair promise, which I did not realise, I would not this day regret having done the like. From Colville I went to the gold mines and made a snug little sum of money, and from -76 to -86 I was with the Canadian Govt. in the Indian Department at a salary of 1000 dollars per annum. I retired after investing all my earnings only to loose [*sic*] it all by the failure of the Commercial Bank. I now find myself a poor man at this my 67th birthday. I would not find it so hard if I was not a victim to sciatica in both my hips. I know you could help me if I was near enough. Months I am laid up in bed. If it was not for this misfortune I would go to the gold fields and make another stake. I must now close with many good wishes for your welfare and prosperity.

I am dear Sir,
Your obedient servant
Peter Erasmus.[2]

SIR JAMES HECTOR, 1903
*(THE WHYTE MUSEUM OF THE CANADIAN ROCKIES,
NA-66-2289, MARY SCHÄFFER)*

The name brought back a flood of memories to the old man. Peter Erasmus, his old friend from the days of the Palliser Expedition, had been hired by Captain John Palliser in the spring of 1858 and assigned to work with Hector—who at the time was a young doctor—as his special assistant and interpreter while in Indian country. Oh, how he had grown attached to and come to rely on Peter for advice and guidance.

The apologetic, almost repentant tone of the letter saddened Hector, as it reminded him of the only unpleasant incident between the two during their brief time together. Only now did Hector realize the anguish, pain, and no end of regret his uncharacteristic loss of temper had caused this gentle man for more than forty years.

Who was this young doctor so admired by Erasmus? James Hector was born in Edinburgh, Scotland, on 16 March 1834, the eldest of six children born to Alexander Hector and his second wife, Margaret Marcrostie. James was also brother to six stepbrothers and stepsisters by his father's previous marriage.

Hector's family was not only affluent but socially prominent. He also inherited something else—significant intellectual genes. His father was a lawyer and well-known writer in the *Signet* and a close friend of author and poet Sir Walter Scott, for whom he acted as secretary, translator of old manuscripts, and transcriber of deeds. His mother was a niece of John Barclay, the first anatomist, teacher, and founder of the Museum of the Royal College of Surgeons in Edinburgh.

Young Hector received his elementary education at Edinburgh Academy, a classical school associated with the best universities in both England and Scotland, and spent four years as a student at Edinburgh High School. At the age of fourteen, he entered his father's office and shortly began a three-year apprenticeship with James Watson, a well-known actuary. At the same time he attended classes at the School of Arts, which would later become famous as the Heriot-Watt College, where he demonstrated an aptitude in chemistry and the natural sciences.

Hector entered the University of Edinburgh in November 1852 as a medical student, not so much with the intent of ever practising medicine but because it was the only avenue that offered him the freedom to pursue his real interests in the natural sciences, especially geology. The historical record is cloudy as to why Hector became interested in geology; it is known he attended "extra-academic" lectures by some of the top men in this field, including mineralogist Stevenson Macadam and geologists Alexander Rose and David Page. He may also have been inspired by the geology courses he took under Prof. Robert Jameson.

Often during his medical studies, Hector would escape to the highlands of Scotland, England, and Ireland on extended field excursions, where he would develop his talents and hone his powers of scientific observation. His instructors read like a roll call of nineteenth-century academia, in particular, botanist John Hutton Balfour, who considered Hector to be his protégé, as well as Edward Forbes, Charles Lyell, and John Goodsir.[3]

As a student, Hector displayed the exuberance and feeling of invincibility so characteristic of youth. Professor Balfour was quick to note his lively spirit, unbounded energy, physical stamina, endurance, and ability to make quick and accurate observations. These were traits Balfour admired; these were leadership traits—traits that would later manifest themselves during Hector's arduous explorations in the wilderness of the Canadian Rockies.

In 1856, Hector, at the young age of twenty-two, took and passed both major medical examinations and received his Doctor of Medicine. The title of his graduation thesis, "The Antiquity of Man," was later borrowed by Lyell for his own classic work written in 1873.[4] For a brief period of time after graduation, he acted as medical assistant to Sir James Simpson, who in 1847 had discovered the anaesthetic properties of chloroform. Hector then set up a medical practice in London but it was only temporary; other things were in the works.

Little did Hector know that Professor Balfour had recommended him to Sir Roderick Murchison, the director of the British Geological Survey and Museum of Practical Geology and the president of the Royal Geographical Society, for the position of naturalist-geologist on a proposed expedition into western Canada. Balfour thought highly of his protégé and felt that "his competence in scientific botany was not in doubt, while his special interests in geology and other aspects of natural history gave him knowledge of up-to-date trends in scientific thought in the whole range of problems with which the Expedition would be concerned."[5] In addition, his medical training could prove invaluable in the wilderness. When offered the position on what was to become known as the Palliser Expedition, Hector could hardly contain his excitement. It was an opportunity of a lifetime. He would become the youngest member of the expedition.

Perhaps Erasmus's letter awakened in the elderly James Hector some long-forgotten memory of days spent in the Canadian Rockies, days that were among the most rewarding of his life. Perhaps Erasmus had reminded him of his own mortality. After all, he was the only original living member of that storied expedition. Gone was not only the respected leader of the expedition, Captain John Palliser, but also the "jolly botanist" Eugene Bourgeau, secretary and astronomer John Sullivan, and even fiery Lieut. Thomas Blakiston, who caused so much tension on the expedition.

Suddenly, a powerful voice from deep within beckoned. It was calling his Blackfoot name: "*Natoos,* come back, come back to the *Usinee Wutche,* the Shining Mountains."

Suddenly, he had a longing to return.

I MEAN TO SEE MY GRAVE!

EVERY NOW AND THEN, THE SILVER-HAIRED PROFESSOR WOULD reread Erasmus's letter. He had had three years to contemplate its contents, and his desire to return to the Canadian Rockies was greater than ever.

Then, in 1903, F. W. Godsal, a rancher from Pincher Creek in the District of Alberta (then part of the North-West Territories), visiting his brother in New Zealand, happened to be introduced to Hector during his visit to Wellington. Godsal, well aware of Hector's explorations in the Canadian West, suggested that a return to the Rockies would be a wonderful idea and invited Hector to visit his ranch in southern Alberta.[1]

Hector realized that if he was going to return, it would have to be soon. He was entering his twilight years and his aging body constantly reminded him that those youthful years of pushing his body to the limit had finally taken their toll. As luck would have it, the Canadian Pacific Railway (CPR) was in the midst of a massive promotional campaign to lure tourists to its majestic mountain playground. Former CPR president William Van Horne's simple philosophy, "If we can't export the scenery, we'll import the tourist," had resulted in a grand and glorious scheme whereby the CPR established first-class hotels and hostelries amid magnificent settings throughout the mountains to attract these wayfarers.

Three quaint hostelries were established in British Columbia between Calgary and Vancouver, and train schedules were arranged to coincide with the best times for scenic viewing. One was Mount Stephen House at Field, about four miles west of Kicking Horse Pass; another, Glacier House, was located in the Selkirks, just below the summit of the Rogers Pass; and a third, Fraser Canyon House, was located at North Bend, near the eastern entrance to the spectacular Fraser Canyon. All three catered to every need of their guests.

The CPR contemplated inviting prominent persons to promote its enterprise, and two names were at the forefront: Sir James Hector of the Palliser Expedition, who had "discovered" the Kicking Horse Pass, across which the railroad had been constructed at considerable expense; and Edward Whymper of Matterhorn fame. Whymper was the most famous mountaineer of his time, having been the first to climb the Matterhorn, although his accomplishment was overshadowed by a mishap during the descent that caused the death of four colleagues. Even though Whymper was well past his prime in 1903, the CPR wanted to take advantage of his worldwide prestige in an attempt to lure guests to its establishments in the Rockies.[2] The plan was for the two famous men to meet on 16 August 1903 at Glacier House, where they could entertain the guests with their exciting tales. In the spring of 1903, Sir Thomas Shaughnessy, the president of the CPR, formally invited both men to his Rocky Mountain playground.

It is not known how much influence Erasmus's letter or Godsal's prodding had on Hector, but his mind was made up; he would return to Canada and his twenty-six-year-old son, Douglas, would accompany him. The CPR was delighted and planned an elaborate and triumphal return of the "Grand Old Man," with celebrations planned at both Kicking Horse Pass and Calgary.

Father and son set sail from Wellington, New Zealand, arriving at Vancouver, British Columbia, on 7 August 1903. Hector was totally unprepared for what he encountered after a forty-year absence. Seeing the bustling metropolis of Vancouver at the mouth of the Fraser River, he joked that his absence made him feel like "a regular Rip Van Winkle." Vancouver was the western terminus

"I'LL FIND MY GRAVE!"
(SEAN DOYLE)

of the CPR and from here they would travel aboard the *Atlantic Express* to the planned celebrations at Kicking Horse Pass.

At 2:00 PM on 11 August, the *Express* left Vancouver. It would take more than twenty-two hours for the train to reach Glacier House, near Rogers Pass. The CPR had arranged James's schedule to allow him a few relaxing days at Glacier House in the magnificent surroundings of the Selkirk Mountains. He would meet Edward Whymper at Glacier, where the two would entertain guests with their tales of exploration and mountain climbing.

The *Express* wasted little time as it sped past Port Moody before entering the savage defile known as Fraser Canyon, where the track was laid on ledges and trestle supports against the sheer face of the rock, sometimes one hundred feet above the foaming Fraser River. In some places the track pierced solid rock, running through tunnel after tunnel. As early evening cast its shadows along the canyon walls, passengers marvelled at the human ingenuity of its construction. The train slowed appreciably. As it inched along the canyon walls, stones were dislodged, rattling down the face before plunging into the raging waters below. At times, it seemed as if the entire train was suspended in mid-air.

The train arrived at the small hostelry called Fraser Canyon House around 7:15 PM; a brief half-hour stop allowed the passengers to indulge in a quick quaff of their favourite beverage. Just beyond North Bend, the rails left the Fraser to follow the Thompson River and, as night fell, the express gained speed and quickly passed through the arid region surrounding Kamloops on its way to Revelstoke. It had been a long and eventful day for the aging professor and the gentle rocking of the Pullman car soon had him in a deep sleep.

Just before entering Revelstoke, the rail line crossed Eagle Pass. Passengers were informed that it was here, in 1885, that work crews from the east met those from the west and Lord Strathcona hammered the last spike. An inquisitive passenger was intrigued by the name of the pass, and a knowledgeable conductor was more than willing to elaborate on its origin.

"According to legend," he said, "Walter Moberly had just crossed the Columbia and was confronted with the problem of running the track through the next mountain range. It seems that he then spotted some eagles flying in a certain direction. Moberly knew that eagles always follow a stream or river when making for an opening in the mountains, and following the eagles, he saw them make a big curve. He had found the pass he was searching for. Appropriately, he called the place Eagle Pass."[3]

The *Express* raced down the eastern slopes of the pass and entered Revelstoke. Archie Bell once described Revelstoke as "the city that precedes the great plunge into the ravine and canyons of the Selkirks. It is where the locomotive receives its water and fuel, where the train crew is changed, and where the passenger on the transcontinental trains from the West recovers from the surprise and wonder of what he has seen, takes a deep breath and launches boldly into one of the colossal amphitheaters of the earth."[4]

Revelstoke occupies a site in the valley next to the great Columbia River, with a commanding view of snow-capped peaks on either side. Passengers had time for a quick breakfast and to reflect on the beautiful surroundings before they were whisked back on board. Revelstoke resented the slight attention it received from the passenger trains, but it could be forgiven for feeling that way; perhaps Sir James would be able to visit this quaint little town another time.

Now began the relentless pull up the valley containing the surging waters of the Illecillewaet River. When the *Express* reached Albert Canyon, it stopped long enough for the passengers to visit the rim of the great gorge through which the Illecillewaet raged far below. It is here that the main stream is joined by its north branch to surge through a deep cleft in the mountains, and it was here that many of the passengers tossed stones down into the raging torrent to test the common belief that blasts of air near the surface are so great that the stones never reach the water. Douglas Hector kicked a few stones over the edge to test this hypothesis, but his father knew better; the laws of physics just don't work that way.

It wasn't long before the *Express* plunged into the cool confines of a magnificent valley clothed in primeval forest. Gigantic cedar, spruce, pine, and Douglas fir were festooned with yellow and black lichens, which hung from the branches like an old man's beard. These giant conifers seemed to dwarf the train and were in turn dwarfed by the magnitude of the mountains. Sir James was awestruck by both the girth and height of these forest titans, but saddened by the sight of charred remains, which stood like ghostly sentinels and spoke volumes of man's careless contact with nature during the construction of the railway.

Sheltered from view was an almost impenetrable undergrowth, with its innumerable fallen trees in every state of decomposition. This dense undergrowth, which rendered travel almost impossible, reminded Hector of his descent from Howse Pass to the Columbia in 1859. He remembered how his small party had hacked its way through such chaos, despite the fact they only had one axe between them. And then he remembered that horrible plant *Echinopanax horridus,* the scourge of beast and man alike—the dreaded "devil's club." Its scientific name aptly describes its notorious reputation.

What a horrid experience is the devil's club! Many a traveller would comment on encountering this plant and curse its existence. In 1885, naturalist Ernest Ingersoll was moved to comment on his first encounter with the plant:

> The far-famed Devil's Club is a tall plant, bearing large, palmate leaves at the summit of two or three scraggy branches and presenting a very pleasing appearance at a distance. Close contact teaches you that these ugly stems and leaves are studded with horrible spines, sharp as needles, strong as rose thorns, and twice as numerous as either. Dense jungles of this malicious weed grow as high as one's head in many places, and make travel in the woods, where the foot slips at every step … not only toilsome but a most painful task. Moreover, the prickles are sharp and acrid not only, but barbed as well, so that they work their way into the flesh and make bad sores unless quickly extracted.[5]

The locomotive belched thick, black plumes of smoke as it struggled to haul the *Express* up the Illecillewaet Valley. It creaked and groaned at an excruciatingly slow pace until finally, with a huge blast of steam that seemed to signify relief, it screeched to a halt. It had reached the tiny hamlet of Illecillewaet, beyond which the track curved in huge loops to overcome the steepness of the grade leading to the summit of the pass. It was here that an extra locomotive would be added to help push the *Express* up this unrelenting gradient, which in places exceeded 2.2 percent.

While the extra locomotive was being added, the passengers had time to peruse their surroundings, and they were appalled by what they saw. Here they were greeted by what could best be described as a typical "frontier" village and a landscape adulterated by man's inhumanity to nature. When the Reverend Spotswood Green passed this way in 1888, he described this scene: "Burnt black trunks alternated with wooden houses, some of which stood on legs in swampy pools only half reclaimed from the overflow of the river by piles of empty meat cans, broken packing cases, &c., which were littered about everywhere."[6] Little had changed in nearly twenty years!

Aided by the extra locomotive, the *Express* began its relentless journey to the summit of Rogers Pass. It was less than twenty miles to the summit but the gradient would require almost an hour and a half of serious work to over-come this obstacle. The pace allowed passengers ample time to savour each breathless moment as the train crossed torrents on trestles that seemed to be suspended in space.

The *Express* crossed five spectacularly high trestle bridges, all located near a series of gigantic loops nearly nine miles in length, before the height of land was gained. Ahead, as if rising from a sea of ice, appeared Mount Sir Donald, its mighty promontory reaching for the sky. The view was overwhelming, prompting Sir James to wonder how they had ever constructed the railroad over the Kicking Horse Pass. After all, neither he nor Palliser ever considered the Kicking Horse as a potential route for any type of conveyance.

The *Atlantic Express* struggled to meet its schedule; it was Thursday, 13 August, and the train was due to arrive at Glacier House at 11:40 AM.

Glacier House, located in perhaps the most spectacular setting of all, was nestled at the foot of Mount Abbot in the heart of the Selkirk Mountains, and it was the first of the CPR's hostelries to open, in 1886. At first, pending the construction of a more elaborate structure, Glacier was nothing more than a dining car on a siding near the summit of the pass. In 1887, a modest wooden structure with six or seven small bedrooms, a kitchen, a reception room, and a large dining room where meals were served was erected. On its doorstep was the "Great Glacier," the Illecillewaet, which seemed to tumble some three thousand feet in great white cascades of ice out of the sky to the very foot of the valley.

Since 1887, the original "Swiss Chalet" of Glacier House had undergone a number of expansions in order to accommodate an ever-increasing number of visitors. By the turn of the century, it had expanded from a quaint hostelry of six or seven rooms to a large hotel, with an additional fifty-four rooms, baths, a billiard room, a bowling alley, and even an elevator. By 1903, this enchanting domicile, so distant from civilization, had become the "shrine" of the mountaineering community. Julia Young, or "Mother Young" as she was more affectionately known, was Glacier's manager, a position she had held since 1893. Everyone who stayed at Glacier House remembered her keen sense of humour and the endless number of stories she entertained with every evening in front of the great stone fireplace. All summer, she had been meticulously preparing for her two important guests, even down to brewing her famous mulled port, which she usually prepared only at Christmas. She wanted everything to be perfect.

MT. SIR DONALD AND THE GREAT GLACIER, CA. 1925–30
*(CANADA. PATENT AND COPYRIGHT OFFICE / LIBRARY
AND ARCHIVES CANADA, PA-058226)*

MARY SCHÄFFER

(WHYTE MUSEUM OF THE CANADIAN ROCKIES, V653 NG 961)

It was a curious group of onlookers that had gathered at Glacier Station to wait for a man few had even heard of. Many questions went unanswered as the whispering grew louder. Who was this man they were waiting for? It came as no surprise that hardly any of those gathered on the platform that warm August day had ever heard of the Palliser Expedition and even fewer had heard of a geologist named Sir James Hector. In those days, very few people had access to and even fewer had read the expedition's massive *Report*. Even most Members of Parliament, to whom it was presented, stashed the report away and never read it.

Finally, the *Atlantic Express* pulled into Glacier Station and, after an absence of more than forty years, the snowy-haired traveller stepped onto the station platform. As soon as James Hector stepped off the train, the fresh scent of the alpine—a scent that one only gets in the mountains—suddenly invigorated him. His back, stooped from years of hardship, began to straighten as best it could, as those gathered pressed to get a closer look at the aged explorer, who, they were told, had mapped five major passes in the Rockies: the Vermilion, Beaverfoot, Pipestone, Bow, and Kicking Horse. How small and frail he appeared!

Hector's party eventually made its way to the hostel to be greeted by the ever-charming Mrs. Young. Mary Schäffer and her husband, Dr. Charles S. Schäffer[7], were also there that day, trying to complete Dr. Schäffer's work on the flora of the Canadian Rockies. Mary's chance meeting with Charles at Glacier House in 1889 had led to their marriage the following year, even though Charles was more than twenty-five years her senior. Dr. Schäffer, an ophthalmologist by trade and an avid amateur botanist, kindled her interest in the Rockies.

Mary Schäffer had taken a keen interest in the history of the Canadian West and was acutely aware of the role the Palliser Expedition played in its exploration. She was also keenly aware of the role a young doctor named James Hector played in the success of that expedition and considered it a great tragedy that so few of those gathered at Glacier Station were aware of his exploits in the Rockies.

Imagine her surprise when one of her historical heroes suddenly walked through the front door of Glacier House!

"I was sitting quietly in the small rotunda of the little hotel, sketching, I think," recalled Mary, "when my ears caught the remark: 'I mean to see my grave!' Then came the profound thump of a fist on the counter of the office. One naturally takes an interest in anyone who is on the hunt of his own grave and as I was always looking for anyone who had any history at his tongue's end, I slipped from my chair and quietly went to the desk to see if I could discover anything new. The charming hostess of many years' standing was listening to a rather undersized and very emphatic man, rather stout, who looked at least 70, though later I wondered if his work might not have aged him.

"Knowing my love discovering historical people, she looked at him and said: 'Sir James, may I introduce you to [Mrs. Schäffer], who takes such an interest in this special western part of Canada?' I do not believe I gasped, but was profoundly astounded to discover I had come in touch with the famous doctor who had helped write Palliser's Journal and who had done so much toward opening a part of the Rockies."[8]

When Hector proclaimed, "I mean to see my grave!" one might have looked at the elderly man and wondered if he might have harboured some morbid death wish. In fact, far from it, Hector was referring to a site near where he had had his famous accident so many years ago and where he was very nearly buried alive.

Mary could hardly believe her good fortune and was thrilled when she and her husband were invited to hear Hector's amazing story of exploration later that evening. She leaves little doubt in her later recollections of this event that her chance meeting with Dr. Hector fired her imagination for wilderness exploration later in life.

"Our first evening with him," would be, Mary wrote, "one of intense interest listening to little sketches of that expedition which began in 1857, ended in 1860, and whose hardships started on landing at Fort William, extending directly west and finally reaching what is now Golden via the Columbia. The extreme limit of the expedition was conducted by Dr. Hector himself in his search for a pass" that would not entail crossing the international boundary.

Mrs. Young had been meticulous in her preparations that evening. She had instructed the chef to prepare a special meal of boiled salmon, beefsteak, mashed potatoes, and an assortment of fresh vegetables. Fresh, hot huckleberry pie would be served for dessert. And there would be plenty of her mulled port, of course. The meal was as hardy as it was sumptuous, but for some reason Douglas Hector did not find it appealing; he had lost his appetite.

After supper, those present began to congregate around Glacier House's blazing great stone fireplace. It was here that guests always gathered to swap yarns, but tonight would be special; Sir James Hector had agreed to recount tales from the Palliser Expedition. As usual, Mother Young began the festivities with one of her numerous stories—and then it was Hector's turn.

Silence engulfed the room as everyone strained to hear the frail old man as he began to speak of a time few had even heard of. Soon he would captivate them with tales of running buffalo, Blackfoot Indians, hardship and starvation, and, of course, the kicking horse incident, which had become part of the folklore of the Rockies.

Hector began by recounting how they had gained the favour of the Indians. It all began with sickness at an Indian camp, he said. "We were certainly lucky. After a few days' deliberation, dysentery became rife in the Indian camp close by and they came to me for 'medicine.' I had carried quite a lot of material from England with me and among the stuff I found exactly what was the most necessary thing to give them. First I moved their camp to completely clean and new quarters, insisted they use only water from a certain stream and applied my medicine for the trouble. All the sick grew well in no time and I became a 'great medicine man.' Our troubles were over. After that the mountains were mine and any guide I chose."

Now that he had their interest, Hector's tale of Captain Palliser and the storied expedition that carried his name slowly began to unravel. It began with the story of how Palliser came to lead this ambitious exploration mission.

Douglas sat back, proudly listening as his father enthralled those present with his story. He tried to remain motionless because, every now and then, even the slightest movement would cause him to wince from a piercing pain in the lower right portion of his abdomen. He had first noticed this dull pain the day he boarded the *Atlantic Express* in Vancouver, but thought nothing of it as it had quickly disappeared. Gradually, the pain had returned with increased severity, but Douglas found it quite manageable and hence failed to inform his father. Now, however, it was a different matter; the pain was becoming almost unbearable and to make matters worse he was sweating profusely and felt nauseous.

But James Hector noticed none of this as he continued to tell his story.

PART ONE

TRAIL-BLAZING, 1858

CAPTAIN J'S PLAN

STANDING ON THE DOCK AT MANDAN POST ON THE UPPER MIS-
souri in the late summer of 1848, a tall, handsome, adventurous bachelor,
barely into his thirties, was about to board the American Fur Company
steamer *Martha* in preparation for his return to civilization. He had just
spent an exhilarating year hunting in the wilds of North America and was
returning to Comeragh House, his home in the Irish county of Waterford,
with all manner of trophy and many unanswered questions.

Captain John Palliser would later confess, I "left the Indians and the
Upper Missouri with great regret, and it was with a sigh that I embarked with
all my buffalo robes, grisly [*sic*] bear and wolf skins, elk horns, &c. &c., and
steamed away for St. Louis. . . . Boucharville and my faithful followers accompanied me on board, and after many a hearty shake of the hand and mutual
good wishes, away dashed and splashed the Martha, rounding the point, and
concealing the Minitaree village from my view as the last cheer of my hunting
companions fell faintly on my ear."[1]

Palliser was the well-to-do heir of a socially prominent Irish family and spoke fluent French, Italian, German, and Spanish. Yes, he was a captain, but not a captain of the regular army. He was a captain in the Waterford Artillery Militia, a position inherited from his father.

In the wilds of a land known only to the Indians of the plains, adventurous fur traders, government military personnel, and a few scientists and missionaries brave enough to venture into this dangerous land, this cheerful and lighthearted bachelor had received his education in wilderness survival.

Palliser would value this education above academic pursuits. After all, he had been less than a stellar student at Dublin's Trinity College, which he had attended only intermittently without ever graduating or achieving a degree.[2] He as much as admitted his distaste for academic interests before leaving for North America:

> With all the eagerness of a college student, who casts aside his dull books and duller tutors for a burst after the partridges, or for the more noble and exciting pursuit of the antlered lords of the forest and mountain, had I looked forward to a visit to the New World; determined to make acquaintance with our Trans-Atlantic brethren, and to extend my visit to the regions still inhabited by America's aboriginal people, —now, indeed, driven far westward of their rightful territories, and pressed backwards into that ocean of prairies extending to the foot of the Rocky Mountains.[3]

His excursion into the wilderness had only temporarily sated his lust for travel and adventure. It left him with more questions than answers. How far did the prairies extend? Was the land suitable for agriculture? Where did the plains meet the mountains? Did a practicable route through the mountain barrier exist? Where was the actual boundary between the United States and British Territory? These burning questions and a zest for hunting only fuelled his imagination and desire to return, although it would take nearly a decade for his plans to be set in motion.

John Palliser was born on 29 January 1807, the eldest son in a family of five boys and four girls, to Colonel Wray Palliser and his wife, Anne Gledstanes. A lust for travel and adventure seems to have been an inherited trait in the Palliser family. Two of his brothers, Edward and Frederick, were big-game hunters in Ceylon, while another, Wray Richard Gledstanes Palliser, had rescued a French damsel from pirates in the South China Sea. John's passion

CAPTAIN JOHN PALLISER AND
DR. JAMES HECTOR, 1860

(LIBRARY AND ARCHIVES CANADA, C-009190.)

for adventure may have been spurred by the exciting tales of big-game hunting on the Grand Prairies of the Missouri of his future brother-in-law William Fairholme. Adventure and excitement came to dominate the Palliser family's way of life, and this eventually led Palliser to travel across the Atlantic to explore America and Canada.

Even aboard the *Martha*, fresh out of her American port, Palliser had already begun contemplating his return. He was well aware of American expansionist plans in North America. The Oregon Territory had already been lost by Britain, and expeditions financed by the Americans were exploring the mountains for plausible transportation routes across the barrier. At least two survey parties were known to have crossed the forty-ninth parallel into sovereign British Territory. Wasn't it time to search for usable travel and trade routes *north* of the parallel? Little progress had been made since David Thompson's time in finding viable transport routes north of the border and south of the historic Athabasca Pass (which Thompson discovered in what is now the southwest portion of Jasper National Park). Native peoples in the region were well aware of these more southerly passes and had even guided a handful of men, including George Simpson, James Sinclair, a couple of "secret" British military agents, and a Jesuit priest, across the Continental Divide. But would these passes be suitable for travel by conveyance?

It had been fifteen long years since Palliser had visited the wilds of North America and still many of these important questions remained unanswered. Why, Palliser wondered? And then he remembered a fortuitous meeting he had had with James Sinclair while on the Upper Missouri. In 1841, Sinclair had successfully led a group of emigrants bound for Oregon across the mountains, and he later informed Palliser that an even better route existed farther south of the White Man Pass route he had used that year. The existence of this "unknown" pass intrigued Palliser and whetted his appetite for adventure. He even came up with a name for the pass.

"This pass I have called Kananaskis Pass, after the name of an Indian, of whom there is a legend, giving an account of his most wonderful recovery from the blow of an axe, which had stunned but had failed to kill him, and the river which flows through this gorge also bears his name. Of the existence of this pass I had learned from my friend, the late Mr. James Sinclair, a half-breed gentleman, formerly resident in Red River; this gentleman had informed me of this pass so long ago as the year 1848, and told me that he intended to try it the next time he made a trip across the mountains."[4]

In a fit of patriotism, Palliser decided that if his government wasn't interested in finding this elusive pass, then he would search for it himself; it was his destiny! He began to devise a modest plan—a solitary mission that he hoped to accomplish within the confines of one season, relying on the knowledge of local guides and his own intuition. Fortunately, this would not be necessary.

One advantage of being born into an affluent, socially prominent, and politically influential family is the powerful friends with whom one tends to become associated. One influential friend of the family was Sir Roderick Impey Murchison of the British Geological Survey and the Museum of Practical Geology and the president of the Royal Geographical Society. The society was already actively involved in numerous expeditions around the globe, and Palliser had an inclination that they might be interested in his plan.

There was another advantage: the powerful society was capable of persuading government officials to sponsor such expeditions. However, there was a stumbling block; Palliser was not a member of the society.

The project excited Murchison, but in order for the society to sponsor such an expensive mission Palliser would have to become a member. Murchison quickly took charge. On 10 November 1856, Professor Charles Nicolay nominated Palliser for membership and Sir Francis Galton seconded the nomination. These men were not only friends of Murchison but also powerful members of the society. On 24 November, Palliser's membership in the society was confirmed; election to such an elite organization in just two weeks was unheard of at the time. Such is the influence of powerful friends.

On 8 December, a distinguished group of society members headed by Murchison gathered to consider the modest proposal submitted by Palliser. The council minutes for that meeting had a simple entry entitled "Palliser J.'s Plan for the Survey of a large portion of North America," which the group immediately referred to the Expedition Committee. Ten days later, Palliser was invited to outline his proposal. He began by rolling out John Arrowsmith's latest map of North America (a wise gesture as Arrowsmith just happened to be one of the committee members), on which he had drawn two blue lines and a caption that read, "The Blue line indicates route across the Prairies, the dotted lines probable route from Rocky mountain Westward."

On the map, Palliser had painted "a straight blue line running a fraction south of west, a little below the 50th parallel of latitude, from the Red River Settlement to near the headwaters of the '*Moo-coo-wans*' [Oldman] River. Here a second blue line from the north-northwest to south-southeast (south of the international boundary) along the eastern edge of the Rocky Mountains. From this, two dotted lines indicate supposed routes across the mountains, converging on the western side at a northward bend of the 'Flat Bow [Kootenay] River.'[5]

The members of the committee were convinced. They not only approved Palliser's plan in principle but also extended the duration of the expedition to two years and proposed an allotment of five thousand pounds to cover expenses. The committee also suggested "that considering the great importance attached to the accurate determination of the physical features of the Boundary Line of the 49th Parallel, between Great Britain and the United States of North America, the President be requested to communicate, as speedily as convenient, with Her Majesty's Secretary of State for the Colonies, on the subject of the proposed Expedition."[6]

This meant that Murchison was instructed to inform Secretary of State for the Colonies Henry Labouchere of their recommendations. The Undersecretary of State was John Ball, who happened to be an old friend and companion of Palliser.

Murchison clearly outlined the goals of the expedition in a letter to Labouchere on 13 January 1857:

> I have the honor to inform you, that the Council of the Royal
> Geographical Society having taken into consideration a plan for the
> Exploration of a large part of British North America, are desirous of
> recommending it to your favourable attention, with a view of procur-
> ing from Her Majesty's Government, the funds necessary to enable
> them to equip an Expedition. ...
> The chief objects of the Expedition would be: —
>
> 1st.   To survey the watershed between the basins of the Missouri and
> Saskatchewan; also the course of the South Branch of the
> Saskatchewan and its tributaries; and, at the same time, should it be
> thought desirable by Her Majesty's Government, examine the actual
> line of the frontier on the parallel of 49°.
>
> 2nd. To explore the Rocky Mountains, for the purpose of ascertaining
> the most southerly pass across to the Pacific, within the British
> Territory. The Athabasca Portage is not only too far north, but totally
> useless for horses; and consequently we have at present to depend

on the courtesy of the United States Government for access to their portion of the Continent to Vancouver's Island & the Western British Territories on the Pacific.

3rd. To report on the natural features and general capabilities of the country, and to construct a map of the routes and surveys.

The Council propose to entrust the command of the Expedition to Mr. John Palliser, a private gentleman and member of this society, who is well known for his travels among the Indians of North America, — for his knowledge of their habits, and his ability to deal with them.

This gentleman is willing to forego personal emolument, and will combine astronomical observations with his responsibilities as Leader....[7]

In addition, it was proposed to add two scientific assistants, two privates of the Royal Engineers, and at least seventeen men (to be engaged in the field) to the party.

Palliser's modest proposal had now become a major scientific undertaking and, with great zeal, Undersecretary John Ball immersed himself in overseeing the project. Ball not only accepted the daunting task of carrying out the detailed work on the plans, formulating instructions, and finding scientific personnel but was also instrumental in prompting the Colonial Office to underwrite the total cost of the expedition. He immediately began inviting suggestions from eminent scientists of the day for qualified scientific personnel who might be willing to join the expedition.

Impatiently, Palliser awaited final approval of his project. Finally, on 28 March 1857, a letter from the Undersecretary for the Colonies informed him of his appointment as leader of the expedition, with special instructions to follow. Ball also informed Palliser that "to assist you & to promote the scientific objects of the Expedition, Mr Labouchere has been pleased to appoint Mr Bourgeau as Botanist, Mr Sullivan as Astronomical Assistant, and he trusts to be able to secure the valuable services of Lt Blakiston of the Royal Artillery, and of Dr Hector who combines the qualifications of a Geologist with those of Medical Man."[8]

With that, forty-year-old Captain John Palliser became the unlikely leader of what was to become known as the Palliser Expedition. He immediately set about making the necessary preparations.

What type of professional qualifications did Palliser possess to be chosen as the leader of such an important undertaking, which had suddenly become a major scientific expedition? He had little scientific background and no professional expertise and was a poor businessman. Even his leadership qualities during his captaincy in the militia were drawn into question, since his regiment appears to have been "disembodied" for much of the time during his first years of service.

Despite these weaknesses, he had strength of character and was kind and generous to a fault. He hated disputes, believed in teamwork, and achieved results with his easygoing style. According to Irene Spry, "He treated his associates not as inferiors to be ordered about but as colleagues, working together on a shared project. His strength lay in enlisting cheerful co-operation, not in dominating subordinates."[9]

Peter Erasmus always considered Palliser to be a tall, imposing figure. He always held himself erect with a straight-backed military appearance, which accentuated his stature and suggested strict military obedience. But his was a quiet authority and when addressing the men in a smooth voice, "he expressed each word with exact and clear pronunciation. He seldom raised his voice higher than ordinary conversational tone but when he spoke his voice carried further than any other speaking at the same time."[10] His easygoing style would draw the ire of Thomas Blakiston during the expedition, but perhaps his weaknesses were really his strengths, which would ultimately lead to the success of the expedition.

On 31 March 1857, Palliser received his special instructions from Labouchere, which outlined his duties as leader. In part, they read:

At the commencement of the season of 1858 you will start, as soon as the weather is sufficiently open and favourable, to explore the country between the two branches of the Saskatchewan River and south of the southern branch, and thence proceeding westward to the head waters of that river, you will endeavour, from the best information you can collect, to ascertain whether one or more practicable passes exist over the Rocky Mountains within the British territory, and south of that known to exist between Mount Brown and Mount Hooker....

Great care must be taken that the Expedition shall return to Fort Gary [*sic*] in sufficient time to allow them to reach England, via Fort Pembina and the United States, in the fall of 1858....

The result of your surveys and observations should be embodied in a Journal of the Expedition, to be kept with the utmost practicable regularity....

In full reliance upon your ability and discretion, Her Majesty's Government have not hesitated to entrust to you the conduct of the Expedition, with the express understanding that the scientific gentlemen of your party will consider themselves subject to your authority...

In the event of any unforeseen accident which might deprive the Expedition of your services as leader, the command of the party may be entrusted by you to either Lieut. Blakiston or to Dr. Hector and you will furnish a duplicate copy of these Instructions to whichever officer you may select for that purpose.

In conclusion, I cannot too earnestly impress upon you the necessity for the utmost caution in the selection of the line of route to be taken by the Expedition, and in avoiding all risk of hostile encounters with any native tribes who may inhabit the country through which you may pass....[11]

On 14 May 1857, an excited Palliser wrote to the Colonial Office: "Having engaged accommodation on board of Royal Mail Steamer *Arabia* I beg to report that in company with Doctor Hector, Mr. Sullivan, and Monsieur Bourgeau I leave London tomorrow morning for Liverpool on my way to North America."

Nine years after that fateful trip on the *Martha*, "Palliser J.'s Plan" had been set in motion.

FIRST ENCOUNTERS

THE FIRST SEASON'S EXPLORATION WAS AT AN END, AND MUCH OF Sir James's tale up to this juncture was nothing more than a blur to those in attendance at Glacier House. *Cotteau des Prairies,* Touchwood Hills, or *La Roche Percée*: these were unfamiliar landmarks to those present at Glacier House. But now, as the expedition made plans to reach the Rocky Mountains, the small group of climbers, explorers, and wilderness visitors gathered around the snowy-haired old man would be able to follow his every footstep. He was approaching territory they were all familiar with. This is the story they wanted to hear.

Palliser was content with the expedition's progress to this juncture. He noted in his report that in the first season, they had "carried on the explorations from the valley of the Red River westward along the boundary line, examined all the country drained by the Assiniboine and Qu'appelle River …also the lower portion of the South Saskatchewan, to beyond the elbow, up to 109° of longitude. Traversed in several directions that region of country between Fort Ellice and Fort Carlton, and containing the Touchwood Hills, Swan River, Fort Pelly, and the lakes district."

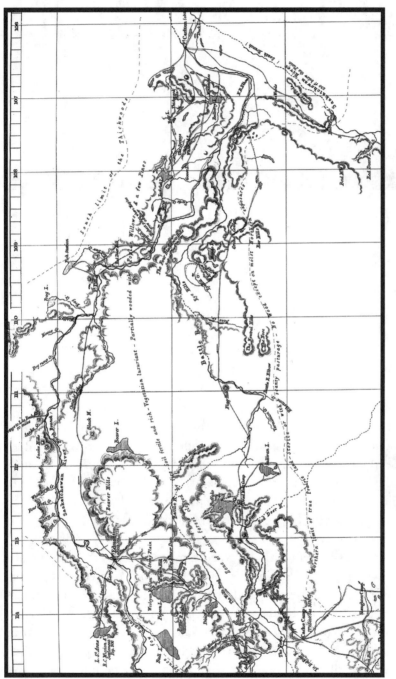

HECTOR'S 1857 ROUTE FROM FORT CARLTON TO FORT EDMONTON AND
THE EXPEDITION'S ROUTE FROM EAGLE HILLS TO SLAUGHTER CAMP IN 1858 (SOURCE: MAPS)

Palliser had wanted to continue pushing west, but the lateness of season and fear of venturing into hostile Blackfoot country with a small contingent of men forced him to curtail activities. Winter quarters would be at Fort Carlton, and by the time they reached Carlton on 8 October, all had grown weary of the plains.

The Blackfoot question would become a major concern as the expedition moved westward across the plains toward the Rockies. This was Blackfoot country, and the name alone summoned fear in the hearts of the Blackfoot people's Native enemies as well as the fur traders.

The Blackfoot Nation consisted of three distinct tribes: the *Siksika,* the actual Blackfoot tribe; the *Kainai,* meaning "Many Chiefs," who were known as the Blood; and the north and south *Piikani,* meaning "rough-tanned robes," known as the Peigan. Although these tribes shared the same language and customs and often intermarried, they retained their separate identities but were closely allied for strength, security, and warfare.[1]

By the end of the eighteenth century, the Blackfoot Nation had become masters of the northern plains. At the height of their powers, they controlled a vast area that extended from the North Saskatchewan River south to the Missouri River in Montana and from the Battle River westward to the Rockies. Historians are uncertain about the origins of the hostilities that existed between this powerful nation and the Stoney and Cree peoples. Rivalries created as a consequence of the fur trade; competition for limited resources, especially bison; protection of hunting grounds; and fallout from horse stealing all contributed to a seemingly endless hostility between the Blackfoot and the other peoples of the northwestern plains. Allan D. McMillan and Eldon Yellowhorn state: "Warfare was a passion, and the only route to prestige for a young man. The honour of dying in battle was impressed upon boys from the early age. Times of peace were rare, and even then a chief had difficulty restraining young men from setting out on raids."[2]

The Blackfoot were the most aggressive, warlike, and feared enemies of the Stoneys, Shoshonis, Flatheads, Pend d'Oreilles, and Kootenay peoples. They wreaked terrible revenge on their enemies, attempting to inflict as much injury as possible on their foes. Rarely did they take prisoners. Stories of their ferocity were legendary. John C. Ewers reports that: "A Blackfoot warrior whose father, brother, or best friend had been killed by the tribe he was fighting was not content merely to take the scalp of his fallen enemy. He mutilated the body of his foe—cut off his hands, feet, and head, or even literally hacked him to pieces."[3] In 1848, Paul Kane writes of a Blackfoot massacre of a party of Cree. Among the slain, wrote Kane, "was a pipe-stem carrier, whom they skinned and stuffed with grass; the figure was then placed in a trail which the Crees were accustomed to pass in their hunting excursions."[4]

Is it any wonder that the members of the Palliser Expedition viewed their proposed journey west to the mountains with mounting trepidation? How would the Blackfoot treat them? As friend or foe?

Fort Carlton had been established by the Hudson's Bay Company (HBC) on the Saskatchewan River in 1795. The location of the fort changed several times before moving in 1810 to the south bank of the North Saskatchewan River, near a spot referred to by the voyageurs as *La Monté*, meaning "the crossing place," which is about forty-five miles north of present-day Saskatoon. Situated on this high bench, it was an ideal site for a trading post—above the flood plain but close to the river and in a good defensive position against Indian attack. It was also strategically located where dozens of trails crossed, approximately halfway in the thousand-mile trek between Fort Garry and Fort Edmonton. Carlton served as a rendezvous point for fur traders, a base for buffalo hunters, and a supply depot for pemmican and dried meat. Palliser had chosen this as the ideal site for the expedition's winter quarters.

Only now did the vastness of the country begin to sink in. Palliser was overwhelmed and began to grow apprehensive about the expedition's goal of achieving its mandate in just two seasons, especially since the difficult mountain section still lay ahead. Realizing that his original proposal was now in jeopardy, he began to design a new plan to persuade government officials that a third summer was vital to the success of the expedition.

Many of the expedition's instruments had been damaged "through sheer work, accidental breakage, and wear and tear from the circumstance that these instruments had frequently to be packed on horses' backs," and Palliser determined to affect their repair in New York. In addition, HBC Governor George Simpson had indicated a problem with the expedition's bills and Palliser wanted to meet with the governor in Montreal in order to clear matters up. He left Fort Carlton on 11 October and reached Fort Garry on 1 November. Here he remained for a few days, before departing on 4 November for St. Paul, Minnesota.

When Palliser arrived at Montreal in early December, he quickly settled expedition accounts with the HBC and was royally entertained by Sir George. But he hadn't forgotten his most pressing concern.

In a dispatch to the Secretary of State for the Colonies dated Montreal, Canada East, 8 December 1857, Palliser conveyed his concerns:

> The country the Expedition will have to traverse next year in order to fulfil its objects will be so great that it would be impossible to fulfil my orders of sending the Expedition back in time to reach St. Paul's [Minnesota] in the fall of 1858.
>
> Under these circumstances, I think it of great importance that Her Majesty's Government should communicate to me further orders; and I should suggest that my services be taken for another season, and that the Expedition should winter in the country between the forks of the Red Deer River, and the Rocky Mountains in the winter of 1858. Thus all the objects in investigating and exploring the country, for both physical and scientific purposes, would be fully attained....
>
> My address [he was leaving for New York] will be, St. Nicholas Hotel, New York, U.S.; and anxiously awaiting your further commands.

Palliser promptly left for New York, where he could have the instruments repaired while he awaited word from the Colonial Office regarding his proposal. He grew restless and decided to visit his friends in New Orleans. By February, he had not received a reply and assumed that officials were leaving matters to his best judgment. Without hesitation, Palliser left for Fort Carlton, ready to launch his second year of exploration and determined to ultimately spend a third summer in the field.

Meanwhile, winter at Fort Carlton had been especially harsh and trying on the men relegated to the mundane tasks of updating journals, tending to the horses, and gathering tedious scientific data. At times like this, personality conflicts are bound to develop between men living in close quarters, and a bitter rift ensued between Thomas Blakiston and John Sullivan—a rift that threatened to tear the expedition apart.

Blakiston was a perfectionist with enormous talents, but he was impatient with others' shortcomings and resented any disagreement with his decisions. He was restless, moody, and edgy and was his own worst enemy. Thomas Blakiston was born at Lymington, Hampshire, England, on 27 December 1832, the second son of Major John Blakiston. When not quite fifteen years

LIEUTENANT THOMAS BLAKISTON
(THE GALT MUSEUM ARCHIVES, UID 1977026700)

old, he entered the Royal Military Academy as a gentleman cadet where, aided by a great gift of mind, courage, and tenacity, his military career flourished. From the Royal Military Academy, he obtained a commission in the Royal Artillery in 1851, becoming a first lieutenant in 1854 and serving with distinction in the Crimean War.

Blakiston was upset from the moment he arrived at Fort Carlton on 23 October 1857, after travelling from York Fort on Hudson Bay in charge of the expedition's delicate instruments. Only Bourgeau was there to greet him! He was also upset that Palliser had not clearly defined his position in the expedition and had not left explicit instructions for carrying out his work. Blakiston was used to precise military protocol. At the recommendation of the Royal Society he had been attached to the expedition for the purpose of obtaining magnetic and geographical observations. He wanted to know his exact role and position in the expedition, and Palliser's absence to greet him rankled the young lieutenant. For some reason, this immensely gifted but difficult person would begin to vent his anger on one particular member of the expedition: John W. Sullivan, astronomer and secretary to the Captain.

Poor Sullivan! Blakiston questioned everything from his work ethic to carelessness in his magnetic observations and calculations. He questioned his character and even told Hector that he could "no longer treat Sullivan as a gentleman." When Sullivan went off to visit a fishery at Jackfish Lake in February, Blakiston accused him of desertion and later of pilfering government stores to satisfy the needs of the starving men. Sullivan saw it differently, writing to Hector while he was away at Edmonton, "During your absence, Blakiston would not take charge of anything, so Bourgeau and I have done jointly what you would have done yourself, had you remained among us, that is, given the men what is necessary and looked to their employment."[5]

Blakiston became so bitter and resentful of Sullivan that Hector thought there was no possibility for reconciliation and that their mutual antagonism could ultimately affect the co-operative nature of the expedition. Palliser would have a major conflict to resolve upon his return.

Sullivan had been recommended to act as astronomer and secretary to the expedition by Dr. Edward Purcell of Trinity College in Dublin. Sullivan was born at Devonport, Devonshire, on 4 June 1836, the son of an able-bodied Irish seaman.

He had an exceptional aptitude for mathematics and, on 18 March 1856, was appointed acting assistant master in the Nautical School, the highest branch of the Greenwich schools. In December of that year, he resigned this position and was appointed to the expedition. Besides his extensive mathematical qualifications, Sullivan appears to have had more than an adequate grasp of French and later took responsibility for translating expedition botanist Eugene Bourgeau's almost illegible report into a readable form. Sullivan also found time to compile remarkable and extensive vocabularies of four Indian languages.[6]

For his part, Sullivan seemed to keep his head above the allegations and bitterness directed at him by Blakiston and even took the trouble to review doubtful astronomical calculations. Hector believed that if Palliser dismissed Sullivan on the basis of Blakiston's unfounded accusations, the expedition would "lose a most tractable" observer and suggested that this bitterness and conflict would affect the "character" of the expedition in the coming year.

In a confidential letter he gave to Palliser upon his arrival at Fort Carlton, Hector stated, "I can only say, that I found no difference in Sullivan since last year, except perhaps he has been stimulated to be even more active & anxious to do his work. You will find that he has brought up your accts. & papers into beautiful order, that he has kept up the Journal with great regularity, & that he has taken quite a flood of observations, including Lunars & all sorts of things & all in addition to his share of the hourly observations, & what more was there for him to do, poor devil."[7]

By mid-December, provisions at Carlton had become so alarmingly scarce that Hector decided the time was right to visit Fort Edmonton. Here he would recruit men familiar with the hardships of wilderness travel, as directed by Palliser. Besides, it would allow him to escape the unbearable tension created by Blakiston. Accordingly, he made arrangements with John Foulds, a Company man, and an Indian lad named Peewinagous to be his guides. Both were experienced travellers and would introduce Hector to winter survival. Even though it was bitterly cold the night before leaving, the young doctor was so excited he spent the night in the sled, rolled up in buffalo robes. On 14 December, they left Fort Carlton.

Hector had a lot to learn. First was mastery of travel by dogsled, with all of its intricacies. "The harness consists of a collar made of an iron ring, with a pad on it," he would write, "which passes tightly over the dog's head, but fits his shoulder well; to this is attached two long straps of dressed hide, kept up by a band across the dog's back; to the collar and back band are generally attached rows of bells, the merry jingle of which enlivens the journey, and gives spirit both to the dogs and drivers. . . . Four dogs are attached to each sled, and they are driven solely by voice, no reins being used." A good blow to the nose of an obnoxious dog, he observed, produces, for a few minutes, "the same effect as a dose of chloroform."

The first day, the three men covered thirty-three miles before encamping. "The first step on halting is of course to untackle the dogs," Hector reported, "which for to-night were all tied to trees, less they should return to the fort. As it is no use tying an Indian dog by cord, the method is, to tie a stick about four feet long close under its neck by one end, while the other is attached to the tree, so as to prevent him gnawing either cord, and so making his escape.

"One man then busies himself clearing away the snow, and cutting willow twigs on which to lie, which he spreads out in a square space just large enough to hold the party, who lie side by side with their feet to the fire; another employs himself cutting firewood, tree after tree being cut into logs six or eight feet long, the great secret of a comfortable winter camp being to have good firewood and plenty of it."

Kettles were arranged as soon as there was a roaring fire, and all became "busily engaged changing [our] moccasins, a good voyageur being as partic-ular about damp feet in camp as any mamma could wish her darling boy to be. The penalty of travelling with damp feet next day might be the loss of some of the toes by frost-bite, so that one has good reason to be careful. Besides care on this point, a great secret in making your feet last you on a long trip, especially with snow shoes, is to have large mocassins, and instead of attempting to wear knitted socks, wrap your feet in a square piece of blanket, as it is the fashion of the country. Too much covering on the feet only increases the chances of their being injured by pressure, without increasing the warmth, for keeping up which exercise should alone be trusted to."

That night they were entertained by a magnificent display of northern lights, as streamers of crimson and green flashed across the sky in gigantic arches.

Six days later, on 20 December, they reached Fort Pitt, still some two hun-dred miles from Edmonton, where they were greeted by James Simpson, the HBC officer in charge of the fort. He decided to join them when they left four days later.

Christmas Eve was bitterly cold; at sunset, the thermometer fell to –9°F, and it was all the small group could do to keep from freezing and enjoy them-selves. On Christmas Day, they were greeted by magnificent sun dogs and managed to cover thirty-three miles. They killed an old bull buffalo for the dogs; at least they would enjoy a Christmas dinner! That night their spirits were lifted by a magnificent display of the aurora borealis.

Two days later, they were attracted by a noise from an immense Cree camp, whose inhabitants were in a high state of excitement. They had succeeded in driving a large herd of buffalo into a "pound" and were in the process of a massive slaughter. Hector described the carnage:

> The scene was more repulsive than pleasant or exciting. The pound is a circular strong fencing, about 50 yards in diameter, made of stakes with boughs interlaced, and into this place were crammed more than 100 buffalos, bulls, cows, and calves. A great number were already killed, and the live ones were tumbling about furiously over the dead bodies of their companions, and I hardly think the space would have held them all alive without some being on the top of others, and, in addition, the bottom of the pound was strewn with fragments of carcasses left from former slaughters in the same place. . . . The entrance to the enclosure is by an inclined plane made of rough logs leading to a gap through which the buffalo have suddenly to jump about six feet into the ring, so that they cannot return. . . .
>
> When first captured and driven into the pound, which difficult manner is effected by stratagem, the buffalo run round and round violently, and the Indians affirm always with the sun. Crouched on the fencing were the Indians, even mere boys and young girls, all busy plying their bows and arrows, guns and spears, and even knives, to compass the destruction of the buffalo.
>
> After firing their arrows they generally succeeded in extracting them again by a noose on the end of a pole, and some had even the pluck to jump into the arena and pull them out with their hands; but if an old bull or cow happened to observe them they had to be very active in getting out again. The scene was a busy but a bloody one, and has to be carried out until every animal is killed to enable them to get the meat. I helped, by trying the penetrating power of the rifle balls on the shaggy skulls of the animals, with invariable success; and it is the least cruel way of killing them, as they drop at once.

The young doctor also observed a superstitious custom related to the whole business, noting that the Cree "always consider their success in procuring buffalo in this manner to depend on the pleasure of the Manitoe, to whom they always make offerings, which they place under the entrance of the pound, where I saw a collection of Indian valuables, among which were bridles, powder horns, tobacco, beads, and the like, placed there by the believing Indians, only to be stolen by the first scamp in the camp who could manage the theft adroitly."

They also hung offerings on a tall pole, placed in the centre of the pound, "to which piece of idolatry I was in a manner accessory by giving them my pocket handkerchief to convert into a flag," wrote Hector. After trading for an additional sled dog, Hector's contingent continued their trek to Edmonton.

On 30 December, just after daylight, they came in sight of Fort Edmonton, "standing on a most commanding point" high above the North Saskatchewan River, where they encountered a large assemblage of people enjoying the festive season. Discounting the four days spent at Fort Pitt, the journey had taken thirteen days' hard travel and they had covered 393 miles from Fort Carlton. At last they would have a belated Christmas dinner. Afterward, Simpson remained at Edmonton on Company business.

Informed that most of the men he had hoped to engage for the expedition from the Lake St. Ann's region were off buffalo hunting on the plains, Hector decided "in the meantime to make a trip to Rocky Mountain House, which is situated about six days further up the Saskatchewan. With me I am to take my own man Foulds, and two of the Company's, all having dog trains like myself."

On 9 January 1858, "having received my provisions from the store, con-sisting of pemican, [sic] a little dried buffalo meat, with a small stock of tea and sugar, we started by crossing the river at 10 a.m. The track at once leaves the Saskatchewan, and does not meet it again till at the mountain fort." It was bitterly cold, as temperatures dropped below −20°F. The bitter north wind bit into their faces and chilled them to the bone, but somehow they managed to travel more than seventy miles in just three days.

On 13 January, just before evening, as they passed over a high knoll known as Gabriel's Hill, Hector got his first glimpse of the Rocky Mountains. The sun had already begun to set so that his view was limited to a vague outline bounding the horizon. Still, he was struck by their great height and darkness, which was broken here and there by streaks of white. The next morning at sunrise, the view improved. "The effect was quite exhilarating as they became lighted up rapidly by the pinky hue of morning, and then I found that the black appearance which they presented the evening before arose from the

Winter Camp

Fort Edmonton

North Saskatchewan. Lignite and gravel beds, near Edmonton.

SKETCHES MADE BY HECTOR
ON THE WAY TO FORT EDMONTON

immense proportions of abrupt cliffs which they present, on which the snow cannot rest. We got quite excited with the view, and went on without halting for about 30 miles, when my men said we were about seven miles from the fort, and they must halt and wash; so they made fire and spent fully an hour dandifying themselves to appear before their friends."

They reached Rocky Mountain House (also known as the Mountain House), which was situated about half a mile above the mouth of the Clearwater River, on 14 January. Hector was not impressed. Unlike Edmonton, it was "a roughly constructed group of log huts, consisting of a dwelling house, stores, and workshops, and all surrounded by a palisade. The woodwork is very old and rotten, and the whole place is tumbling to pieces. I established myself in one of the rooms in the dwelling house, while the men found quarters for themselves in the huts. There were many Indians camped round the fort, waiting for the return of Mr. Brazeau, who had promised to bring up a further supply of rum with him from Edmonton."

Here Hector would spend eleven days, tramping through the nearby woods, studying the geology, making elaborate sketches, and experiencing the effects of Chinook winds, "soft winds from the west, which cause a rise in the thermometer, sometimes even to above the freezing point," and the rapid disappearance of snow. A number of Blackfoot Indians had arrived at the fort and from a distance carefully observed his actions. They were convinced that the doctor, clamouring up the hills with his scientific instruments, was performing some type of "medicine dance."

Hector noticed that the Company men were more than willing to induce the Blackfoot to part with their furs and scanty supply of meat. Their trading practices appalled him: "The desire for rum, however, soon induced them to part with some of their scanty supply, and now the environs of the fort presented a dreadful scene of riot and disorder. The Blackfoot Indians are more easily rendered violent by the liquor than the Crees, so that it is always watered for them, even being diluted to the extent of 11 water to 1 of spirit ..." How would he ever carry on meaningful talks with them, he wondered?

Rumour travels quickly throughout Indian country, and the Blackfoot were already aware of the expedition. Moreover, they "were surmising the most absurd reasons for our visiting their country next year; so I thought it right to give some account of ourselves, and thus gain the good-will of the chiefs by allowing them to have the information to distribute to their people."

Hector was disappointed when only a few of the chiefs came to speak, "the

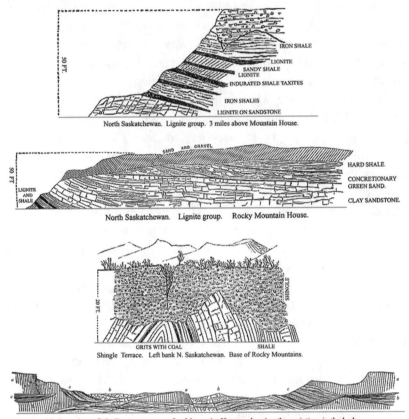

IRON SHALE
LIGNITE
SANDY SHALE
LIGNITE
INDURATED SHALE TAXITES
IRON SHALES
LIGNITE ON SANDSTONE

50 FT.

North Saskatchewan. Lignite group. 3 miles above Mountain House.

HARD SHALE.
CONCRETIONARY
GREEN SAND.
CLAY SANDSTONE.

50 FT.

LIGNITE
AND
SHALE

SAND AND GRAVEL

North Saskatchewan. Lignite group. Rocky Mountain House.

SHINGLE

20 FT.

GRITS WITH COAL   SHALE
Shingle Terrace. Left bank N. Saskatchewan. Base of Rocky Mountains.

Ideal section of the lignite group at the Mountain House, showing the variation in the beds.
a, coarse-grained sandstone: *b,* concretionary greensand; *c,* shales with lignite.

FIGURE 1: GEOLOGICAL SKETCHES MADE
BY HECTOR NEAR ROCKY MOUNTAIN HOUSE

rest being still the worse off for their debauch. When the Blackfoot Indians came to a fort one chief always remained sober, to keep the peace, and in turn receives a gratuity of rum to take away with him, so that on returning to his camp he may make up for his temperance. Without this very sensible precaution there might often be bloodshed, either among the Indians themselves, or between them and the people of the fort. The sober chief of this band, called *Pee-to-Pe*, or the Perched Eagle, seems to be a fine fellow, and insists on sleeping on the floor in my room, partly as a compliment to me, but more because he will consider it an honour to brag of among the others afterwards. At night one of the chiefs I spoke to in the morning harangued the other Indians from the palisades of the fort, upon the necessity of their good behaviour to us white men, reminding them that they get nothing but good at our hands, and not to confound us with the 'Big Knives,' as they term the Americans, who, he said do not treat them well, but are deceitful."

This admonition seemed to have its desired affect, because early the next morning ten or twelve of the principal chiefs crowded into Hector's room for a conference. They had wonderful names that rolled off his tongue: *A Ca-oo-mah-ca-ye* (The Old Swan), *Natoos-a-pee* (The Ancient Sun), and *Ma-coo-yeh-o-mabi-kan* (The Swift Wolf). On the advice of Brazeau, the HBC officer in charge of the post, Hector prepared papers for each of them.

"These papers merely mentioned the name of each, and stated that he had promised to aid us in every way in passing through their country," Hector reported, "but the main benefit we would derive is from each having a note of the character that particular Indian bore among the traders at the fort, so that we might be better able to judge which to trust to us as guides, and also that we might at once recognize the real chiefs on meeting them in the plains, which is not always an easy matter, and to mistake is sure to give offence."

Pee-to-Pe began to speak. Felix Monro, part Blackfoot himself and a Company man fluent in their language, translated for Hector. *Pee-to-Pe* remarked that "his tribe saw so little of the whites, that they might not know how to behave so well as other Indians, but that when we come among them, we will find them a great people with singleness of heart. That there were no doubt some of the young men who would do us harm if they could, and steal our horses; but that the chiefs would prevent them, as with them the chiefs were not like those of the Crees, but had power over their young men." Hector was impressed with his sincerity and promised *Pee-to-Pe* that if he would join them in the summer, he would be one of their guides.

While at the Mountain House, Hector would receive word of a very remarkable hunter, a Stoney who was said to be most knowledgeable about travel in the mountains. "As he is known to be one of the best hunters in the tribe, and his Indian name, which signifies, '*the one with the thumb like a blunt arrow*,' is so unpronounceable, I called him *Nimrod*, which name has stuck to him ever since." Nimrod was a member of the Mountain Stoney, a name derived from the term *Assinipwat*, or "Stone People," because of their method of using hot stones in their cooking. Peter Erasmus contends that "they were the best trackers of any of the Indian people, and they developed the use of medicines to a degree unsurpassed by any of the other tribes. It was largely through their knowledge of medicine plants that the Cree looked to them as friends and never bothered them when they went to hunt buffalo."[8] They were a spiritual, peaceful, and hospitable people, who were reputed to be excellent hunters and the most reliable mountain guides.

Hector desperately needed a guide of Nimrod's qualifications for the coming summer, but, try as he might, could not locate the man. Then, just as he was about to depart for Edmonton, Nimrod amazingly appeared, having arrived at the post to trade. Hector managed to convince the Stoney to act as his guide, and Nimrod promised to rendezvous with him at the Old Bow Fort in the first week of August. Hector returned to Edmonton on 29 January.

While at Edmonton, he had occasion to document a rather curious medical condition prevalent among many of its inhabitants. "Goître is very prevalent among the residents here and at the Rocky Mountain House, but in a modified form, and which I have only seen one case where there is any approach to cretinism. I tabulated the details of 50 or 60 cases, but have not discovered any one condition of habit of life that is common to all who suffer from this complaint. The only curious feature seems to be that children born at one fort are never attacked till removed to another, and it again disappears on their return to their native place."

On 12 February, Hector accompanied John Sinclair, an apprentice postmaster in the service of the HBC, to the Catholic mission at Lake St. Ann's, some fifty miles west of Edmonton, to try to engage needed recruits for the expedition. The weather had turned bitterly cold and the temperature continually dropped to −30°F, with worse to come; that night was the coldest Hector had ever experienced, as his mercurial thermometer remained frozen at −47°F. When they arrived at the mission the next morning, they were suffering severe frostbite to their faces, but were thankful they hadn't frozen to death. Warmly received by "M. Le Combe" (Father Albert Lacombe) and Father Frain, they attended Sunday service in the mission's little chapel. To his dismay, Hector discovered that the men he had hoped to hire were still off hunting, so he left word that the expedition was hiring and returned to Fort Edmonton.

Back in Edmonton, Hector was introduced to Peter Erasmus by John Swanston, chief factor at Edmonton for that winter. It had been suggested that Erasmus's knowledge of many Native dialects would be invaluable as interpreter for the expedition. At the time, Erasmus was employed by Reverend Thomas Woolsey, who was in charge of the Wesleyan (Methodist) mission near Fort Edmonton. After formally being introduced, Hector said to Erasmus, "Well, well! I hardly expected to find a minister's man of that size holding the easy duties of an interpreter."[9]

Peter Erasmus was an exceptionally well-educated and proud Métis, born at the Red River Settlement on 27 June 1833 to a Danish father and an Ojibwa mother of "mixed-blood." Under the tutelage of Reverend Woolsey, Erasmus became fluent in six Native languages, as well as Latin and Greek. He would become one of those few, but select, individuals who would not only become part of history but would also play a role in the shaping of it. This remarkable man would provide vivid descriptions of the character and disposition of many of western Canada's historical figures and of the Riel uprising of 1885. He would act as translator on behalf of the Indians during the Carlton Treaty negotiations in 1876, and he would always fight for their rights. Sadly, he would also bear witness to the disappearance of the buffalo.

Ultimately, Erasmus would spend only the better part of one year with Hector, as his assistant and sometimes "guide," but it was his role as interpreter that would prove most valuable to the young doctor. It was through Erasmus that Hector would learn much about Indian languages, customs, and folklore.

Erasmus developed an admiration for Hector from the moment they first met. "He had a remarkably retentive memory," recalled Erasmus, "a gift for shrewd observation, and a deep sense of humour. His description of what he called civilized living among the British, the habits and customs of its lesser people as well as those of the titled rich, told in that droll humourous way of his, was a constant source of delight to me." Hector and Palliser were quite different from the Englishmen Erasmus had come to dislike. "Most Englishmen of my acquaintance," he wrote, "considered themselves made of superior cloth; even the most ignorant and pitiably helpless individuals faced with the ways of living of the West all looked down on the native inhabitants as inferior beings, even though they knew that their lives were dependant [sic] on the goodwill and resourcefulness of our people."[10]

Thank goodness, Erasmus said, these Englishmen were different. They did not express a condescending, intolerant attitude toward "the native sons of the land with part European blood in their veins." Erasmus felt at ease with these men and relished working *with* them, not *for* them. He cherished being privy to the lively discussions around the campfire each evening, discussions that included prospects of the land for agriculture and for settlement, as well as scientific matters that he didn't understand. And he never fully understood the time they took gazing at the stars or their passion for collecting specimens. These scientific gentlemen left no stone unturned and nothing seemed to escape their trained eyes; not a flower, insect, animal, or geological specimen went unnoticed.

All preliminaries dispensed with, Hector said to Erasmus, "I'd like to get two saddle horses and pack animals to go out and secure contracts for the summer expedition from the list that the factor has been kind enough to prepare. These men are out on the plains. Perhaps you can find them without too much delay."[11] Since Erasmus's duties were only required by Reverend Woolsey on Sundays, he agreed to Hector's request and eagerly prepared for the journey.

On 7 March, word was received that the men from the mission were returning from hunting on the plains. "This morning," wrote Hector, "I started with a guide, and Peter Erasmus, the Rev. Mr. Woolsey's interpreter, to endeavour to engage men for the Expedition from among the band of 'freemen' that are at present travelling in from the plains to Lake St. Ann's settlement." About forty miles from Edmonton, shortly after dark, near "Hay Lake," they came upon some tents, states Hector. "Only half of the party had got thus far on their return, as they were heavily loaded with the proceeds of their hunt, but the rest were expected to pass this place next day, so we resolved to wait before beginning negotiations. However I did business so far as to engage one man named Plant [*sic*], who very kindly gave us tent-room for the night."

At about eleven o'clock the next morning, Hector continued, "the rest of the band arrived, forming a motley troop with loaded horses and dogs, and travelling in a style hardly different from Indians. The rest of the day was spent winning the good will of their old chief Gabriel Dumont, who has repeatedly crossed the Rocky Mountains, and can also talk Blackfoot; and further when I succeeded in getting him to consent to act as guide for the Expedition, I had no difficulty in filling up my complement from among the young men. He gave me much information about the country to the south, and about the mountains, which I noted at the time, and which proved of much use to us in organizing our plans...."[12]

Hector had arranged to meet the men he had engaged from the Lac St. Ann's settlement at Fort Pitt near the end of May. From there, they would make their way to Fort Carlton in Company boats, as soon as the river was free of ice.

Their duties complete, Hector, Foulds, and one other Company employee prepared dog sleds and left Edmonton on 15 March. On the way back to Fort Carlton, Hector discovered a novel way of travelling on the frozen North Saskatchewan. "The ice was very smooth and free from snow, and in anticipation of this I had borrowed a pair of skates before starting, so that while my companions were slipping and tumbling, I got along with great ease." By Hector's own best estimates, he skated a full thirty-five miles on the river before encamping.

They reached Fort Pitt on 29 March and were back at Fort Carlton by 5 April, where Hector was greeted by his comrades and the Red River men enlisted by Palliser.[13] The influx of the Red River men from Fort Garry had depleted provisions at Carlton, and Hector wisely dispatched them to the Eagle Hills south of the fort, where abundant buffalo would sustain them. He also thought it better not to have the men hired from Lac St. Ann's meet at Carlton as prearranged and went off to Fort Pitt to instruct them to meet the Red River contingent at the Eagle Hills. He then returned to Fort Carlton to meet Captain Palliser, whose presence was expected within the next few days.

By 2 June, the Captain still had not arrived and Hector became worried. With Richard Hardisty, the Company clerk in charge of Fort Carlton,[14] he set off to find Palliser, whom he assumed was making his way to Fort Carlton from Fort Garry, some 550 miles distant. Two days later, during a brief break to rest their horses, "Captain Palliser suddenly walked in on us, silently as an Indian," Hector recalled. "He was walking in advance of his party, as the horses had all broken down, and they were bringing them slowly on, while he kept ahead in order to have a better chance of killing game, on which they were dependent, having no stock of provisions with them."

On the way back to Fort Carlton, Hector informed Palliser of the major rift that had developed between Blakiston and Sullivan.

On Tuesday, 15 June 1858, with preliminary arrangements completed, all was in readiness for the journey to the mountains. Palliser and his team left Fort Carlton for the Eagle Hills, where they would unite the Lac St. Ann's and Red River brigades. However, they left without the temperamental

Blakiston. Palliser had, for the time being, solved the dispute between Blakiston and Sullivan by dispatching Blakiston to Edmonton "in order to carry on the magnetic determinations at the posts, as well as to bring us supplies overland in carts, ordered up in boats from Norway House last winter, to meet us at the Forks," where the Red Deer and Medicine Lodge rivers converged.

Palliser's intention, once he and his party reached the junction of the two rivers, was to proceed to "an old Fort at the foot of the Rocky Mountains not far from the boundary line, thence I shall trace the boundary line to the westward, and afterwards take a course to the northward in search of a pass practicable for horses over the Rocky Mountains within the British territory."

The second leg of the Palliser Expedition was about to commence.

SLAUGHTER CAMP

EVERYONE KNEW CAPTAIN PALLISER'S REAL REASON FOR DISPATCH-
ing the young lieutenant to Edmonton. The friction between Blakiston and
Sullivan was tearing at the heart of the expedition, and Blakiston's dogged
stubbornness and downright bitterness had prevented any thoughts of reconciliation. They were about to enter dangerous country controlled by the
Blackfoot Confederacy and the last thing Palliser needed was internal conflict.

After first passing the "Stone Indian Knoll" and then "The Elbow," they
arrived at the Eagle Hills on Saturday 19 June. It took two days to gather all the
men, who were roaming, hunting buffalo, and on the following Monday, the
main branch of the expedition—now resembling a huge caravan of thirty-
two men—commenced its trek across the prairies. The journey west was
punctuated by intolerable heat and hail so intense that it stripped most of the
trees of their foliage, while the carts constantly became mired in the quagmire created by the torrential rains. At night, sheet lightning played in the

EUGENE BOURGEAU

(SASKATCHEWAN ARCHIVES BOARD, RA-4982)

northern skies, as feeble light from fireflies lit up the surrounding coppice. Sullivan wrote in his journal: "This little insect is an object of superstitious veneration with all the tribes of North America that we have seen. They regard them as the spirits of their departed friends holding their great feast on the plain, when the nights are quiet and warm and the buffalo are in the best condition."

When the weather did become tolerable, expedition members were plagued by thousands of mosquitoes and attacked by "bulldogs," horseflies hungry for chunks of flesh from man and beast. At times the flies were so unbearable that they necessitated making huge smudges, which the horses would seek in order to feed. To make matters worse, the men were constantly in search of fresh water.

On 5 July, they came in sight of the Neutral Hills. This landmark was the demarcation line between territory controlled by the Cree and that controlled by the Blackfoot, and was approximately twelve miles from present-day Unity, Saskatchewan. Palliser ordered a high alert; they were in Blackfoot country now. He even forbade the men from straying from the main party to hunt buffalo. Mile after dreary mile, always fearful of being attacked, they pushed westward.

All began to grow weary of the prairies, especially Bourgeau. The little man from the French Alps had grown tired of collecting prairie plants and longed for more familiar territory. "I am anxious to reach the mountains as soon as possible. It is now two seasons since I saw mountains resembling the Alpine chains of my native country."[1] He longed for the crisp mountain air and to collect his beloved "alpines."

On Friday, 23 July 1858, after marching for two hours through swamps and pushing their way through dense growths of willows, they reached the Nick Hills at about 8:00 AM. Upon reaching the summit, "we obtained our first view of the magnificent Rocky Mountain chain, which to the northward appeared like a blue line on the far-off horizon, while to the south they seemed more high and massive, their summits clad in snow, which glittered at intervals like silver crowns. Great excitement prevailed among our party at this sudden and unexpected sight and, we looked to the Rocky Mountains as the long desired object which was to relieve us from the monotony of prairie life," wrote Palliser. The Cree called them the *Usinee Wutche*, or the "Shining Mountains"; the Stoneys called them the *Assin-wati*.

The next day, as they passed over Hunter's Hill, the spectacular and

"THE DEVIL'S HEAD"

(*SEAN DOYLE*)

ominous landmark known as the Devil's Head came into view. They travelled south before encamping at the edge of the great prairie.

"I determined there to wait the arrival of Lieut. Blakiston," wrote Palliser, "who was to join us after having gone by the regular cart track, via Edmonton, in charge of ammunition, flour, and a few articles for Indian presents. We waited three or four days, and with difficulty supporting ourselves on deer, which were very scarce, as the Assineboines [*sic*] had hunted there all spring." Finally, the Captain could wait for Blakiston no longer as the scarcity of provisions obliged him to move in search of game. Palliser directed James Hector to return to "the forks," near the junction of the Red Deer, Medicine, and Little Red Deer Rivers, where the trail from Edmonton to Old Bow Fort branches off from the "Wolfs Road." Here he would bury a letter for Blakiston with instructions on how to find them. Palliser had prearranged with Blakiston that instructions on how to find him would be secretly buried in the ashes of one of their abandoned campfires.

As Palliser intended to send part of the expedition to winter quarters at Edmonton using this same route, he established a cache "of all the articles that we could possibly dispense with, in order to lighten the Expedition as much as possible, and enable us to abandon the carts for a time, hide them, and proceed with pack-horses." They nicknamed the site "Cache Camp."[2]

On 29 July, want of provisions forced Palliser to abandon Caché Camp and move south. After about fifteen miles, they halted, encamped, and were preparing dinner when Blakiston, following the directions Hector had buried at the "forks," arrived in camp, well in advance of the rest of his men. "He brought us the news that the boats had not arrived, and he was obliged to leave without the stores; but he succeeded in bringing me some ammunition from Edmonton, which, after all, was the only thing of vital importance," Palliser wrote. Almost immediately, there was a notable rise in tension throughout the camp. The next day, the rest of Blakiston's entourage arrived, and for the first time since leaving Fort Carlton, the entire party was together and ready to move south in search of buffalo to replenish their almost diminished larder.

On 30 July, they moved on and had travelled little more than sixteen miles to the southeast over level prairie broken here and there by elevated ridges when Palliser decided to encamp. Just then, two men whom Palliser had sent to scout for buffalo came charging into camp at full gallop. The excited men informed Palliser that buffalo, in vast numbers, had been sighted about ten miles east of their encampment. Palliser was relieved, as they were now "driven for provisions."

Palliser considered buffalo hunting a noble sport, and he was acutely aware of the dangers involved when "running buffalo." This he had been taught in 1847, during his previous visit to North America, by a masterful hunter named Boucharville. He learned that in the excitement of the hunt, injury to man or mount from a desperate and enraged bull or from a stumble into a prairie dog burrow could be swift and serious. He had been witness to just such events and did not want any of his men, especially his young doctor or lieutenant, to be injured. But at the same time he wanted them to experience the thrill of the sport.

That night, the whole camp was abuzz with unbounded excitement. Peter Erasmus was no exception, even though he had experienced the exhilaration of running buffalo many times. There was so much to remember: loading on the run, singling out an animal, placing a lethal shot close behind the shoulder, and avoiding the charge of an enraged bull. All these practices Palliser explained in detail to Hector and Blakiston. Sleep would not come easily that night.

The next morning, the hunters were astride their mounts before daybreak. Palliser's journal provides a vivid description of the exhilaration of the kill in which the prowess of the hunter is pitted against the survival instincts of the prey:

> Started before daylight; arrived early in the direction of the buffalo seen the evening before; halted for breakfast; the morning was cold and stormy. I allowed the men to wait until noon, by which time the buffalo would begin to lie down after feeding. They are then not so swift as if they were pursued early in the morning. We were now more than two miles' distance from the buffalo, who were not in sight, as we had taken care to take up a position as that they could neither see us or get our wind; they were in such numbers that their peculiar grunt sounded like the roar of distant rapids in a large river, and causing a vibration also something like a trembling in the ground.
>
> We had scouted the animals pretty well, so that all that remained was to eat our breakfast and make for the point of attack. Breakfast finished, our 'runners' saddled and mounted, the whole party moved slowly on, the carts following in the rear of the 'runner.' Having ascended the slightly elevated ridge we then beheld our game, four or five thousand buffalo, some lying down, some grazing with the old bulls in the outskirts. At our appearance the wolves, who almost

"RUNNING THE BUFFALO"

(SEAN DOYLE)

invariably accompany bands of buffalo, sneaked about and around, eagerly watching our movements, and perfectly aware that the events to come off were to terminate in an abundant meal after the field was left to themselves.

A few antelope were gracefully moving near the buffalo, and over the heads of all noisily soared some crows and ravens, and appeared quite aware that something was in the wind. Soon after seeing us the buffalo were in motion at a steady lope, crowding gradually into a thick black mass, and now the hunters came on a steady canter increasing with the speed of the buffalo into a hand gallop; the old bulls were soon left in the rear as the pace improved, some stood blown and staring after they had made ineffectual attempts at charging the hunters on their headlong way after the swift cows. The run was magnificent, and there was considerable emulation between my Saskatchewan and my Red River men.

Although there was some debate as to the number of animals killed, the best estimate was sixteen or seventeen healthy animals. Several of the party suffered falls, but none was seriously hurt.

That evening was one of jubilation and high spirits as the men set about preparing the slaughtered animals. Drying racks to hang the meat were quickly erected, and many a tall tale, both real and fabricated, was told round the campfires that night. Erasmus was dismayed when both Palliser and Hector predicted the demise of these wonderful beasts. He listened with disgust as the Captain told of the wholesale slaughter of buffalo just for their hides, their carcasses left to rot on the windswept prairies. Sadly, Peter would bear witness to this prediction.

They called it "Slaughter Camp," and situated as it was beside a small tributary of the Bow River in full view of the shining mountains, the men spent a glorious evening watching the sun set behind the snowcapped peaks.[3]

Palliser was now confident that his expedition was well supplied for its trek into the mountains and began to formulate plans for exploration.

On 2 August, he summoned the men to a meeting, at which time he would outline his proposal. He had decided that the most efficient way to explore the vast territory and the possible routes through the mountain barrier would be to split the party into four branch expeditions to search for usable passes.

"I arranged that Dr. Hector should ascend into the mountains in any direction which he thought most conducive to the interests of geological and geographical science; that Captain Blakiston should explore the two passes generally used by the Coutanies [Kootenay], crossing the mountains by the more northerly pass and returning by the more southerly one. I gave Mons. Bourgeau instructions to penetrate into the mountains as far as he thought conducive to the interests of botanical science. And to myself I reserved the exploration of a pass, the existence of which I had heard when in the American Indian country in the year 1848, from Mr. James Sinclair, a very intelligent half-breed, well known and deeply regretted."[4] The staging ground for these branch expeditions would be at Old Bow Fort, near the junction of Fort Creek and the Bow River near the base of the mountains.

Palliser was anxious to learn more about the extent and characteristics of the British Territory south to the international border and he prepared to make a dash to the boundary line himself. This would only slightly delay his search for the mysterious Kananaskis Pass. Sullivan would join him, which would once again separate the two antagonists.

Before the meeting had ended, Blakiston began to question Palliser as to his exact role in the expedition. He also pressed Palliser to name a deputy leader who, in the Captain's absence, injury, or even death, would assume leadership. Blakiston also proposed "that two men should be left at the site of Bow Fort on Bow River (at which point the parties were to separate), for the purpose of constructing a canoe, in which, after returning from the mountains (having calculated the time required), he proposed to descend the Bow River and the south branch to the Forks of the Saskatchewan, thereby getting a knowledge of the whole length of the river and the country through which it flows."[5] This seemed like a reasonable request and the meeting ended with Blakiston fully expecting Palliser to accept his proposal, as it had been favourably entertained. Palliser retired, saying that he would consider this idea at length and report his decision to the lieutenant the next morning.

Palliser spent an uneasy evening contemplating the day's proceedings and the proper course of action. He did not want to appoint a second-in-command, sensing that doing so would cause even more friction. Palliser may not have been the most astute when it came to making scientific observations or recording data, but he was a shrewd judge of character. He had already made a mental note of Blakiston's shortcomings, many of which had caused tension among his colleagues. Senseless quarrels with Sullivan and a lack of proper judgment when dealing with other members of the expedition had been duly noted. Blakiston's quick temper also did not endear the young lieu-tenant to the Captain. Palliser had even made a mental note of his lack of friendliness to the staff and servants of the Company men at Fort Carlton.

The Captain had made his decision, and he fell asleep comfortable that he had made the right one. Early the next morning, Palliser met the young lieu-tenant and informed him that since the Bow was an unknown river, he had rejected his request as being too risky. "I was moreover, told (after having at last demanded to know my position in the expedition)," wrote Blakiston, "that I was to consider myself under the order of another member [Hector]; immediately making which declaration, Captain Palliser rode off on an exploration of the southward, and I accompanied the remainder of the expe-dition to the site of Bow Fort . . ."

Blakiston was dumbfounded at Palliser's rejection and could hardly con-tain his anger. After all, had he not been added to the expedition on the rec-ommendations of General Edward Sabine and Major John Henry Lefroy, two immensely powerful men at the War Office? Both had vouched for Blakiston's stern conscientious sense of duty and enormous ability. He seemed perfectly suited for the position of magnetic observer, which required him to make tedious hourly observations of Earth's magnetic field, in order to determine deviations in magnetic north from true north.

But it was obvious to Palliser that the objectives of the expedition could not be carried out under Blakiston's command. Later Palliser explained that "when Blakiston 'thought proper to adopt a course of conduct' which left him no option, he decided that Hector, with his longer field experience, his steady judgment, and his ability to get on with the other members of the expedition and with the men, should have the responsibility."[6] In his mind, there was no doubt; Hector was the correct choice.

Palliser, having satisfied himself that he had made the best possible deci-sion and the best arrangements in organizing the branch expeditions, accompanied by John Sullivan, James Beads, Baptiste Gabriel, two other men, and thirteen horses, left on 3 August to explore the land between the British Territory and the international boundary. In his wake, he left behind an embittered and angry young lieutenant under the command of a civilian, a circumstance that would come back to haunt him.

OLD BOW FORT

PALLISER LEFT THE MAIN BRANCH OF THE EXPEDITION ON THE morning of 3 August. Hector, seemingly unfazed by the course of events between Palliser and Blakiston and armed with Palliser's explicit instructions, prepared for the trek into the mountains. Their sharp outline on the western horizon and the thought of finally being rid of the dreary prairies raised everyone's spirits, everyone's, that is, except Blakiston's.

Blakiston did not share this joyous mood and appeared even more sullen and withdrawn as he began deliberating his options. At times, he appeared so removed that he became oblivious to the other members of the party. He couldn't understand how Palliser could put an officer of the Royal Artillery under the command of a young and inexperienced civilian. His mind was in turmoil! How could he respond to Palliser's abrupt rejection both of him as deputy leader and of his plan to explore the Bow River? How could he regain his honour?

The disjoined party continued its relentless push toward the mountains.

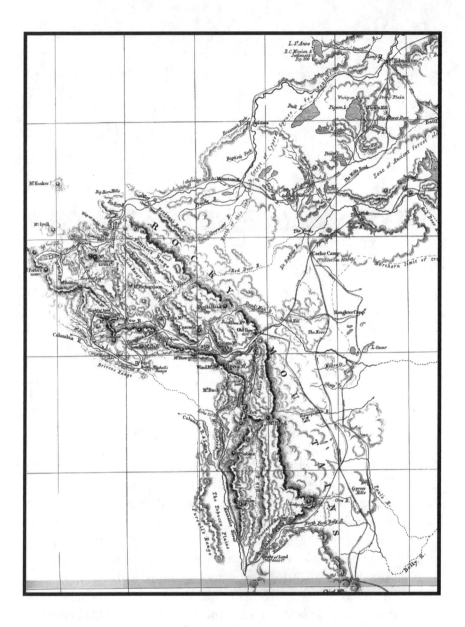

HECTOR'S AND PALLISER'S ROUTES IN 1858 FROM OLD BOW FORT
ACROSS THE ROCKIES AND BACK TO FORT EDMONTON
(*SOURCE:* MAPS)

On 6 August, as they traversed a magnificent plateau covered with brightly coloured wildflowers, they were rewarded with a magnificent view to the west. Hector could hardly contain his excitement. "The snow of the mountains with the foreground sharply lined by projecting ledges of rock was quite exhilarating, after the dreary monotony of the arid plains."

Intoxicated by the view, Hector rushed ahead, descending a succession of hills to reach the Bow River. The water was swift, cold, and clear. Protruding from its banks were layers of shale and sandstone, as well as seams of coal. To the northwest, the Wildcat Hills formed ridges lying parallel with the mountains. He paused long enough to make some detailed sketches.

"I got some fine trout from the river," Hector noted, "caught by some Indians that I met, and at night joined the carts before encamping under Dream Hill. Our camp was in a most picturesque position surrounded by well timbered hills except to the west, in which direction a level plain seemed to sweep up to the base of the mountains, foremost among which rose the craggy knob called the Devil's Head."

The next day's travel was a dawn-to-dusk affair over difficult terrain. "Half an hour after starting this morning we came to Deadman's River [Ghost River], and found that the plain we had been admiring the previous evening was really the valley of that river, which rises near the 'Devil's Head,'" Hector reported.

Near the junction of the Ghost and Bow Rivers, the group encountered considerable difficulty moving the carts down the steep embankment, before finding a shallow rapid where they were able to ford the river. Once on the left bank of the Bow, they headed west on terraces, following an ancient and rough Indian trail.

"As we travelled along we were met by a number of Stoney Indians who continued to accompany us during [the] day," wrote Hector. "At noon the valley commenced to become contracted and rocky, and we were much delayed by the carts getting repeatedly upset. Where we halted the river is hemmed in closely by rocks and forms a succession of rapids, and as the lands are well wooded the scenery has assumed quite an alpine character."

In the afternoon, they resumed their journey and the rough trail caused no end of problems. However, "with the help of the Indians, who were very well disposed, we reached the site of the Old Bow Fort at sunset, and encamped on a fine level shelf a few hundred yards up a creek that joins the Bow River at this point and elevated about 90 feet above the water."

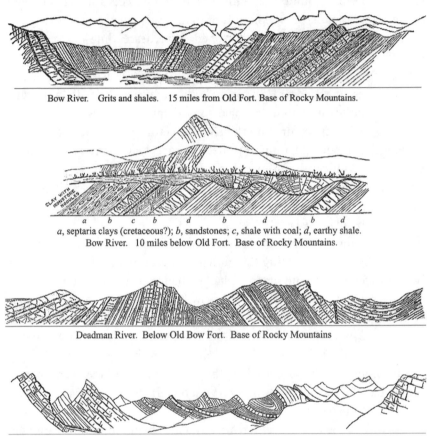

Bow River.   Grits and shales.   15 miles from Old Fort. Base of Rocky Mountains.

a, septaria clays (cretaceous?); *b*, sandstones; *c*, shale with coal; *d*, earthy shale.
Bow River.   10 miles below Old Fort.   Base of Rocky Mountains.

Deadman River. Below Old Bow Fort. Base of Rocky Mountains

Bow River. First longitudinal valley.

FIGURE 2: GEOLOGICAL SKETCHES MADE BY
HECTOR NEAR OLD BOW FORT

Old Bow Fort, situated at the foot of the mountains high on the north bank of the Bow River near the junction with the Kananaskis River and not far from Deadman's (Ghost) River, was the traditional staging site for parties entering the mountains. The fort was the brainchild of Governor George Simpson after the merger of the North West Company with the HBC in 1821. Simpson's plan was to lure the Peigan trade away from the Americans by constructing this new post on the banks of the Bow River.

In 1832, John Rowand, chief factor at Fort Edmonton at the time, chose the site situated above the Bow at the mouth of Old Fort Creek, about 210 miles by trail from Edmonton (just west of present-day Morley, Alberta). Henry Fisher was placed in charge of constructing the post, which under the command of chief factor John Harriott, opened for business in the fall of the same year. It was called Peigan Post in the hope that it would entice the Peigan to trade with the Company rather than with the Americans. The first season was a disaster. The Peigan had already traded most of their furs with the Americans, while the Bloods, Blackfoot, and Sarcees resented not being able to trade at the fort, instead having to travel to Edmonton to trade their wares. All became increasingly unruly. Fear of the Indians and a disappointing lack of trade forced the closure of Peigan Post in its first season, and it fell into a state of disrepair.

The HBC, however, was not about to give up so easily on its new post, and by 10 August of the following year, the fort had been completely rebuilt and was open for trade. But, once again, lack of trade and the constant fear of Indian attack made it impractical to keep the post operating, and it was abandoned for a second time on 4 January 1834. It was left to the mercy of the Sarcees, who lost no time in taking possession and dismantling it. The resulting ruins became known as Old Bow Fort.[1]

The main body of the expedition would stay at Old Bow Fort for three days. At the ruins of the old fort, Hector traded tobacco and ammunition for much-needed leather and pack saddles with his newfound Stoney friends. The Stoneys provided Hector with a wealth of information about his chosen route into the mountains, and one elderly Stoney sketched a map for him on birchbark. Erasmus indicated that this map "proved to be an invaluable aid in our search for a pass. This later proved to be near where the doctor met the serious accident with his saddle horse."[2]

On 11 August, Hector was ready to depart Old Bow Fort. He left horses and supplies meant for Palliser in the care of Palliser's guide, "Old Paul." Bourgeau decided to accompany Hector, but where was Nimrod? It had been

VIEW TO THE WEST FROM THE SITE OF OLD BOW FORT
*(H. POLLARD / LIBRARY AND ARCHIVES
CANADA, C-000531, C-000243)*

months and many days' travel since Hector had enlisted the Mountain Stoney's aid in guiding him through the mountains; had the man forgotten his commitment? Hector was greatly relieved that just in the nick of time, true to his word, Nimrod suddenly appeared. As they prepared to leave, the young doctor was completely unaware that Blakiston was meanwhile intent upon actions that would ultimately affect the course and makeup of the expedition.

Thomas Blakiston, preparing to fulfill his own orders, had delayed leaving Old Bow Fort an extra day; he had other things on his mind. Withdrawing to a secluded spot, he sat down and, after some "mature deliberation," penned a letter to the Captain wherein he "threw off his command." He left this letter with Old Paul, with instructions that he was to deliver it to the Captain immediately upon his arrival. On 14 August, the still bitter and resentful young lieutenant departed Old Bow Fort with his men in search of the Kootenay and Boundary Passes.

Palliser, not knowing what was in store for him, was racing back from the international boundary, and on 14 August arrived at the Bow River. "Continuing our ride along the south bank of the South Saskatchewan or Bow River, we passed three successive falls of the river; these falls, like the whole surrounding scene, were wild and beautiful. We were now right in the mountains, which towered majestically above us," he wrote.

Crossing the river above the third falls, they arrived at Old Bow Fort around 2:00 PM. Glancing around, he was inspired by the beautiful scenery. The peaks, their summits glistening from a recent sprinkling of snow, towered above in sharp contrast to the sombre forests at his feet. The Bow surged by "in all the wildness of mountain character, foaming at intervals over ledges of rock in its valley, and then rushing onwards between high banks, clad with luxuriant vegetation."

Palliser was less enthusiastic in describing what remained of the former Peigan Post: "the only portion remaining of this building are [sic] the stone chimneys; the rest of the fort, which was only of wood, has long since been burnt by the Indians." His hunters were relieved to see him for they had been living in dreadful fear of attack by the Peigan. He could see it in their eyes.

And then, Old Paul gave him Blakiston's letter:

Sir,
After our conversation on the 3rd inst., from which I infer that
private matters influence you in your public duties, my position in

Her Majesty's service will not allow of my considering myself any longer in anyway connected with the Exploring Expedition under your command.

I shall, however, carry out to the best of my power what I had undertaken previously to our conversation above referred to, namely, to survey the Kootanie [sic] Pass, and in the event of my reaching Edmonton in sufficient time, proceed with the Red River men by water to Fort Carlton, and arrange for their transport to Red River.

I have, &c.
Thomas Blakiston,
 Lieutenant, Royal Artillery[3]

Palliser's spirits were dashed. What were these "private matters" he referred to? He was dumbfounded! Could this be true? Blakiston had thrown off his command! Palliser couldn't believe that Blakiston had been so adversely affected by the decisions he had made at Slaughter Camp. He read the letter over again, just to be sure. In one brief moment, his excitement regarding the prospects of searching for the mysterious pass in the clouds had been quashed.

Once he regained his senses, he realized the enormity of Blakiston's decision. Originally, Palliser had planned to "proceed westward to Vancouver's Island after crossing the mountains, and leave the men and horses to return to the eastern slope and then to Edmonton, under the charge of Mr. Sullivan. I was aware that Captain (now Colonel) Hawkins[4] of the Engineers was engaged in laying down the boundary line from the Gulph [sic] of Georgia towards the Rocky Mountains, and a Government dispatch received by me last spring expressed a desire that I should communicate with Col. Hawkins." Only now did he realize that Blakiston had "deranged" his plans a little.

To make matters worse, he had to deal with a serious illness that indirectly impacted one of his men. "The wife of one of my hunters was taken very ill with inflammation; I feared she would have died. I blistered her severely, and gave her a great deal of medicine."

He feared she may have contracted the dreaded smallpox. Where was the doctor when he needed him? The next day, he noted: "Joseph's wife's face broken out: I am sure it is small-pox, but do not like to tell them so. She appeared to be better and free from pain, but very weak." Fortunately, she recovered. The source of the sickness is not revealed in the historical record; however, the fact that no other member of the expedition contracted the dreaded disease suggests it was not smallpox.

Palliser remained calm. Yes, he had been sabotaged by Blakiston but he had to remain focused. He instructed the men to prepare caches and bury "dry meat for Blakiston's and for Hector's parties" on their return, "in case they should get short, and not be able to support themselves in the mountains." And, he didn't forget about the welfare of the horses, instructing two men to return to Edmonton to begin putting up hay for the winter. Even under these disruptive circumstances, he remained in control and his thoughts were for the welfare of his colleagues and the horses. On 17 August 1858, Palliser left Old Bow Fort in search of Kananaskis Pass.

THE COLD WATER RIVER

LATE IN THE AFTERNOON OF 11 AUGUST 1858, AFTER PLACING horses and supplies for the Captain under the care of Old Paul, Hector began his journey: "I started at the same time with M. Bourgeau, who also wished to follow up the valley of Bow River. We both chose this route as it allowed of our entering the mountains at once without travelling further in the open country, which yields little of interest either to the geologist or the botanist."

From its icy glacial origins high on the Continental Divide, the Bow River winds a sinuous course over nearly three hundred miles to its confluence with the Old Man River west of Medicine Hat, where it becomes the South Saskatchewan. Originally, the Stoneys knew the river as *Mun-uh-cha-ban*, or "the places one takes bows from"; today, they call it *Mini-thni-Wapta*, the "Cold Water River." The Peigan had another name—*Manachabon sipi*, meaning "where the bow reeds grow." From sketchy, outdated maps, discussions with traders, and local Indian knowledge, Hector hoped to discover its source and a usable pass across this barrier to the Columbia River in British Columbia.

His party was small: "Peter Erasmus, Sutherland, and Brown, all Red River men, and also my Stoney Indian friend, who had promised the previous winter to serve as my guide in the mountains, and who had just turned up in time to keep his word." They travelled light: "I had with me eight horses, three of which served to carry all the little baggage I cared to take, consisting principally of instruments, bedding, ammunition, and tobacco; for I was assured that in the part of the mountains I intended to explore, there was an abundance of game, I did not take any provisions excepting a little tea and a few pounds of grease," and a private cache of pemmican. Hector would come to regret this decision.

Palliser had assigned three Red River men and seven horses to assist Bourgeau in the transport of his scientific and camping equipment. The carts in which Bourgeau had been enduring a bone-jarring journey since the start of the expedition were deemed expendable for mountain travel and left behind. The diminutive botanist, whose short, stubby legs could barely reach the stirrups, was not built to ride horses; his colleagues described him as a "shocking horseman."

Eugene Bourgeau, born in the village of Brizon, France, was forty-four years old when John Ball recommended him for the expedition. Affectionately known as "the prince of botanical collectors," he had few peers when it came to collecting and preserving botanical specimens. His father was a modest sheep herder, and not being born into affluence, Bourgeau did not have the benefit of a formal university education. He learned his botany the hard way—from nature, while tending his father's flocks high on the mountain slopes in the French Alps. Perhaps this humble upbringing was responsible for his modesty, a virtue that endeared him to all of his colleagues.

Carefully negotiating the steep ravine from Old Bow Fort to the Bow River, the small party soon passed the impressive falls on the river and "after three miles we saw the track leading to the ford by which the Bow River is crossed to reach Kananaskis Pass," wrote Hector. This was the *Ozade Chagu*, or the "Forks Trail," the traditional Stoney pack trail to the Kananaskis Lakes.

"Up to this point our trail passed through fine open woods of young pine, over high terraces," Hector wrote. "On reaching the first point where the valley narrowed, we had to cross over heaps of loose rounded stones that had been swept down by the torrents, so that we got on very slowly; our horses with their tender feet being quite unfit for such rough ground. We had, indeed, fixed light plate shoes on some of their feet, but these only seemed to

Bow River. Mountain. East side of first valley.

Bow River. First range. 3,000 ft. above the eye.

Bow River. Second range. 3,500 ft. above the eye.

Bow River. Cascade Mountain. 4,500 ft. above the eye.

FIGURE 3: GEOLOGICAL SKETCHES MADE BY
HECTOR IN THE BOW RIVER VALLEY

increase their discomfort. Above the contracted part of the valley we plunged into a labyrinth of dense forest, some of the black spruce trees being of great size, and struggled on through fallen timber till we reached the rocky spur of the mountain on our right, which above the torrent hems in the river so closely that we had to make a considerable ascent in order to pass over it. In the gorge thus formed there has been a great accumulation of shingle, not of the kind that forms terraces, but of larger and more angular fragments. This damming back the river has given rise to several lakes (*Lacs des arcs*) that occupy the width of the valley, except the channel of the river, with which they only communicate at flood season. The scene that opened up to us on crossing the point was very striking." Nimrod was following a trail that led to a traditional Stoney campsite known as "Indian Flats," near present-day Canmore, Alberta.

From the summit of a spur, near The Gap west of present-day Exshaw, Alberta, they were presented with a magnificent view. "Just beyond a second spur like the one we were upon, we had a peep into a valley so wide and extensive that it appeared to us hemmed in as we were by precipices several thousand feet in height, that we were looking right through the range into comparatively open country. The peaks on either hand were of bold grotesque, caused by the varying power of resistance which the contorted strata composing the mountains present to the atmosphere." The geological prospects excited Hector and he lingered to make a few exquisite sketches. Meanwhile, Bourgeau could think only of collecting alpine plants. A faint trail descended the spur, and they encamped at 9:00 PM in an open, rocky spot beside a small lake.

Bourgeau referred to the Bow River as the "*River des Arcs*" and wrote to his mentor, William Hooker: "In ascending this river, it is found to flow from a large valley in the interior of the mountains, which I have named the *Valley des Arcs*, as far as the second lake, there being a first and second *Lake des Arcs*. The high peaks of this valley bear the following names: —*Pic des Pigeons, Pic de la Grotte, Pic du Vent*, the last being so named from the storms which begin on its summit."[1] Wind Ridge, north of *Pic du Vent*, caught his eye and would become his favourite collecting site.

Bourgeau found the work difficult and demanding. "There are considerable obstacles to travelling in the mountains," he wrote. "The forests suffer almost every year from fires; the trees fall in all directions on the ground and thus form innumerable barricades to the progress of horses and even of men. To ascend to the summit of a mountain, a very hard day's work is needed to cross the forest region. This description holds good in all the localities which I have visited."[2] He would remain in this beautiful valley, collecting specimens, for only seventeen days. He would cite "weighty reasons" for his short stay; whatever these reasons were is anyone's guess, but his fear of the Indians and a possible lack of provisions, coupled with his distaste for travel on horseback, were probably incentive enough.

Bourgeau and Hector would part company on 12 August, but not before spending an exhilarating morning together on the lower slopes of Grotto Mountain. At dawn, they began their ascent. Hector reported: "After ascending 500 feet we got out of timber, but more by getting onto rugged surfaces of rock, as large trees were growing at least 800 feet higher in favourable situations. At this point Bourgeau began to get alpine plants in abundance, among which was a saxifrage with a denticulate leaf. We followed up the rocky bed of a torrent till our progress was stopped at a point where the stream commences by a trickling fall, several hundred feet in height, into a clear pool with green mossy banks, and in which we performed our morning abulations [sic]. On one side of this little valley is a great deposit of angular blocks of rock, mixed with calcareous clay, forming the sides to a height of 150 feet. In this deposit we found a large cave, with a high arched roof and narrow mouth, and like Robinson Crusoe's one, with its old goat for a tenant, but in this case he had long been dead. The floor was quite battered hard by the tracks of sheep and goats.

"Turning from this point, which was 1,000 feet above our camp, we descended by another spur of the mountain to breakfast."

In a way it was a bittersweet breakfast they shared, as Bourgeau would remain to botanize on the slopes of Windy Mountain. Hector was disappointed at leaving his cheerful companion, whose wonderful attitude and cheery disposition were so infectious that they were an inspiration to everyone, in complete contrast to Blakiston's vitriolic nature. Palliser was so impressed by Bourgeau's work ethic that he was moved to state that Bourgeau "has been a most active energetic and excellent companion, always hard at work in which his whole soul seems engrossed and no matter what his fatigues or privations may be his botanical specimens are always his first care. ... Little Bourgeau is a Brick his collections to me (who know nothing of Botany,) very pretty and the colours as vivid after the specimens are saved as they are in Life—He is most indefatigable and always at work."

Bourgeau's collections consisted of dried and pressed plants, seeds, and roots for culture, and vegetables cultivated and used by the Aboriginal peoples. "The collection of flowering plants and ferns consists of 819 species, belonging to 349 genera and 92 orders, which is more than two-fifths of the total flora of North America."[3]

Bourgeau could hardly wait to finish a meal before he was off in search of plants, and each evening he would spend hours meticulously preparing his specimens. This infectious attitude even moved Erasmus. "The Botanist's enthusiasm was almost as great as a gold miner in the discovery of a big nugget," he wrote. "It gave me a lot of amused satisfaction to watch his delight when he found a new species. I watched for new plants in my travels with Dr. Hector and when I was fortunate enough to bring an addition to his collection I was treated to a lesson that was most instructive.

"I knew that the Indians sought out plants that they used in their medicines with remarkable effect. I could never again heedlessly trample plants without reminding myself of this man's gentle and almost reverent handling of a rarity in plant life."[4]

At noon on 12 August, Hector took leave of his companion and followed a track that led over the spur of Grotto Mountain before emerging into a magnificent valley. "We passed some singular masses of the concrete that forms the terraces left standing like the spars and chimneys on the sloping face of the deposit. At dark we camped by some old Indian wigwams where the valley is wide and flat, and with fine patches of level prairie along the river for our horses. Just opposite our camp there is a mountain with three peaks which form a striking group, while a little further up the valley there is a cross valley or nick bounded by a very lofty precipice. Being right in the middle of the valley we were about 1 ? miles from the mountains on either side."

"Wishing to give Nimrod a chance to get us some meat, of which we already stood in need," Hector decided to remain at "Indian Flats" for three days. Besides, the lush prairie grass would provide excellent fodder for the horses. In the meantime, the young doctor occupied himself by scrambling up the lower slopes of peaks on the north side of the valley to collect fossils, make geological notes, and sketch. He cast a wishful eye at the beautiful ridge arching to the sky directly above their camp but lacked time to ascend it. Perhaps he'd get another chance, he thought.

A distinct chill was in the air when they commenced their journey up the valley on the morning of 15 August. "Here the shingle deposits were again greatly developed, and travelling on the terraces we kept well from the river till we reached a beautiful little prairie at the base of the 'Mountain where the water falls,' as the Indian name has it, or the Cascade Mountain." Nimrod referred to the thread-like stream of water cascading down the face of the mountain, which had acted as a landmark for many generations, by its Stoney name, *Mini-ha-pa*. They encamped in the beautiful little prairie at the base of the falls.

That evening, an "old friend," the one who had sketched a map for them, came wandering into camp. The old Stoney, "from the Indian camp we had left at the old Bow Fort, joined us this evening," wrote Hector, "having come through the first range by a pass to the south of the 'Devil's Head,' in which he says there is a lake the length of half a day's march, where they catch the finest trout and white fish in the country. At the upper end of the lake which sends a stream to the Bow River just below where we are camped, he says there is a 'height of land' to be crossed, and from the other side of which rises Deadman's [Ghost] River." This was the traditional route into the mountains past lake *Minnee-wah-kah*, the Stoney term for "Lake of the Water Spirit." It was not only a much safer route, because it avoided land controlled by the Blackfoot, but also contained abundant game. Sir George Simpson and James Sinclair had used this very route in 1841 when they crossed the mountains. The old Stoney also informed Hector that he had used this route in 1847 when he guided the Reverend Robert Rundle to this little prairie at the base of Cascade Mountain.[5]

According to Nimrod, the route ahead was a mess of fallen timber, so they decided to delay at the little prairie, sending the men in advance to clear a reasonable track. This would give the young doctor time to explore the lower slopes of Cascade Mountain, north of the present-day townsite of Banff. The next morning around eight o'clock, Hector began his ascent. After some vicious bushwhacking, he broke clear of timber about one thousand feet above the valley and stopped to search for fossils. This was a good excuse to catch his breath. Suddenly, to his amazement, he writes, "a humming bird, blown by a strong west gale, flew against my face, but I did not succeed in capturing it. This is the first I have seen since leaving Red River settlement, and it certainly seemed quite out of place among the alpine vegetation."

Following the base of a precipice, he found that he could not pass without descending into "an immense corrie," from which he startled a large band of sheep. He stopped to observe:

> These animals are singularly matched by nature with the colour
> of the grey limestone rocks, so long as they are looking towards the
> observer, when it requires a skilful eye to detect them; but the

moment they turn to flee they become very conspicuous, as every part of their body as seen from behind is pure white. It is often quite startling in ascending a mountain and gazing as you suppose at nothing but grey rocks, when suddenly a flock of white objects appear fleeing away from you, and as suddenly they seem to vanish when their inquisitive habits make them wheel in a mass to have another look.

The bottom of the corrie was filled with large angular blocks of rock, and patches of snow remained almost converted into ice, but not worthy of being termed glaciers. Among the blocks of rock the sifleurs or mountain marmots kept whistling in a very loud shrill note answering one another, and I also heard the squeaking note of the little Pica or tailless hare, which is very common here. This is one of the most comical animals I have seen. It is about the size of a small rat, but made exactly like any other rabbit, excepting that it has round open ears. It sits up on its hind legs and calls its note in the most impudent fashion faster and faster as you approach, but always ready to pop out of sight so quickly that you can hardly shoot them, at least with a flint gun.

The sifleur generally plays the same trick, but he is not impudent, and does not allow you to come so close before he dives among the rocks.

Hector ended his adventurous day slipping, sliding, and thrashing his way through stunted evergreens and undergrowth so dense that he sometimes found it easier to slide over their tops. Finally reaching the bottom of the valley, he stumbled back into camp just in time for supper. It had been an exhausting but exhilarating day on Cascade Mountain.

Shortly after sunrise on the morning of 17 August, all were ready to resume their journey. Instructing Sutherland, Brown, and Erasmus to take charge of the pack horses and follow the trail cleared the previous day, Hector and Nimrod "set off to see a fine fall on the river, which lay about three miles out of the direct course. A high hill stands out in the centre of the valley, and it is in breaking past this that the river is compressed into a very narrow spout-like channel, and then leaps over a ledge of rocks about 40 feet in height."

After this brief visit, they hastened to rejoin their colleagues, but not before encountering a band of sheep from which they culled two ewes. They would provide a nice addition of fresh meat for their larder. Above the falls, the river became dilated and sluggish, the valley became filled "with large swampy lakes," and the animal track they were following became so muddy they were forced to seek drier ground high on the lower slopes of Mount Norquay.

From his vantage point, Hector made note of many of the prominent geological features of the valley. "The Terrace Mountain, which overhangs the first longitudinal valley, corresponding to Cascade Mountain on the other side of the river, is composed of the same limestones and shales dipping at 50° W.S.W.

"This direction of the dip prevails throughout the range, but it is probable that the limestones which are thrown up almost vertically on its western flank are the lowest beds, the whole group forming one synclinal trough, that has been completely overthrown.

"Looking up the valley to the W.S.W. we had before us a truncated mountain, evidently composed of massive horizontal strata, and which I named Mount Bourgeau. The pass Sir George Simpson crossed the Rocky Mountains by in his journey round the world lies to the south of this mountain, and I half thought of crossing the river and following it, but we found so much 'white water' in the streams from the south, showing that they were in flood, that the old Indian who still travelled with us said we would fail in getting through that way, as the valley is so bad at one place as to require travelling actually in the stream, between perpendicular walls of rock, for half a day, and if it is flooded this becomes impossible. I, therefore, determined to continue up the same side of Bow River, until opposite an old neglected pass that used to be used by Cree war parties, and known as the Vermilion Pass."[6]

Finally, they came upon the cleared track and were able to make much better progress, joining the rest of the party shortly after noon. By now, the midday heat had become so oppressive that they decided to halt and seek some shade, rest the animals, and feast on some of the fresh mutton they had killed earlier that morning.

"The meat was in fine order, and had no particular flavour," wrote Hector, "yet it made not only myself but also other two of the party very sick. This, however, was the only time I ever saw this kind of meat disagree with the stomach, so it may have been due to some ailment in that particular animal, as we all soon came to consider the wild mutton of the grey sheep as the finest food we could get."

Two hours later, the heat had subsided and so had their indigestion. Once again they were fit for travel and, crossing a low point of rocks near the river, entered another great valley along the eastern side of which ran "a wall of vertical beds, of light grey limestone, the serrated edges of which at once suggested the name of Sawback Range for them."

Hector observed a noticeable change in the character of the mountains. "On the west side we have quite a change in the features of the mountains. The strata which compose them are nearly horizontal, and the mountains form cubical blocks or ranges of battlement-like precipices, while super-imposed masses resemble towers and bastions." This was in complete contrast to the dip-sloping so characteristic of the peaks comprising the eastern slopes.

The path ahead was a nightmare: in some places a quagmire, in others a spongy morass covered with scrubby pine and spruce. When given a choice between making their way through a quagmire or chopping their way through the deadfall higher upslope, they chose the swamp, and the horses suffered miserably. The swampy conditions and the intense heat of the valley bottom began to try their patience and drain their energy. After some time they managed to extricate themselves from this morass, and finding a nice spot with rich pasture, they encamped.[7] It had taken seven hours of hard work to reach this spot, which Hector thought to be "a fair day's work in the mountains."

That evening, Hector's eye was drawn to two more interesting geological features in the Bow Valley. "There are many caves in the limestone precipices of the Sawback range, some of them at a great altitude above the valley. Seeming to stand out in the centre of the valley is a very remarkable mountain, still at a distance of 12 miles, which looks exactly like a gigantic castle." His excitement began to mount with the realization, from the information and the map received from the old Stoney, that they were nearing the pass that offered a possible route across the backbone of the continent.

Shortly after breakfast on the morning of 18 August, they broke camp, fully expecting to be at the base of their objective by nightfall. "Soon after starting this morning we came to a hill, about 400 feet high, from which I took a set of bearings, and got a fine view of the mountains," Hector noted. "Through a deep valley to the southwest is a very massive mountain, completely snow capped. To the S.E., down the valley there is also a snow-capped mountain, but up the valley there is quite a number of peaks, none of them prominent, but all glittering white. Castle Mountain I now saw to be connected to the east side of the valley."[8]

After travelling for about three more hours, they spotted Nimrod frantically waving from the top of a hill, trying to get their attention. He had wounded a moose and in his haste to pursue the animal had fallen and broken his knife. One of the pieces had hurt his back, but nonetheless he had continued to track the animal for about four miles and knew where it was hiding. He invited Hector to finish the beast off. "Advancing against the wind without disturbing a branch we got within 40 yards of him, standing with his long nose straight out, and his antlers laid back on his flanks. I gave him the benefit of both my rifle barrels, which was the first notice he had of our proximity. After that he only bounded about 70 yards before he fell. When we approached him, however, he showed fight, and got up again, but it would not do, as he was going fast."

It was a splendid young bull still in velvet, which stood more than six feet at the shoulders. They butchered the animal on the spot and, after slinging pieces of its carcass over the pack horses, made their way back to the main party. Erasmus would not feast on the fresh moose nose that evening, however; in the heat of the day, he had gone off hunting and become lost. It was becoming painfully obvious to the young doctor that he would have to rely on Nimrod's skills as hunter and guide if his small contingent was to survive in the mountains.

It required three more laborious hours of hacking through deadfall that rose breast-high on their horses before they finally reached the base of Castle Mountain. Here, Hector writes, "we camped by the side of a small clear stream, and for the first time put up the little wigwam I had traded for from the 'Stoneys,' as I intended to remain here a couple of nights and prepare the moose meat."[9] Erasmus returned to camp tired and exhausted after spending a cold night in the mountains without a coat.

On 19 August, all of the men excepting Hector and Sutherland busily occupied themselves preparing the previous day's kill. The carcass was sliced into thin strips, hung on drying racks, and smoked. This would prevent spoilage. Hector had little time for such mundane tasks. Accompanied by Sutherland, he slipped off to explore the lower slopes of Castle Mountain. Hector later described their expedition:

> We had a tedious walk through the woods for five miles, before we made much of an ascent, but then we began to rise very rapidly. At 1,000 feet above the valley, before we had got quite out of the woods, we came to a cliff, about 80 feet high, composed of quartzite and indurated sandstone of a pinkish hew; the beds were nearly horizontal, and as they seem to continue so all the way to the top of the moun-

Bow River.   Second. longitudinal valley.   Mt. Bourgeau.

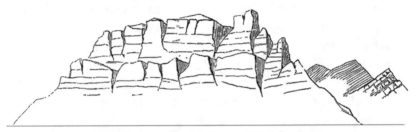

Castle Mountain, in second longitudinal valley.   5,000 ft. above the eye.

Vermilion Pass.   Third range.

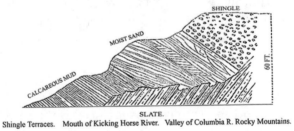

Shingle Terraces.   Mouth of Kicking Horse River.   Valley of Columbia R. Rocky Mountains.

FIGURE 4: GEOLOGICAL SKETCHES MADE BY HECTOR FROM CASTLE MOUNTAIN TO KICKING HORSE RIVER

tain, which is at least 3,000 feet higher, these quartzites must be the lowest beds I saw.

On this cliff we first heard the call of the sifleur. Above the point is a grassy slope, having an inclination of 33°, and so slippery that it was only with great trouble that we got over it; it would seem to indicate the occurrence of some soft beds that have weathered into the slope. After this we reached the first of the cliff ranges that are so conspicuous from the valley below; it was composed of quartzite, passing into a conglomerate of pebbles of milk quartz and other rocks.

When 2,000 feet above the valley we passed round to the N. side of the mountain, and found that a deep valley separated it from a lower spur composed of splintery shale of a dull red colour. The mass of the mountain, which yet rose 2,000 feet above us, seemed to be composed of thick bedded limestones, and these breaking away as the soft shales below them seem to have been destroyed has given rise to the castellated appearance.

We saw several bands of sheep, but did not get a shot; however, we killed two of the marmots or sifleurs. It is the size of a badger, with coarse short hair and no proper fur. It has large incisor teeth like those of the beaver; it lives among the rocks, and has a large nest, in which it lays up stores of provisions for winter, during which season it never comes aboard; but whether it hybernates [*sic*] or not the Indians do not know. It returns to its hole late in September, at which time it is very fat, and quite as good eating as the beaver, having the same rat flavour.

Hector and Sutherland were tired men when they returned to camp around eight o'clock that evening, having had twelve hours of hard walking. Boiled moose nose and fresh marmot were eagerly devoured by the hungry hikers, who hadn't eaten anything substantial since breakfast. While enjoying a cup of muskeg tea, prepared from the leaves of the Labrador tea plant, "which makes a capital beverage in absence of a better," Hector meticulously studied the rudimentary map and asked many questions of the old Stoney.

Soon the calming effects of the tea combined with the physical exertion of the day took their toll, and the young doctor fell fast asleep and dreamt of discovering a usable route across the Great Divide.

THE KICKING HORSE INCIDENT

IT IS UNCLEAR WHY HECTOR ABANDONED THE BOW VALLEY IN favour of the route the old Stoney had sketched for him. Perhaps he had been convinced it would lead directly across the Great Divide to the Columbia River. In any event, he chose to follow the route outlined on the crude map.

The map indicated a line of travel away from the Bow toward the height of land that led to the *Usna Waki-Cagubi,* or "where the red clay spirit is taken" (the Paint Pots), and this intrigued Hector. This is where the Kootenay Indians obtained the red ochre pigment, an important item of trade. This red pigment was a powerful symbol to the Stoneys, who believed it was made by *Waheambah,* or "the Sun," and had the power to yield the life-strength of blood.

On the morning of 20 August 1858, Hector and his party began their trek. "The moose meat having been sliced and partially smoked, we started to cross the river at 9 a.m., having spent the morning searching for a ford. The place where we crossed the river is only 60 yards wide, but very rapid, and

"KICKED BY A HORSE"

(*SEAN DOYLE*)

taking our horses above the girth if they kept the oblique line of the ford we had discovered, but some of them that turned to go more directly were obliged to swim."

A difficult and steep ascent followed. "We at first followed the brink of a valley, which the creek has cut through the superficial deposits. We then struck through the wood to the south-west, which clothe the gentle sloping and wide valley that leads to the height of land. Finding the lowest ground of the valley to be rather soft, although we were away from the creek a considerable distance, I kept more on the mountain side, so that we had to make a descent to the real watershed, the position of which so near the Bow River and so slightly elevated, took me quite by surprise."

After six hours of travel and, by Hector's reckoning, not more than twelve miles, they passed a deep blue lake, only to find they were considerably above the actual pass. After a steep descent, they found that "the small stream along which we ascended here ends in two small lakes, the water of which is beautifully clear; and 200 yards further on, and at 17 feet above the level of the upper lake, we came on a rapid and turbid stream, flowing to the S.W., which was the head of the Vermilion River, the principal branch of the Kootanie River."[1] These were the first waters they had encountered flowing *toward* the Pacific and here they encamped.

Hector was not the first man to cross this watershed, nor did he ever claim responsibility for its discovery, but he was the first to record crossing the Vermilion Pass, and he was astonished by the ease with which he had reached the height of land. "The ascent to the watershed from the Saskatchewan [Bow River] is hardly perceptible to the traveller, who is prepared for a tremendous climb by which to reach the dividing ridge of the Rocky Mountains," he wrote, "and no labour would be required, except that of hewing timber to construct an easy road for carts, by which it might be attained."

In their final report, Hector and Palliser would conclude that "of all the passes traversed by our Expedition, the most favourable and inexpensive to render available for wheel conveyances would appear to be Vermilion pass, as the ascent along it to the height of land is the most gradual of them all."

Leaving the men to set up camp, Hector set out to explore the lower slopes of the peak to the east (exactly which peak this was is uncertain—possibly Storm Mountain). After reaching the treeline and studying the landscape, he concluded that the peak "is a mere spur from a large central mass of snow-capped mountains to the south-east, which I named Mount Ball, after the Under-Secretary of State for the Colonies [in 1857]. On the opposite side of the valley I saw that the Vermilion River rises from a glacier of small size in a high valley of Mount Lefroy."[2] Hector quickly lost track of time and only with considerable difficulty stumbled down the slopes to reach camp long after dark. Once again, there was a late supper enjoyed beneath the canopy of a brilliant Milky Way.

The next morning they awoke to a heavy mist, which had soaked all their supplies, including the dried moose meat. It was the first moisture they had encountered since entering the mountains, and it was a bad omen. After breaking camp, they began the long descent of the western side of Vermilion Pass, a descent that took four hours and, by Hector's reckoning, covered only about six miles in a straight line. "The dense woods often compelled us to cross and recross the stream, it being so much easier to travel on the shingle in the channel than chop our way through the forest; but there is no want of level land on both sides of the stream along which a trail might be cut, which might be followed in any state of the stream."

Finally, around noon, "we arrived at a sudden bend which the river makes to the south-east, changing its course at right angles. Here, in the corner of the valley on the right side, is the Vermilion Plain, which is about a mile in extent, with a small stream flowing through it. Its surface is entirely covered with yellow ochre, washed down from the ferruginous shales in the mountains. The Kootanie Indians come to this place sometimes, and we found the remains of a camp and of a large fire which they had used to convert the ochre into the red oxide which they take away to trade to the Indians of the low country, and also to the Blackfeet as a pigment, calling it vermilion." This was the *Usna Waki-Cagubi*, where three cold mineral springs heavily laden with iron-oxide stain the soil its brilliant colour. The Indians considered this a place of "great medicine," where the *Macoya Debe*, or "Little People," watched over these soils, acting not only as their guardian but also bringing the soils to the surface where they could be found.

The next three days were occupied in the descent of the Vermilion River. The journey was marked by all manner of difficulty as they searched in vain for a suitable track. As they hacked their way through fallen timber and an almost impenetrable growth of cedar, they were plagued by drenching rains. "Every bush and tree was loaded with moisture, it soon did not matter much whether we went into the river or not, so that we frequently saved a difficult turn by accepting a ducking." Unknown to the men, their dried moose meat was rotting away.

Just before entering a gorge (Hector Gorge), they encountered a thick deposit of white, gritty, calcareous material, where in many places "the banks showed the marks of teeth, where the white goats had been gnawing it, and their wool was plentiful on the bushes all round." Nimrod suggested that the men collect pieces of this soft slate, as it would make excellent pipes.

After passing through the gorge, they entered a wide valley, encamping in a lovely meadow where the Vermilion joins the Kootenay River. "There is some confusion," noted Hector, "as to which is called the Vermilion and which the Kootanie River in the accounts given by the Indians, so I have thought it better to confine the former name to the large stream by which I descended, and consider the smaller stream into which it flows as the Kootanie River. This accords better with [the] nature of the valleys, as the Kootanie River, although an insignificant stream, before receiving the Vermilion River flows S.E. through a magnificent valley from three to five miles in breadth."

Hector thought of following the Kootenay River south, but Palliser had explicitly instructed him to confine his explorations to the waterline of the mountains and to return to Edmonton by early October. Furthermore, they were now "beginning to be pinched for provisions" as they hadn't encountered any game to replenish their depleting larder. He turned north into territory completely unfamiliar to Nimrod, in search of the headwaters of the Kootenay, hoping that it would lead to the Columbia.

As they broke camp on the morning of 24 August, Nimrod, who had been off early to hunt, "returned shortly as white as it is possible for a red Indian to be with fear. He had been chasing a deer, and had suddenly come on a panther [mountain lion], but further than saying that he had wounded him, we could get him to tell us nothing." These secretive carnivores were so seldom seen by the Indians that they feared them even more than the grizzly, "although there is no comparison between the ferocity of the two animals," wrote Hector.

Suddenly they found the route extremely difficult if not impossible, and according to their itinerary, they made no more than four miles. Hector gave up and encamped. He sent Nimrod and Erasmus ahead to search for a suitable trail. They came back, having discovered a faint animal trail higher on the terraces that led up the valley. The next day they had another encounter with a mountain lion. "Shortly after passing two streams, one from each side of the valley, we encamped in some burnt woods by the side of a morass. As we were encamping, we heard the cries of a panther, which are exactly like those of an infant. Nimrod says that they call in this manner when they come on the tracks of men and horses, and he seemed to think it might come close, or even into our camp during the night; so when he lay down to sleep, he kept his '*dagare*,' or big Indian knife, close to his hand."

That evening they discovered the disastrous effects the dampness had had on their moose meat, which, "although well enough prepared to keep in the dry climate of the east slope, had within the last few days completely rotted." This was serious, as they hadn't encountered any game since leaving Vermilion Pass days earlier.

On 26 August, they reached the height of land dividing the headwaters of the Kootenay and Beaverfoot Rivers. "The watershed is in a large morass, with several lakes occupying the bottom of a deep wide valley, common to the two streams, although flowing in opposite directions," Hector recorded. "The line of the watershed is so little marked that it is impossible to cross even on foot between the two streams without going in water." The serenity of the valley, the beauty of the lakes, and the warm waters beckoned the weary travellers; besides, it had been some time since they had had a bath!

"The day had cleared up, and the scene where we encamped on the margin of the upper lake was fresh and charming," Hector noted. "Its shallow waters were thrown into waves by a stiff westerly breeze, and splashed on a shore of pure white sand; but when we entered the lake to bathe, we found that a few yards from the shore it had a muddy bottom that was almost unfathomable."

While basking in the sunshine, Hector had time to reflect on their route. "A road for carts down the valley of Vermilion River, from the height of land to the Kootanie River, could be cleared without difficulty, for, supposing the road to follow a straight line along the river, and the descent to be uniform, which it almost is, the incline would only be 40 feet in a mile, or 1 in 135.

"The absence of any abrupt steps, either in the ascent or descent, together with the small altitude to be passed over, form very favourable points in the consideration of this pass as a line of route." (He was correct; in the fall of 1922, this route became Highway 93, the Banff-Windermere Highway.)

On 27 August, they began the long descent of the Beaverfoot, and the swampy conditions encountered in the valley made travel almost impossible. Hector named two glittering peaks on the northeast side of the valley Mount Goodsir and Mount Vaux, while the unbroken wall on the opposite side of the valley he named after Captain Brisco, Palliser's valued friend and fellow sportsman. Intuition told him that the river they were following must be a tributary of the Columbia, which was probably just across the unbroken wall to the west. Nimrod disagreed, stating that "he recognized a mountain which he knew to be upon the North Saskatchewan, and accordingly said we were descending a branch of that river. I however thought that hardly possible, as the vegetation was too luxuriant for the east side of the mountains, and we were already at too low an elevation for the rapid stream that we were upon to be any feeder of the Saskatchewan." Hector's deduction would prove to be correct.

It took three days of constant struggle to descend the Beaverfoot. The band of men, now weary from chopping their way through deadfall, extricating their horses mired in mud, being wet from constant rains, and starving from lack of food, finally emerged from their predicament on 29 August. Their horses had fared no better, emerging cut and bruised from constantly leaping over deadfall. Lack of good pasture not only tried their patience but made them very testy. But where were they? Fate was about to intervene!

"We had travelled a few miles when we came to a large flat, where the wide valley terminated, dividing into two branch valleys, one from the north-west and the other from the south-west," Hector later recalled. "Here we met a very large stream, equal in size to the Bow River where we crossed it. This river descends the valley of Beaverfoot River, turns back on its course at a sharp angle, receives that river as a tributary, and flows off to the south-west through the other valley. Just above the angle there is a fall about 40 feet in height, where the channel is contracted by perpendicular rocks."[3]

Now it was necessary to get the outfit safely across the river, a difficult and tedious process at the best of times, but even more difficult when dealing with animals whose patience was wearing thin and who resented fording an unknown and angry torrent.

It was here, at around 11:30 AM on 29 August 1858, that James Hector suffered the near-fatal mishap that would be immortalized in the name of the Kicking Horse Pass.

Hector wrote of the incident: "A little way above this fall, one of our pack horses, to escape the fallen timber, plunged into the stream, luckily where it formed an eddy, but the banks were so steep that we had great difficulty in getting him out.

"In attempting to recatch my own horse, which had strayed off while we were engaged with the one in the water, he kicked me in the chest, but I had luckily got close to him before he struck out, so that I did not get the full force of the blow. However, it knocked me down and rendered me senseless for some time. This was unfortunate, as we had seen no tracks of game in the neighbourhood, and were now without food; but I was so hurt that we could not proceed further that day at least. My men covered me up under a tree, and I sent them all off to try and raise something to eat." Sutherland managed to get a rope around the beast and pull the horse from the eddy to safety.

Hector's account of this accident makes it appear as if he remained in control of the situation, despite being rendered "senseless for some time"; however, the account by Peter Erasmus paints a more dire picture of the situation.

According to Erasmus, Hector was unconscious and remained so for some time. "We all leapt from our horses and rushed up to him," recalled Erasmus, "but all our attempts to help him recover his senses were of no avail. We then carried him to the shade of some big evergreens while we pitched camp. We were now in serious trouble, and unless Nimrod fetched in some game our situation looked hopeless. One man stayed and watched the unconscious doctor."[4]

In Erasmus's version of events, confusion reigned as men yelled and tried frantically to bring the horses under control. The commotion only served to confuse the animals even more and they bolted in total disarray. It is under such circumstances, when panic sets in, that time passes rapidly. Sometime thereafter, which Erasmus estimated to have been at least two hours, the men had gathered their senses, but had given up all hope for their young leader. Erasmus lent an ear to Hector's chest and, unable to detect any sign of life, declared the obvious. Stricken with grief, the men began to dig Hector's grave.

All of a sudden "Sutherland yelled for us to come up; he now was conscious but in great pain," wrote Erasmus. "I woke in time to behold my grave yawning for me," Hector later recalled. "My friends had decided I was dead and they were doing the last respectful act—putting me under the sod." Legend has it that as he was about to be buried, Hector regained consciousness and, looking skyward, winked; this drew the attention of Sullivan and saved Hector from an untimely interment. "I did not use that grave. Instead, they named the river the Kicking Horse, and gave the Pass, which we made our way through a few days later, the same name."[5]

When the doctor regained consciousness, the pain in his chest was unbearable and he could hardly move without fainting. Barely able to talk, he directed Erasmus to retrieve his medical kit and instructed Peter to prepare a medicinal concoction from ingredients he always carried.[6] He knew from experience that this preparation would ease the pain. Erasmus became concerned that he might make a mistake preparing the medicine and would be held responsible for the doctor's death, so "I had him sign a document stating the facts of the accident in case his illness might prove serious. He readily agreed that it would be the proper thing to do." The narcotic had its desired effect and Hector dozed off.

All the turmoil had agitated the men, and in their flustered state, they began to discuss their situation. They were in serious trouble; not only was their leader injured but they were also out of food and Nimrod wasn't sure where they were. When Hector regained consciousness, the powerful properties of the drug had eased the pain but he was still unable to move. He could see the panic in the eyes of his men. Quickly, before he dozed off again, he sought to restore order and gain control. Nimrod, Sutherland, and Brown were dispatched to hunt for game, while Erasmus was instructed to ascend a low mountain in the angle of the valley to obtain bearings. Hector still held aspirations of continuing west in search of the Columbia, but deep down he knew that his unfortunate accident had left him unfit for the task. Better to find a way out of their predicament!

Alas, that evening the hunters returned empty-handed. They had followed tracks of deer and wapiti but had encountered nothing. Nimrod, however, did return with a bit of encouraging news, having found two faint trails, probably left the previous summer by "Shouswaps or Kootanies [sic]," that appeared to follow the river and "go high up over the mountain." Hector was encouraged by the news. Perhaps Nimrod's discovery would be their salvation.

Although Hector thought that the horse's blow had broken some of his ribs, this could not have been the case, as severe pain and respiratory difficulties would have continued for weeks after the accident.[7] However, one thing was evident: he was in no condition to ride. By noon the next day, his condition had greatly improved but, still unable to ride, he sent the men off to hunt. Once again they returned empty-handed, although they reported sighting a large herd of goats. But Nimrod had fallen while tracking a bighorn and had run a sharp spike into his foot, rendering him unable to hunt. It was Erasmus's turn to prove his prowess. Unfortunately, Erasmus had never professed to be a good hunter.

Erasmus later wrote of his experience:

Nimrod gave me directions to where he had last tracked the sheep. I had not yet reached the place when I spotted some of the animals across a deep ravine. They had not seen me or scented my presence. Taking advantage of every cover I could, crawling on my knees for the

most part, I reached a point directly opposite. Trembling with
excitement and weakness, I slowly raised my head above the cover
and looked. There in plain sight was a big sentinel sheep, his head
raised watching something in the opposite direction. He was standing dead still. I slowly pushed my gun across a dead log and tried
to take aim, but my eyes watered and the gun shook so I had to wait
to calm my nerves.

Biting my lips in vexation at my foolish nerves, I finally got a grip
on myself, took aim, and fired. He gave a tremendous leap and landed
nearly twenty feet below, tumbling and rolling to the bottom of the
ravine. I knew the sheep was dead. The others disappeared in a twinkling
of an eye. I lay for a moment stunned at the effectiveness of my long shot,
then with a yell that echoed back from the mountain, scrambled and
slid down the slope after my kill.

It was hard to keep from dancing and holding my gun in triumph as
I had seen some of my Indian friends do after some extraordinary shot.
I quickly skinned the animal, cut off a thigh for my carrying sac and hit
back for camp, anxious to carry the good news to the others. Nimrod got
up and hobbled over to where I had placed the meat. After examining
the meat he turned to me in disappointment. 'No good, Peter. No good.
Can't eat.' Then I remembered: I had killed a buck, and at that time of
year, during the rutting season, they were not fit for human consumption.[8]

Erasmus lowered his head in embarrassment, disappointed that he had
let his colleagues down. Nimrod did his best to prepare some of the meat for
consumption, and in their famished state, some of the men attempted his
offerings, but to no avail. It only made them nauseous. Erasmus sat in silent
misery.

"We were now in a bad way," understated Hector, "as, although I had kept
a private caché of about five pounds of pemican [*sic*], which I now produced,
it was only enough for one meal for us all. I intended however to make it last
for three days, by which time we should, from the look of the stream which I
intended to ascend, be able to reach the height of land, and get back to the east
slope of the mountains, where we would be sure to find game." Some of the
men talked openly about sacrificing one of the horses, but Hector stubbornly
resisted. Who would shoulder the extra packs? No, Hector was determined to
get out of this predicament without resorting to such a drastic measure, at

least not until all the pemmican was exhausted and they had no other option.

On the last day of August, summoning all the strength he could muster, Hector was lifted onto his horse and began the arduous ascent of the stream his men had named the Kicking Horse River. He had barely recovered enough to walk and didn't know how much jostling his body could endure, but he was convinced of one thing: to delay would mean to perish. He scribbled in his journal: "My recovery might have been much more tedious than it was, but for the fact that we were now starving, and I found it absolutely necessary to push on after two days."

Travelling as fast as their jaded horses and Hector's painful chest would allow, they followed a trail blazed by Nimrod the previous day. Hector now realized that their only hope of survival was to reach the Bow Valley as soon as possible, where he hoped they would once again encounter abundant game. They reached a point where the valley pinched in dramatically and terminated in a steep slope, covered with a heavy growth of evergreens. Ahead, the river descended in a series of cascading, turbulent falls. They began a rapid ascent, following a rugged, perilous animal trail that traversed steep and dangerous slopes high above the river. Slowly, the steepness of the slope sapped their resolve and they paused only long enough to feast on a profusion of juicy blueberries. They relished the sweetness, but it did little to satisfy their craving for "real food," as the berries were "not very substantial food, when we had been fasting altogether for the past day, and living on only very short allowance for the previous five."

It is at times like this that exhausted, starving men are prone to errors in judgment and accidents occur. Soon, they were one thousand feet above the valley and the steep and dangerous trail they were following was barely wide enough for the pack horses. Erasmus had to summon all of his courage. He didn't particularly enjoy mountain travel; the overhanging cliffs were claustrophobic and the narrow ledges tested his spirit to the limit. He confessed, "I never conquered my fear of precipitous heights and felt buried in the dark spaces among the big trees that shut out a view of the open skies above."[9] Unlike Bourgeau, Erasmus actually longed for the prairies!

Hector should have foreseen what was about to happen. However, in his weakened state, he could be excused for his lack of judgment. He does not elaborate on the difficulties they now encountered; perhaps in his weary state, he just wasn't aware of the danger. This was the part of the valley that, many years later, would become known to the railroad builders as the "Golden Stairs." The trail was barely wide enough for a man on foot, let alone fully loaded pack horses. It required nerves of steel, as well as the utmost concentration, to traverse this section, where the slightest misstep would dislodge boulders into the abyss far below. Just to look down made a man dizzy and tried his frayed nerves. Erasmus was petrified!

In their weakened condition, they were an accident waiting to happen. Just as the horses attempted to negotiate a particularly steep and slippery section, Hector writes, "One, an old grey, that was always more clumsy than the others, lost his balance in passing along a ledge, which overhung a precipitous slope about 150 feet in height, and down he went, luckily catching sometimes on the trees; at last he came to a temporary pause by falling right on his back, the pack acting as a fender; however in his endeavours to get up he started down hill again, and at last slid on a dead tree that stuck out at right angles to the slope, balancing himself with his legs dangling on either side of the trunk of the tree in a most comical manner."

The situation was anything but comical, however, as the dangling horse carried the party's essential supplies and scientific instruments. It took some time for the men, with great peril to their lives, to detour around the animal and scramble up the slope to approach the terrified beast from below. With much difficulty, they managed to get a rope around the battered and bruised beast, remove its pack, and extricate it from the tree trunk. With some furious pulling from above, they shouldered the animal back up to the trail. Right then and there, Hector decided that if a horse had to be sacrificed to stave off starvation, then the old grey would be the first to go!

After eight laborious hours and one near-catastrophe, five beleaguered men and eight spent horses finally reached level ground and open forest. Writes Hector: "We passed many small lakes, and at last reached a small stream flowing to the east, and were again on the Saskatchewan slope of the mountains. The large stream we had been ascending takes its rise from a glacier to the east of the valley through which we had passed. We encamped in a beautiful spot beside a lake,[10] with excellent pasture for the horses. I had killed a grouse, and we were glad to boil it up with some ends of candles and odd pieces of grease, to make something like a supper for the five of us after a very hard day's work." A hard day's work indeed! In their famished state, they devoured every last morsel, even the bones. It was 2 September 1858, and it had taken three laborious days to reach the height of land that would later become known as the Kicking Horse Pass.

They were camped 4,075 feet above sea level, where night temperatures always seem to drop below freezing, especially in September. Their hunger only accentuated the cold, and the men spent a miserable night attempting to keep warm in their crude sleeping blankets. When they awoke the next morning, they were greeted by a landscape covered with a glistening white frost. The ponds were covered with a thin layer of ice and the plants touched by the frost crunched underfoot as they attempted to stamp some warmth into their freezing bodies.

The next morning, they began their descent from the pass. The injured doctor was feeling much better now, perhaps relieved that they had survived a terrible ordeal and confident that they would find some game on the eastern side of the watershed.

"As I was now nearly recovered from the accident, I started with Nimrod at daylight to hunt, leaving the men and horses to follow a prescribed course to the east," Hector remembered. "We took our horses with us and after a few miles we came to a large stream from the west, up the valley of which we saw a great glacier.[11] Following it down, we came after five miles to a large river, which Nimrod at once recognized as Bow River, and then I began to recognize the mountains down the valley, 15 or 20 miles to the east, as the Castle Mountains. The descent from our camp at the height of land of the pass which we had just traversed is very slight to Bow River, and cannot amount to more than 100 feet. We crossed Bow River, and leaving our horses tethered in a swamp, set off to hunt on foot. We saw several fresh moose tracks, and followed one for more than two hours, but failed in coming up with it."

Toward noon, they rejoined the rest of the party at the mouth of Bath Creek and Nimrod, much recovered from his own accident, set off once again to hunt.

Shortly thereafter, Hector writes, "we heard [the] most furious firing, and in a short time he returned in a high state of glee, having shot a moose. We at once moved our camp to where it lay, about one mile distant, in a thicket of willows. It was a doe, and very lean, but, notwithstanding, we soon set about cooking and eating to make up for our long fast. It was not till we got the food that we all found how depressed and weak we were, as desperation had been keeping us up. I had three days before promised that if nothing was killed by to-day I would kill one of the horses, and this evening, if Nimrod had not killed the moose, the old grey that fell over the cliff would have been sacrificed."

Hector now revealed why he had so adamantly resisted the earlier wishes of his men to kill one of the horses. "I had refrained from killing a horse sooner, as I have been warned by experienced travellers that once the first horse is killed for food many more are sure to follow, as the flesh of a horse out of condition is so inferior as merely to create a craving for large quantities of it, without giving the strength or vigour to induce the hunters to kill other game. The prospect of starving is then looked on with indifference, as they know it will be avoided by killing another horse, until at last too few are left to carry the necessities for the party, who then undergo great sufferings, and, as in the case of several American expeditions, some may even perish."

The next morning they were unexpectedly visited by a Stoney, who had been drawn to their camp by the smoke from their fire and no doubt by the pleasant odour of the roasting moose meat. The Stoney informed Hector that they were close to an encampment of his people, about six miles to the northwest. Quickly breaking camp, they slung the moose meat over the horses and set out to find the Stoneys.

"Immediately on our arrival at the camp, which was in a pretty secluded spot, by the side of a mossy lake,[12] the squaws took the whole management of our affairs, —unpacked the horses, put up the tent, lined it beautifully with pine foliage, lighted a fire, and cut wood into most conveniently sized billets, and piled them up ready to hand. They then set about cooking us all sorts of Indian delicacies, —moose nose and entrails, boiled blood and roast kidneys, &c." They were treated royally by the Stoneys, who like them had arrived in the valley starving. However, this valley had plentiful game. They had slain six moose in just the past two days. For the first time in several weeks, Hector's men were able to relax and enjoy the pleasant companionship of their newfound friends.

"At evening a half-breed arrived, who was tenting with these Stoneys. He was a brother of Paul, our chief guide, and whom I had left at the Bow Fort to go with Captain Palliser," Hector recalled. "He was very glad to see us, and got all the news, and made me a present of a fine buck moose; he had just come from hunting, and offered to go with my men for the meat to-morrow. Other Indians also returned, and altogether they had killed three more moose to-day. They had however, gone long distances." It appeared to them to be a veritable hunter's paradise.

That evening they built a huge roaring fire to celebrate and gave thanks for their good fortune. But Hector's run of bad luck had yet to follow its course; later that evening, after everyone had retired, the spruce tree hanging over Hector's tent caught fire. The burning spruce produced a magnificent blaze, "the roar of which luckily wakened me up, and, without waiting to see how much was burning of the forest, I caught our powder and my trowsers [sic] and bolted right into the swamp. It did not communicate with the other trees," Hector wrote, "however, after brilliantly illuminating the forest for half an hour, and having consumed the foliage and resinous bark, it died out, leaving the charred trunk and branches as sturdy as ever. The glare of light which this fire threw on the dark forest and swarthy faces of the Indians, who gathered round to watch its progress, was very striking."

Hector was as determined as ever to continue his explorations, regardless of his physical condition. Old Paul's brother informed him that it was possible to follow the Bow River to its source high in the mountains and then descend the other side into the valley of the North Saskatchewan. He was also informed that along the way he would encounter magnificent peaks and valleys filled with great expanses of ice. This only whetted the intrepid explorer's appetite; he decided he would seek the source of the Bow River.

Old Paul's brother also informed Hector that the way was marred by terrible muskeg, swamp, deadfall, and a scarcity of game. Even the white goats abundant in the region would be out of season and unsuitable for eating. It mattered not to the young explorer; he was possessed by ambition and, this time, the Stoney women would properly prepare a suitable supply of moose meat. No matter the hardship, he said, "I determined to try that route, and to trust to our stock of dried meat lasting until we got to the eastern ranges, where there are plenty of grey sheep. A young orphan boy in the camp, who wished to join some friends at a camp on the North Saskatchewan, I allowed to join our party, as he will be useful." With some shrewd bargaining he even managed to get rid of "our old friend 'the grey' horse with the bruised countenance, and by giving a little 'to boot,' got a very good animal in exchange."

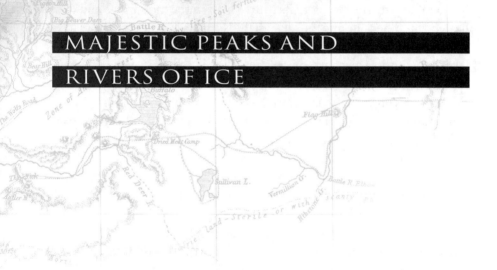

MAJESTIC PEAKS AND
RIVERS OF ICE

ON 8 SEPTEMBER 1858, DR. JAMES HECTOR AND HIS FELLOW explorers waved goodbye to their Stoney friends and, beckoned by the tales of huge mountain peaks and rivers of ice, struck through the woods to follow the infant Bow. Hector had recovered admirably from his injuries and was ready to continue his mission, but almost immediately, his group was forced to hunker down after being attacked by a violent snowstorm.

Once the storm had passed they resumed their trek. After they crossed a large tributary stream, the valley suddenly became quite contracted, and Peter Erasmus once again had to fight an anxiety attack that comes with a feeling of being "bound to a small place and crowded in." Fortunately, the valley soon opened up and "right before us Goat Mountain stood out at right angles from the western range, causing us to bend to the east," wrote Hector. "In the angle thus formed is a large lake, from which flows the tributary just mentioned, and at its head a glacier, of small size, nearly reaches the water level. Bow River was now a stream of very small size, but very rapid. We soon crossed to the left bank, and after passing round Goat Mountain the valley became much expanded. It was bitterly cold all the afternoon, and the night was clear, with sharp frost. We did not put up our tent, which, when pitching in a regular manner, we generally flung over a shed of poles, but this night we made a regular winter encampment with pine foliage under us. The mountains to the north of our camp had a very curious outline, the men saying that they were like an old woman's jaw."[1]

The next morning, they wasted little time breaking camp and moved quickly through the subalpine environment, with its stunted growth of alpine fir. The orphaned Stoney boy the group had informally adopted produced several fine trout by shooting them with arrows. He also demonstrated to the team how to snare a spruce grouse. "He took a short piece of sinew twine and made a noose, which he fastened on a slender pole, and advancing slowly to the bird gently passed the noose over its head, and pulled it off the tree," wrote Hector. "The grouse did not seem frightened in the least, but sat gravely looking at him all the time, and actually when the noose was close dodged its head into it." It was a good lesson and "we often adopted this plan of catching them afterwards, and I have never found much difficulty in effecting it where the forest was dense."

The ease of the gradient was much appreciated, unlike that of the Kicking Horse. Before long, Hector's party had reached Bow Summit. "An hour's ride brought us to where the Bow River dilates to form a narrow lake, the water of which is a bright green colour. Two miles further we reached a second and larger lake, being two miles long and one broad. Along its western shore the mountains rise precipitously, except at one point where a narrow valley allows a short glacier to reach the water's edge, being fed from the perpetual ice and snow that mantle the mountains in that direction. We kept along the east shore of the lake till it was terminated by an open prairie..."[2]

Hector was stunned by the beauty of the place. The stillness of the lake provided a perfect mirror for the surrounding peaks. Behind the lake, Bow Glacier glistened in the noonday sun as it tumbled from the Wapta Icefield. Old Paul's brother was right; magnificent peaks and valleys filled with rivers of ice were everywhere.

Shortly they reached the height of land. "There is a small stream, however, which flows into this lake from a fine plain which forms the upper part of the valley. Following up this, we came to where it rises from a group of springs, and, a few yards further on, a second group gives rise to the waters of the north branch. We dined at this watershed, which is the highest point we

"BOW LAKE, 1915"

(*WALTER WILCOX* / CAMPING IN THE CANADIAN ROCKIES)

passed over with the loaded horses, being 6,347 feet above the sea. Snow was lying under the shade of the trees, not withstanding the clear midday sun." Here at Bow Summit, which separates the waters of the North and South Saskatchewan drainage systems, they lingered for several hours, revelling in the majestic landscape. In a classic understatement of one of the most spectacular views in the Rockies, Hector simply stated, "The view from this point was very fine."

"The descent to the valley below, unlike that we had ascended, is very sudden, and the angle of the mountain on either hand jutting in successively from the sides of the valley formed a vista for at least 25 miles. We did not at once commence the descent of the slope, but kept along the right or east side of the valley for fully a mile, and then took down a break-neck trail that winds through the woods to its bottom."

The rapid descent of nearly one thousand feet in less than six miles from Bow Summit quickly brought them to a large stream. Hector named it the "Little Fork" and, descending it, "got occasional peeps of a lofty peak to the east, which I named Mount Murchison, occupying, however, such a central position among other high and precipitous mountains that we saw it only at intervals. The Indians say it is the highest mountain they know of . . ." They followed the Little Fork northwest "through a rugged valley between Mount Murchison and Mount Balfour,"[3] before reaching a beautiful lake where they encamped. "This lake is closely wooded on all sides to the water's edge, except at one point on the west shore, where a spout-like glacier reaches through the woods almost to the shore. The surface of this glacier is very steep, as it descends at a very high angle from the ice-fields, which are 2,000 feet above it. It is a perfect ice cascade, and is broken at several points by fissures both longitudinal and transverse."[4]

On 10 September, "keeping along the 'Little Fork' of the North Saskatchewan we passed two shallow lakes, into which it dilates."[5] Hector deduced that they were formed by the detritus of a terminal moraine that stretched across the valley. Moving now to the left side of the valley, they had to make a considerable ascent to avert "a great slide of stones" that had obliterated much of the forest. Finally, they reached the dense woods on the other side of the slide and commenced hacking their way through deadfall strewn in every direction. As nightfall approached, they reached the Howse River just above its confluence with the North Saskatchewan and here came across "a very distinct trail, much more so than any we had seen in any other part of the mountains. This evening, September 10th, after we encamped, we observed the comet for the first time, as hitherto our view to the westward had been blocked by the mountains."[6]

That evening, the fatigued men spent a restless night, their sleep continually interrupted by "a great noise, like distant thunder, at intervals, which Nimrod said was caused by ice falling in the mountains." Hector questioned this explanation, finding it difficult to fathom that falling ice could create such a thunderous sound; on the other hand, there had been no thunderstorms that evening. Perhaps Nimrod was correct.

Early the next morning, they began following the newly discovered track until it disappeared and they promptly became lost searching for a new trail. A large feeder river from the west looked enticing, so they followed it up and were immediately plunged into one of the densest growths of forest they had ever encountered. Deadfall lay in every direction. They hacked their way through until "a little way further through the woods brought us to a large lake, which occupied the full width of the valley excepting a narrow margin along its north shore, and which was very much encumbered with fallen timber."[7] Suddenly, as they were chopping their way along, the same horse that had plunged into the water at Wapta Falls jumped into the water and swam off into the lake. "We had to leave him alone, lest our endeavours to get hold of him should only start him for the other side of the lake, which was a mile wide. After a time he turned to land again," wrote Hector, "but his pack was so soaked that we had to halt for the night where we were. To occupy the remaining daylight I sent two men on to cut out a track, while I tried to dry and save the few skins and plants I had collected, and which had been unfortunately packed on this horse.

"Our camp was the most curious I have seen, as the fallen trees on the slope of the hill were so large and so intertwined that it was with difficulty we found places to stretch ourselves here and there among them. We fished, and set lines in the lake, but without success. It appears to be very deep, and the south shore is almost precipitous. In the afternoon violent gusts of wind occasionally blew down the valley raising the water into large waves; but the evening was calm, and the reflection of the opposite mountains was wonderfully clear. Trying to shoot some bats that were flitting in numbers over the water, we found that the noise was echoed in a most wonderful manner by the successive points from side to side of the lake, the report being thus repeated in a sharp distinct manner six or eight times."

It took another day to reach the western extremity of the lake at the foot of a great glacier that descended from an immense icefield, which would later be named the Lyell Icefield. The Indians referred to this place simply as "The Ice." Whipped by chilling winds off the toe of the glacier, it would be their home for two days. Hector had never before explored a glacier and his meagre knowledge of the dangers it posed had been garnered from textbooks. Whether he was unaware of these dangers or simply chose to ignore them, he set his sights on exploring the ice. From their camp it appeared to be an easy ascent; however, with lack of proper equipment and training, the jaunt would be risky, foolish, and dangerous—some would say downright insane. Still, the young, inexperienced explorer had to satisfy his curiosity. He just couldn't pass up this glorious opportunity.

Hector asked Nimrod to accompany him, but Nimrod didn't have to be reminded of the many sad tales of hunters venturing onto the ice and falling into deep crevasses, never to be seen again. Even if they did escape, he told Hector, they were "sure to be unlucky afterwards in their hunting." No, Nimrod would not dare venture onto the ice. Sutherland volunteered to accompany him on his foolhardy escapade instead.

At sunrise on 13 September, they began their risky adventure. "After crossing single flats for about a mile," Hector recorded, "we reached a high moraine of perfectly loose and unconsolidated materials, which completely occupies the breadth of the valley, about 100 yards in advance of the glacier. Scrambling to the top of this, we found that to our left a narrow chasm, with perpendicular walls, brought down a stream from a glacier, descending by a lateral valley from the south, but the greater bulk of the water that formed the river issued from ice caves, that were hollowed beneath the great glacier of the main valley."

Numerous transverse crevasses prevented them from gaining the glacier along its southern border, forcing them to "wade through several streams issuing from below the ice, till we found the surface forming a uniform slope unbroken by crevasses. This was immediately beyond a point where a great longitudinal fissure seemed to divide the glacier into two halves up the centre of the valley; that portion to our left being pure ice much crevassed, but free from dirt on its surface; while to our right the surface we now ascended was less steep, smooth, and unbroken, but so discoloured by foreign matters, that at a little distance it might have passed for a talus of rocky fragments. It was very cold work for our feet as we merely wore mocassins, without socks of any kind. The mocassins, however, gave us one advantage, which was the securing of a sure foothold."

Carefully they toiled up the glacier until it levelled off, at which point

Hector determined that they were approximately fifteen hundred feet above the terminal moraine at the toe of the glacier. He later described the scene:

I now saw that the glacier I was upon was a mere extension of a great mass of ice, that enveloped the higher mountains to the west, being supplied partly through a narrow spout-like ice cascade in the upper part of the valley, and partly by the resolidifying of the fragments of the upper *Mer de Glace*, falling over a precipice several hundred feet in height, to the brink of which it is gradually pushed forward.[8]

A longitudinal crack divides the glacier throughout nearly its entire length, sharply defining the ice that has squeezed through the narrow chasm, from the portion of the glacier that has been formed from the fallen fragments, the former being clear and pure, while the latter is fouled by much débris resting on its surface, and mixed in its substance. The more rapid melting of the dirty portion of the glacier gives it a smooth undulating surface, which is much lower than the adjoining surface of the pure ice, which besides is much cut by crevasses and ice valleys, through which flow considerable streams, that often disappear into profound chasms.

We had to go a great way round to avoid one of these rents, and at last had to jump it when about four feet wide, and, as I found, by timing the fall of stones, 160 feet deep. . . . The precipice at the head of the valley stretches for more than two-thirds of its width; the remainder is occupied by the ice cascade. The blue pinnacles of ice, tottering over the edge of the cliff, were very striking, and it is the noise of these falling which we had mistaken for thunder a few days before when many miles down the valley.

On coming fairly in view of the precipice, when about two miles from the foot of the glacier, I found, by watching the fall of these pinnacles, and observing the interval till the crash was heard, that I was a little over four miles distant, so that the lower part of the glacier is about six miles in length.[9]

A small peak north of the glacier drew Hector's attention. It looked like an easy scramble. "After examining the surface of the glacier, and arriving at its upper end close to the precipice, we struck off to the north side of the valley, to ascend a peak that looked more accessible than the others. With some difficulty we got off the edge of the glacier, and climbing through some scrubby pines of low stature, soon came to the surface of naked rock. Here we found traces of where a bear had been digging roots of alpine plant. The mountain was almost precipitous, and formed of nearly vertical beds of soft white slate and quartzose rock.... We reached the top of the mountain at three o'clock. My aneroid [barometer] had ceased to work some time before reaching the summit, its lowest reading being 22.11 inches. We were probably about 4,000 feet above our camp at the foot of the glacier. The summit consisted of a narrow ridge sloping to the S.W., at an angle of 40 to 50 degrees, while, to the N.E., it presented a sheer precipice more than 1,000 feet in height. We only got along by crawling at some points, while sometimes an abrupt nick in the knife-like edge had to be passed by dangerous climbing."[10]

Standing on the summit, they had a magnificent view of the Lyell Icefield. The peaks and ridges appeared to stand "out like islands through the icy mantle." The view was intoxicating. Massive icefields and lofty peaks were everywhere. One particular pyramidal giant to the south, completely wrapped in snow, he named in honour of one of his eminent professors. "Mount Forbes, which lies between the Glacier Lake and the great fork of the north branch, I found to have an altitude of 13,400 feet."[11]

A bitter wind, which pelted their faces with snow whipped off the ice, quickly brought Hector to his senses. Now would be a prudent time to abandon their isolated perch for safer ground. "Descending again to the glacier in the midst of a snow storm, with a cold wind from the N.E., we skirted along the north edge, passing where the stream from the northern glacier passes under the great glacier by an immense cavern, the floor of which sloped at an angle of 30°. At one point we thought at first we should require to turn back, and gain the surface of the glacier, as we came to a precipice that was closely hemmed in between a wall of ice and one of rock. However, by knotting our leather shirts together, and taking off our moccasins, which were now frozen, we managed to get past the difficulty, and pushing on rapidly reached our camp at eight o'clock."

It didn't get any better than this! The glow on Hector's face from the intense rays of the sun reflecting off the surface of the ice hid his immense satisfaction. It had been a truly remarkable if not foolhardy feat. He and Sutherland had been on the ice and rock for nearly twenty hours; they were famished, as well as dehydrated. However, much to their disappointment, the hunters had been unsuccessful and "we were now limited to the dry lean moose meat, which has not much more nourishment in it than chips of parchment."

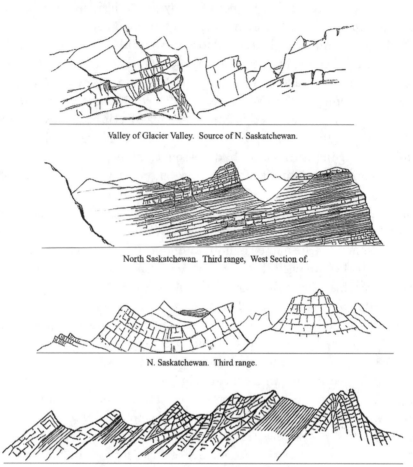

Valley of Glacier Valley. Source of N. Saskatchewan.

North Saskatchewan. Third range, West Section of.

N. Saskatchewan. Third range.

N. Saskatchewan. Second Range.

FIGURE 5: GEOLOGICAL SKETCHES MADE BY HECTOR
ALONG THE NORTH SASKATCHEWAN RIVER

That night, the glare from a large fire down the valley at the lower end of the lake drew their attention. Hector became alarmed. Had they caused the fire? After all, they were the only ones in the valley and there had been no recent lightning strikes.

Early on the morning of 14 September, they began to retrace their steps—since the immense Lyell Icefield blocked their way and was not an option—and on reaching the eastern end of the lake found, much to their consternation, that they were in fact the guilty party. The fire had already destroyed a large portion of the ancient forest and a bitter scent of burning spruce and pine hung in the air. "The wind was luckily from the west, so that by keeping close to the stream, and going in the water whenever practicable, we got along; but, as sometimes we were forced to pass over the smouldering ground, our horses' legs suffered a good deal."

Hector made a short side trip up the Middle Fork, while the men encamped among some sandhills on the banks of the North Saskatchewan. He was convinced this valley must lead to Howse Pass, which he had seen on John Arrowsmith's map. He longed to find it, if only the season weren't so late. Perhaps he would get another chance. Regretfully, he returned to camp. Nimrod had taken the young Stoney orphan across the river to hunt and was absent all night.

It was now mid-September, and as the men resumed their journey, they were hailed by Nimrod, who was waving frantically from across the river. He and the young boy had been successful in bagging some white goats. They tried to eat some of the meat, "which was that of a fine young kid, and was fat and exceedingly good-looking, but in spite of our hunger none of us could retain it in our stomachs, as the rank musky flavour gave rise to intense nausea."

After recovering from their nausea, they once again resumed their journey and found a good track. Hector's itinerary recorded: "Cross the river, which is 130 yards wide and almost too deep to ford. Go very fast along the left side of a very wide valley, through the dense woods till on reaching 'Pine Point,' where we crossed over a rocky promontory and turned sharply to the north and west four miles along the river to the Kootanie Plain."[12]

This historic open plain, which is approximately eight miles long by three miles wide at its widest point, with splendid pasture, Hector reported, "is called the Kootanie Plain, as at the time the Kootanie Indians exchanged their furs with the traders of the Saskatchewan forts, before there was any communication with them from the Pacific coast, an annual mart was held at this place, to which the Kootanie Indians crossed the mountain, while the traders came from the Mountain House. This accounts for the well-beaten track which runs along the valley." Here, wild game abounded.

They spent two days at this historic site. While Nimrod and the other men went hunting, Hector returned to the rocky promontory "to examine some pines I had noticed there. They grow on sand-hills, and have much the appearance of Scotch firs, the trunks and branches being twisted, and of red colour. The cone is large, and covered with a fragrant balsam."[13] The breathtaking mountain panorama enhanced by the brilliant fall colours of the aspens and the crisp mountain air signalled the approach of autumn. They would have to move fast if they were to reach Edmonton before the onset of the early winter the Indians were predicting.

On returning to camp, Hector was pleased to learn that the hunters had been successful in killing four large rams. However, the steepness of the terrain had prevented them from recovering all but small portions. As they were low on provisions, it was decided that a determined effort would be made the next day to salvage the rest of the carcasses.

Early the next morning, they made their way up the rocky chasm to the sheep carcasses, and leaving the men to butcher the animals, Hector decided to scramble up a ridge that led to the top of an adjoining peak. "The highest point I reached was about 4,300 feet above our camp at the Kootanie Plain. Although snow was lying in sheltered spots far below this altitude, yet there were no true glaciers, which shows the most remarkable difference, at which I have always been astonished, between the altitude of the snow line in the eastern portion of the range from those valleys that communicate with the western slope."[14]

Their larder was now bulging with an ample supply of fresh meat, but would it be enough? Edmonton was still more than two hundred miles and many days distant. On 18 September at 8:00 AM, they commenced their trek eastward following the North Saskatchewan. After making about fourteen miles, they crossed the *Wapa teehk*, or White Goat River.[15] "Through this valley Nimrod said a trail runs to Jaspar [*sic*] House, known as 'Old Cline's' trail," Hector noted. "Cline was a trader that every summer travelled through the mountains from Jaspar House to the Kootanie Plain, and then returned through the woods by their eastern base, collecting, during this tour, enough provision to support him at the trading post of Jaspar House during the winter."

At four o'clock that afternoon, Hector passed out of the mountains and

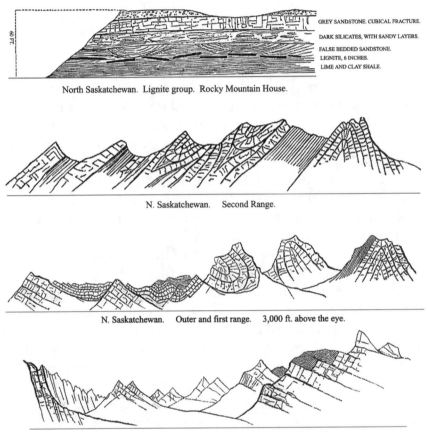

60 FT.

GREY SANDSTONE. CUBICAL FRACTURE.

DARK SILICATES, WITH SANDY LAYERS.

FALSE BEDDED SANDSTONE.
LIGNITE, 6 INCHES.
LIME AND CLAY SHALE.

North Saskatchewan. Lignite group. Rocky Mountain House.

N. Saskatchewan.   Second Range.

N. Saskatchewan.   Outer and first range.   3,000 ft. above the eye.

N. Saskatchewan. Second longitudinal valley. 5,500 ft. above the eye.

FIGURE 6: GEOLOGICAL SKETCHES MADE BY HECTOR
ON RETURN TO FORT EDMONTON

entered the foothills east of the Brazeau Range. It had been thirty-eight event-ful days since he had departed Old Bow Fort, and he lingered to make some elegant sketches of the magnificent view unfolding behind him. The Brazeau Range seemed to form an unbroken line etched against the horizon. Suddenly, engrossed in his thoughts, he was overtaken by a terrific thunderstorm.

"The fall of rain and hail was so severe that the horse tracks were quite obliterated, and I was pushing on very fast in doubt of whether I had passed them or not, when suddenly my horse shyed [sic] at a bush, and immediately out sprang a splendid panther. I did all I could to pull off the leather cover from my rifle, but it was so soaked with the rain that I found it immovable. He stood a few seconds within 12 feet of me, lashing his tail, and as if in doubt whether to spring, while my horse danced about in a state of disquietude, till at last he made off into the brushwood again." Shaking from fright, Hector could hear his heart pounding through his buckskin jacket. He only had time to remark about "the great width of his face, and the length of his tail." Quickening his pace, he followed the sounds of distant gunshots, fired as signals to indicate the location of his men.

The next day they reached Big Horn Creek, where there was splendid pas-ture and abundant game. Here, finally out of the foothills, they would recu-perate for seven days before beginning their final push toward Edmonton. However, the sight of fresh snow covering the mountains meant winter was fast approaching; they couldn't afford to waste too much time. Two days after arriving at Big Horn Creek, they were joined by Chief Sampson and his band of Stoneys, who were on their way to winter camp near Old Bow Fort.

"Our horses are improving rapidly," wrote Hector, "as it was merely food and rest for a few days that they required, with the exception of one that had been severely burned in passing through the fire at the Glacier Lakes. I man-aged to exchange him with the Stoneys, however, for another that was sound, though perhaps not so fine a horse otherwise." Hunting was exceptionally good and they were relieved. Their Stoney friends converted a splendid but lean buck into "pounded meat," reserving only the bone marrow, which they devoured raw after the Indian fashion. Perhaps the long journey to Edmonton would not be as trying as they had envisioned.

On the morning of 27 September, "after giving away everything we could spare as presents to our Indian friends, and leaving them with the boy that had accompanied us from Bow River, we started to continue our journey to Edmonton. The seven day's [sic] rest had greatly improved the horses, and without it I doubt if we should ever have got them to winter quarters."

Three days later, Hector's party reached Rocky Mountain House, but unlike on his previous visit less than a year earlier, "The place had a deserted look, the parchment windows being torn, the doors standing ajar, and the court-yard choked with weeds. We established our camp in the kitchen, and tearing down some of the half-rotten pickets, soon made a blazing fire, but did not feel nearly so comfortable as if we had been camped as usual." They stayed for only one night.

They were still more than one hundred miles from Edmonton, and the early winter the Indians had predicted hit with a vengeance. The temperature plummeted below freezing as snow buffeted by bitter north winds bit into their faces. By 4 October, only sheer willpower was keeping them going. Hector remembered an old survival trick that John Foulds had taught him the previous winter; "as it was very cold, I tore up my blanket for the general good, to make wrappers for our feet." At least they would not suffer from frostbitten toes as they forced their way through the deep snow and drove their spent horses into the raging north wind.

Hector appeared to be in a tremendous hurry to reach Edmonton ahead of the weather. Erasmus watched as he paced back and forth, impatiently waiting for the horses to feed. Nimrod even remarked, "The chief for the first time is in a hurry. He doesn't stop to say his prayers to the sun, like he always does. Surely the devil must be riding behind him."[16] This observation was not in reference to some form of pagan worship, but to a belief by the Indians that Hector's constant heavenly observations were based on some religious rite. Erasmus was always left to explain the real purpose of his actions. Nimrod never doubted Erasmus's explanation as he was completely convinced of the doctor's ability to "keep directions and obtain locations with his instruments," no matter the circumstances.

Finally, around noon on 7 October, they reached Whitemud Creek, where they halted to wash and make themselves presentable before arriving at Edmonton.

Hector noted, "At 4 [PM] we reached the river, and soon attracted the attention of the inhabitants of the fort, and I had the satisfaction of distinguishing Captain Palliser and the rest of our party awaiting me on the other bank. The swimming of the horses was a troublesome work, as some of them were very weak."

Palliser was much relieved that his intrepid explorer had finally returned and was safe. Hector could only wonder if the Captain would ever believe the story he was about to recount.

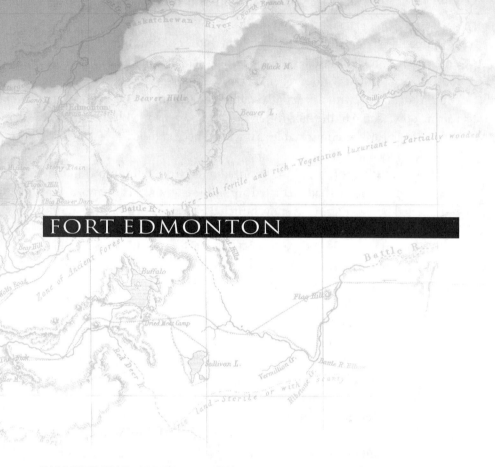

FORT EDMONTON

PALLISER HAD ARRIVED AT FORT EDMONTON FROM HIS BRANCH
expedition on 20 September; Bourgeau had preceded him and was busy
preparing his botanical specimens. The Captain had found "his" Kananaskis
Pass and wrote glowingly to Lord Stanley, the Secretary of State for the
Colonies, that "this pass will connect the prairies of the Saskatchewan with
Her Majesty's Possessions on the west side of the Rocky Mountains. The pass
is situated precisely where I had long supposed ..." History would prove him
wrong.

The Captain waited impatiently for the rest of his colleagues to return,
eager to learn of both their safety and findings. Gradually they filtered in;
Blakiston returned on 1 October, while Hector was the last to arrive on 7
October. Palliser was relieved that all had returned safely, and he was proud
of their achievements.

Palliser was rejoiced to report to Lord Stanley that the expedition had
"discovered" and laid down numerous routes across the Rockies. Blakiston

had crossed and mapped the North and South Kootenay Passes; Hector had successfully explored the Vermilion, Kicking Horse, and "Little Fork" (Bow Summit) Passes; and Palliser himself had found his elusive pass on his way to the Columbia River. He was positive that at least one of these passes was not only practicable for horses but that with little effort could also be made passable to other means of conveyance.

Palliser was quick to lavish praise on his colleagues for their accomplishments. He lauded Hector for the massive amount of geological and geographical information he had amassed in the mountains and wrote that, in addition to being an accomplished naturalist, the young doctor was "the most accurate map maker of original country I have ever seen."

He praised Bourgeau for his magnificent collections and for his "unceasing exertions, not only in his botanical labours, but for his zeal and care as manager of the provisions and stores of the Expedition, and his anxiety to assist me in every possible way."

"I have also to express my satisfaction with my secretary, Mr. Sullivan," he wrote to Lord Stanley, "not only for his zeal and assiduity in carrying on the astronomical observations, but also his assistance and exertions for the interests of the Expedition, particularly with regard to the horses; also by his care and regularity with the accounts...."

Most notable was Palliser's failure to commend Blakiston for his explorations. He took pains to note that after Blakiston had resigned his post in the expedition, he used expedition men, guides, and horses, which Palliser pointed out to Blakiston but said he "would let it pass." Palliser was also annoyed at Blakiston's refusal to share his information. "I was surprised by a positive refusal to give me any maps, or the benefit of any observations whatever. I have nothing further to write on the subject, save to submit Lieut. Blakiston's letter of 11 of August 1858,"[1] wrote Palliser.

The North Saskatchewan River was the highway to the interior, and Fort Edmonton, established in 1795, was the headquarters of the Hudson's Bay Company's (HBC) Saskatchewan trade. It would be their winter quarters.

"Fort Edmonton," Palliser wrote, "the largest fort of the Saskatchewan, is built altogether of wood, consisting of one good-sized house, two stories high, the habituation of the officer in charge of the post; it also contained ourselves afterwards, and some visitors. Adjoining the house are the storehouses of the Company, containing their goods and furs, besides the log-houses inhabited by the men engaged by the Company, together with their wives and families; the whole is surrounded by wooden pickets or piles firmly

FORT EDMONTON, 1870
(CHARLES HORETZKY / LIBRARY AND ARCHIVES CANADA, C-007475)

driven into the ground close together, and about 20 feet high." A sentinel's gallery ran around the entire palisade and at the four corners rose bastions armed with cannons.

The fort, situated as it was high above the river, was a constant source of wonder to all those who saw it for the first time. The famous missionary Father Albert Lacombe once said that it reminded him of a "rude baronial stronghold in the Feudal Ages."[2]

The fort's design was in the shape of an irregular hexagon, "about 100 yards long, and 70 wide; and contains a population of about 40 men, 30 women, and 80 children, almost entirely supported on buffalo meat, the hauling of which, for sometimes upwards of 250 miles across the plains, is the source of great and most fruitless expense. Indeed the labour and difficulty of providing for a consumption of 700 lbs. of buffalo meat daily, and from a great distance, would frequently become very precarious, were it not for an abundant supply of fish from Lake St. Ann's, about 50 miles to the west of the fort, whence they are capable of hauling 30,000 or 40,000 in a season; these are fine wholesome white fish, averaging four pounds weight each," wrote Palliser.

The inhabitants had devised an ingenious method for preserving such large quantities of meat; it was called the "Ice Pit."

"This is made by digging a square hole," wrote artist Paul Kane, "capable of containing 700 or 800 buffalo carcases [sic]. As soon as the ice in the river is of sufficient thickness, it is cut into square blocks of a uniform size with saws; with these blocks the floor of the pit is regularly paved, and the blocks cemented together by pouring water in between them, and allowing it to freeze solid. In like manner, the walls are solidly built up to the surface of the ground. The head and feet of the buffalo, when killed are cut off, and the carcase, without being skinned, is divided into quarters, and piled in layers in the pit as brought in, until it is filled up, when the whole is covered with a thick coating of straw, which is again protected from the sun and rain by a shed. In this manner the meat keeps perfectly good through the whole summer, and eats much better than fresh meat killed, being more tender and better flavoured."[3]

In the middle of the enclosure stood the "Big House," a massive structure approximately seventy feet deep and sixty wide, constructed from squared timber. Two small, brass cannons occupied a grassy plot in front of the structure. From a gallery at the front, "a high stairway led down to the grassy courtyard, about which the Bachelors' Hall or Gentlemen's quarters, the Indian Hall, the men's quarters and warehouses were ranged. Within the Big House this stairway opened upon a wide hall, on either side of which lay two immense rooms, the Gentlemen's mess-room and the ball-room,"[4] wrote Father Lacombe. The living quarters for the chief factor's family were located behind these rooms. Underneath the stairs were the steward's office, the armoury, and storerooms, while above were more offices and bedrooms for guests, where expedition members would be housed during the coming winter.

A windmill, high on a hill, overlooked the fort. According to Hector, its great granite stones, quarried very near the site of the mill, were not very serviceable. "They manage, when they get a gale of wind, to grind some tolerable flour, quite enough to prove that, if the business was properly conducted, it might be a valuable source of support; nine-tenths of the little flour that is consumed in the Saskatchewan is brought either from Red River or all the way from England."

The major industry at the fort consisted of building boats for the fur trade. White spruce used in their construction was cut and rafted down the river from about ten miles west of the fort. Abundant poplar trees along the margins of the river were used only for firewood; about eight hundred cords were required each winter. The blacksmith's forge was stoked with coal stripped from seams surrounding the fort. Meanwhile, the women busied themselves making moccasins, articles of clothing, and pemmican.

Palliser's first order of business once arriving at the fort was the care of the horses, which had suffered terribly in the mountains. Donald Matheson and Samuel Ballenden had worked feverishly to put up seventeen stacks of hay, and once he was satisfied that they would have sufficient feed for the winter, Palliser set about paying the men from the Lac St. Ann's brigade. This was a complex bartering system in which payment for services rendered was calculated in beaver skins and then paid out in kind with various items from HBC stock. It was a task unfamiliar to Palliser and one at which William Christie, who had just been appointed chief factor at Fort Edmonton, proved to be invaluable.

"Mr. Christie, who understood the pricing and value of the articles, very kindly undertook the payment of the men," wrote Palliser, "which is thus conducted:—Mr. Sullivan made an account of wages due to them, deducting advances, &c. I then signed this, and each man presented it to Mr. Christie, who sat in my shop at the fort, surrounded by ready-made clothes, blankets, beds, axes, knives, files, kettles, tea, sugar, tobacco, &c., and the man kept taking what he wanted till Mr. Christie called out '*assez,*' after which the account closed.

"Frequently Mr. Christie would say, 'Now you have but half a skin left,' when his customer would immediately turn to the ribbons or beads for an equivalent of the difference," Palliser continued. "I did not pay any men of my Red River brigade until all the St. Anne's [sic] men were settled with, because they were returning to Red River, where they could get what they wanted on better terms there. The freight up the Saskatchewan was necessarily heavy, all of which was taken into wages account at the time of agreement. Nevertheless, like children at the sight of toys, it was difficult to deter them from purchasing, and I had considerable trouble in laughing them out of the idea of buying an expensive article, in order to carry it back to the place it came from at considerable trouble and inconvenience."

Palliser had greatly underestimated the enormity of the land and the vast distances that had to be traversed. Now more than ever, he realized that a third season would be necessary if the expedition was to fulfill its mandate—but still he had heard nothing from the Colonial Office regarding his previous request for an extension, made some ten months earlier. Privately, he conferred with James Hector and together they discussed what remained to be done. Palliser began to design another plan of action. He had to be quick if he was to receive a reply before the commencement of the next season and penned an urgent letter to Lord Stanley, imploring him to extend the expedition's mandate for another year.

In his letter to Lord Stanley dated 7 October, Palliser not only reviewed the expedition's accomplishments but also added the enticing notion that practicable routes across the mountains existed wholly within British Territory. He suggested that transport routes for carts, even a railroad, connecting the plains with the western side of the Rockies could be constructed using one of the passes they had explored.

Palliser reported that "Dr. Hector informs me, that the water-line of the mountains is not identical with their geological axis; this axis he was unable to reach, and had only opportunity of examining what are called flanking ranges, therefore the most important geological results relating to the Rocky Mountains of North America remain as yet unascertained, because, in conformity with my instructions, I was obliged to order Dr. Hector not to advance further than the axis of the watershed of these mountains; and I take this opportunity of recommending Her Majesty's Government to alter that part of my instructions, and direct my movements in the following manner: —That, as soon as my explorations are completed on the east side of the mountains (for now there remains only 6° of longitude in the country of the boundary line), I should send Dr. Hector to complete his exploration, and then meet me at Fort Colville, whence we could return home to England by Panama, and the British West Indian main steamer from Charges, as a far cheaper route than recrossing the whole continent of North America."

Palliser tried to make his proposal as enticing as possible, but there was the question of funds. "The expenses of next season will exceed £1,500 if anything at all is to be done. But if Her Majesty's Government are really apprehensive of the grant of £1,500 being overdrawn, I have but one course to pursue, that of abandoning the completion of the boundary line, and all discoveries in the Rocky Mountains, and returning home in the beginning of the season." He knew this last comment would raise eyebrows and to alleviate concerns explained that the HBC had promised to purchase all fifty-three of his horses at the completion of a third season's explorations.

He continued, "I feel greatly honoured by the confidence Her Majesty's Government have hitherto placed in me; and should her Majesty's Government consider the importance of ascertaining the practicability of a railroad across the Rocky Mountains, as well as a more extended acquaintance with the geological structure of those mountains themselves, worth the further sacrifice of a few hundred pounds, I would propose that the Government grant me the whole of the £1,500 for expenses in this country alone for the next season [1859–60], independent of salaries and the homeward travelling expenses, the former of which will amount to £570, and the latter, I hardly think, will exceed an equal sum, if I am allowed to adopt the route I propose as most conducive to the interest of science as well as the purposes of economy."[5]

Palliser had his detractors in England and they were growing in number. Those who had believed from the outset that his expedition was nothing more than a glorified big-game hunting excursion were powerful men in positions of influence.[6] Blakiston also fed their appetite for distrust in his own private letters by sarcastically and openly supporting the "hunting trip" accusations. However, due to the efforts of Hector, Bourgeau, and even Blakiston, the expedition actually had become a scientific endeavour. Would his plea fall on deaf ears? Would his letter convince the Home Government to grant him a third year in the field? All he could do was wait; it would take at least nine months for a response to arrive—assuming they even received a response. After all, there had been no reply to his previous request sent off nearly a year ago.

On 12 October, Palliser took leave of his Red River men, "who started down the Saskatchewan in the boats, which also conveyed Lieutenant Blackiston [*sic*] on his way home." Safely tucked away in one of the boats was the packet containing Palliser's plea to Lord Stanley.

Blakiston's bitterness toward the Captain was still evident and the men were glad to see him depart. The young lieutenant was also suspected of absconding with the meteorological data obtained at Fort Carlton during the winter of 1857. All these records were subsequently lost and the allegation was never proven. So great was Blakiston's animosity toward Palliser that later, in an act of complete insubordination and much to the displeasure of the Colonial Office, Blakiston published his own report in *Further Papers*, which was considered an insult to the leader of the expedition.

Another problem arose, but Palliser used it to his benefit. "Before the departure of the boats, our servant, James Beads, received a letter from below [Red River] to say that his brother had been killed that summer on his way from St. Paul's by the Salteaus [*sic,* Sioux Indians]; he therefore asked my leave to return in the boats" to the Red River settlement. "I hesitated for some time before granting this leave, but recollecting that I should require a special mail service next year, in order to receive my commands from Her Majesty's Government, I gave him permission to go, at the same time providing dispatches which should organize means for his return, with my instructions from the Colonial Office for next year."

At last, with the departure of Blakiston, peace had been restored to the remaining members of the expedition. Now they would be able to recuperate from their summer ordeals in tranquility. Each resigned himself to the mundane tasks of updating journals, preparing reports, working up scientific data, and drawing maps.

YULETIDE ON THE NORTH SASKATCHEWAN

DESPITE ALL THE SNOW AND COLD WINDS ENCOUNTERED BY Hector and his men as they raced for Fort Edmonton in the fall of 1858, the settlement actually enjoyed a magnificent Indian summer for a short time. However, by the middle of November, winter had finally set in for good; the streams had frozen over and a permanent covering of snow blanketed the landscape.

Hector was growing restless. Another jaunt to the mountains became an enticing proposition and once again he was off. "With three dog sleighs, and accompanied by Erasmus and [James] Richards, and a Cree Indian I had engaged, known as the 'Fox,' I started to visit the mountains in the neighbourhood of the 'Devil's Head,' as it was necessary to learn something of the nature of the country along their base beyond the mere valleys of the great rivers."

They left Edmonton on 26 November, following the Blackfoot Trail heading south for the Bear's Hill. They continued to follow the Battle River for four days and on 29 November crossed the river to follow the Wolf's Trail (west of present-day Ponoka, Alberta). The weather was bitterly cold and the air filled with ice crystals, "causing a dazzling haze, and which fall steadily, the air being dead calm, and cover the ground and the branches of the trees with a beautiful efflorescence," wrote Hector.

With evening temperatures falling below –37°F, setting up a proper winter camp was a necessity. On one exceedingly cold night, they "had a splendid camp around dry pine woods, and kept up a roaring fire all night, generally having six logs at a time, each about one foot in diameter and eight feet long," Hector reported. The group took advantage of the clear winter sky to indulge in a bit of astronomy. "The stars were wonderfully clear, and, when Jupiter was near the meridian, we distinctly saw, as it were, two irregularities on its margin with the naked eye, and which, with common field glasses were clearly defined as two of the satellites. For several days at this time, even with the small sextant telescope, two large spots were observed on the sun's disc. This phenomenon may have had something to do with the production of the sudden extreme cold which occurred at this time, and which I have since learned was felt all over the central portion of the continent."

Following the Red Deer River, on 5 December they reached the Forks where the Little Red Deer and Medicine Rivers join the main Red Deer River. Here they encamped and dined on porcupine. The Fox demonstrated how to remove the quills. "He extracted them by a very ingenious process, taking advantage of their barbed points. He took his leather gun-cover, and flapping it against the porcupine, then withdrew it with a jerk, which pulled most of the quills out, and left them standing in the leather, and then there was no difficulty in grasping them by their blunt soft roots, and so obtaining them in handfuls." The fat porcupine made a fine meal.

Travel was swift on the frozen river—but not without its pitfalls. "After going a few miles this morning we all fell through the ice, but managed to get out again in safety. However, wet clothes are not to be trifled with when the thermometer is at –20°, so we got on land, made a big fire, and dried ourselves." The next day they were in full view of the mountains, and the Devil's Head stood out like a dark, ominous beacon on the horizon.

On 7 December, they came upon a lonely camp of Stoneys and were greeted by Hector's friend Chief Sampson, whom he had met at the Kootenay Plain. The Fox was not familiar with this part of the country, so once again Hector turned to his knowledgeable Stoney friends for assistance, enticing one to act as guide. He was to be paid a skin a day, with extra skins for any animals he killed. However, the Stoney was ill-equipped for travel in these

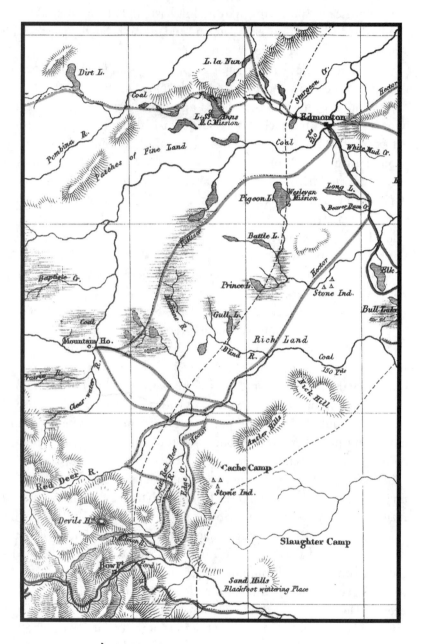

HECTOR'S 1858 WINTER ROUTE TO DEADMAN RIVER

(*SOURCE:* MAPS)

"THE SHINING MOUNTAINS" AND THE DEVIL'S HEAD

(*ERNIE LAKUSTA*)

HECTOR'S SKETCH OF GEORGE SIMPSON'S HISTORIC ROUTE

extreme temperatures, so Hector gave him a large buffalo robe, which he made into a hooded coat, and a second blanket in which to sleep.

Early on the morning of 10 December, they awoke to a splendid aurora of beautiful red and green streamers that were so bright they mistook the display for dawn. Later that morning they reached the *Prairie la Graisse* and the route into the mountains that HBC Governor George Simpson had used in 1841. Hector sketched this historic site.

In negotiating a steep descent of nearly four hundred feet to Waiparous Creek, Hector and his team narrowly avoided disaster. "In effecting this descent, which was exceedingly steep, we untackled the dogs, and each held on by the 'tail line' of his 'sled' and, sitting in the snow, dragged behind to prevent its acquiring an impetus. I was going down in fine style after this fashion, when a young pine tree got between my legs and pulled me up short, the jerk broke the line; and the sled with the instruments and kettles, slid off like a shot. As the slope terminated by a perpendicular cliff of 90 feet, over which I could just see the tops of the tall pines growing up from below, I thought there was no hope, but when just on the brink it struck a rock that whirled it round, so that it buried itself in the snow without further damage." The adrenalin rush that followed this close call quickly erased any thoughts of the disaster that could have been.

They awoke the next morning to discover that they had been completely covered by a heavy snowfall, "and the effect was very curious, as there was not the slightest trace of our camp, —men, dogs, sleds, and fire all being covered by unbroken snow," Hector wrote. "When this occurs I always notice that the additional warmth, and perhaps the knowledge of the extra work on rising, makes us always much later in starting. The dogs also make the most of it as no whistling or calling will make them reveal themselves, and the 'knowing ones' are only to be found by walking round the camp in every direction, till you tramp on them."

Hector explored the country around Deadman's River, but found that the open water and floating ice made it impossible to venture any distance into the mountains. On 13 December, he decided to return to Edmonton using the same track by which they had reached Old Bow Fort the previous summer. It was a bitterly cold journey. On Christmas Eve, at 3:00 AM, they began their last push and, accompanied by another magnificent aurora borealis, reached Fort Edmonton just in time to join the yuletide festivities.

It was a hard life on the frontier, isolated from the outside world. Often, the inhabitants of the fort had to endure extreme winters, periods of starvation, outbreak of disease, drunkenness, and even murder. There were few opportunities during the year to rejoice and Christmas was one of these occasions. It was customary for HBC officials to meet at Edmonton between Christmas and New Year's to discuss business and prepare orders for the coming year. The fort bulged with an influx of visitors from as far away as Fort Chipewyan and Lac La Biche, and as each dog team arrived, the fort became a bedlam. It was also customary, Erasmus wrote, for each employee "to receive a ration of rum the day before Christmas, but by a rule of the Company no-one is to touch it before the next day,"[1] when all were ready to celebrate! Palliser and Chief Factor Christie had arranged for a huge celebration.

Most of the inhabitants attended midnight mass in whichever denomination they chose, which was celebrated by Father Lacombe and Reverend Woolsey. By noon on Christmas Day, each chimney gave evidence of culinary delights as savoury streams of aroma filled the air. By late afternoon, the gates to the fort were slammed shut and the big bell began to ring, summoning everyone to the Big House and the repast.

Many have commented on this yuletide feast. In 1846, artist Paul Kane was present at the festivities and he provides the best description of the repast. Everyone assembled in the huge dining hall, the wooded walls of which were not plastered, but instead, as Kane had described some years earlier, "painted in a style of the most startling barbaric gaudiness, and the ceiling filled with centre-pieces of fantastic gilt scrolls, making altogether a salon which no white man would enter for the first time without a start, and, which the Indians always looked upon with awe and wonder."[2]

Time was regulated by a huge clock that hung on the wall. The wall was also adorned with all manner of pictures and the stuffed heads of buffalo and moose, as well as the horns of many other beasts. A cavernous fireplace with a huge mantel proved to be a gathering place for the gentlemen of the fort.

No fine china or snowy white linen covered tables here, just tin cups and plates. The only hint of opulence was the polished brass candlesticks. At the head of the centre table "was a large dish of boiled buffalo hump; at the foot smoked a boiled buffalo calf. Start not," stated Kane, "the calf is very small, and is taken from the cow by the Caesarean operation long before it attains its full growth. This, boiled whole, is one of the most esteemed dishes amongst the epicures of the interior."[3] Dried moose nose, buffalo tongue and haunches, roast goose and duck, beaver tail, and white fish from Lake St. Ann's delicately browned in buffalo marrow also graced this huge table. Locally grown potatoes and turnips and freshly baked bread and bannock completed the repast.

After dinner, the men gathered round the fireplace to stoke their pipes but, upon hearing the fiddlers strike up a tune, quickly moved into the ballroom. Everyone was welcome, Kane remembered. "Indians, whose chief ornament consisted in the paint on their faces, voyageurs with bright sashes and neatly ornamented moccasins, half-breeds glittering in every ornament they could lay their hands on; whether civilised or savage, all were laughing, and jabbering in as many different languages as there were styles of dress."[4] English wasn't even a second language among this gathering.

Finally the dancing began. It was nothing more than organized bedlam amid the pall of a room thick with smoke from Black Twist tobacco. "The dance itself was but one degree removed from the barbaric Indian dances beside the campfires," wrote Kane. "The tunes were rendered as fast as could be played and the floor was packed with a motley crowd of dancers—Indians, half-breeds, and Hudson's Bay men with half-breed girls and Indian squaws for partners.

"The steps were a mixture of the Red river reel, jig, strathspeys, and hornpipes, interspersed with pow-wows by the Indians gayly bedecked in paint and feathers, and Highland flings by the Scots."[5]

Palliser loved a good party and enjoyed himself immensely as he twirled the ladies around the dance floor.

Spirits flowed freely but never got out of hand. Palliser enjoyed himself so much that he was prompted to write to Governor Simpson. "We have spent a very pleasant Xmas here and was very agreaby [sic] surprised by not seeing a drunken man during the whole of Xmas week—Mrs. Christie and I gave two balls in the large room opposite the dining room. The room was splendidly decorated, with swords bayonets flags etc., Bourgeau and Sullivan were the decorators, they made a splendid wooden Lustre to hang from the ceiling, and lighted the whole place up with candle and reflectors it was a brilliant sight and they all enjoyed themselves very much—a great many came from St. Annes [sic], we had about 200 people, I counted 170 after several had gone. They began at 8 and kept up till 3 in the morning—I intend giving another as soon as the mail starts, but we are all very busy till then."[6]

The grand finale to the week-long festivities was the traditional dogsled races on New Year's Day, after which the influx of men from the outposts returned to their isolated posts in the wilderness. Before long, peace and tranquility once again settled in on Fort Edmonton.

PART TWO

TRAIL-BLAZING, 1859

SEARCHING FOR GIANTS

BY THE SECOND WEEK OF JANUARY, HECTOR WAS ONCE AGAIN growing restless. Now he set his sights on a journey to Jasper House and the legendary Athabasca Pass and a search for the mythic peaks of Hooker and Brown. Once again he was joined by Erasmus and Richards, as well as a voyageur named Paul Louison.

They left Edmonton on 12 January, their sleighs loaded with equipment and enough pemmican to last twenty-eight days. Chief Factor Christie, with two horse carioles and several dogsleds loaded with provisions for a "picnic," decided to accompany them to the "horse guard," about twenty-five miles northwest of Edmonton, where the HBC and the expedition were wintering their horses. After reaching these grounds, the "horse-keeper" gave them the use of his log hut, where they would pass a warm, cozy evening having their "pic-nic."

Erasmus tells of a merry party that night. "The two horse guards had a big slab of ribs, fresh doe meat roasting on a spit in front of the chimney fire, and boiled cold buffalo meat, and to be sure they would have enough, they added two jumbo whitefish to another spit to roast with the doe ribs. You can believe me there was little left of the bounteous feast to throw to the dogs."

The young doctor was adamant that no "class lines," cherished by the Company, would be drawn, and even Chief Factor Christie "lowered the bars to tell some interesting and amusing experiences, under the influence of the doctor's genial and companionable inclusion of all the men in a generous helping of rum, which he highly recommended as the best remedy for all our troubles."

Erasmus noticed that Hector partook very little of his "solicitous recommendations in the matter of drinks, but made certain the factor received his just share." Peter's own refusal to indulge in spirits elicited an eloquent lecture from the doctor "on the faults, illnesses and dire calamities of the whole human race due chiefly to men's refusal to accept known and tried remedies for the faults of obstinacy, stupidity and oddities of a teetotaller. It amused me greatly because the doctor knew for some time of my pledge to abstain at any social function, using liquor for medicine only."[1]

About ten o'clock the next morning, Hector and his men left for Jasper House. It was tedious work tramping through the deep snow over fallen timber and through heavy bush on snowshoes, all the while attempting to keep the dogs in order. Four days later, on 16 January, they reached the Athabasca River and followed it for seven miles before finally reaching the ruins of Fort Assiniboine, an abandoned HBC post.

"We took possession of the kitchen of the fort, and by cutting down some of the old palisades soon got plenty of fire-wood," wrote Hector. Here they would spend their last comfortable night until reaching Jasper House.

Two days later there was a great change in the weather. "In the morning the thermometer was 14°, but during the day it rose very rapidly, with a great storm of wind from the S.W. When we encamped this wind was at its height, and was bringing down the trees all around us. It came in great gusts, sometimes with a few drops of rain." Hector made note of the tremendous rise in the temperature, which by 7:00 PM registered 40°F, only to fall to 1°F by 10:00 PM. He was experiencing a full-blown Alberta chinook!

It snowed incessantly for the next couple of days, making travel difficult for the dogs and exhausting the men. Louison "stupidly smashed his sled," necessitating rearranging all the loads on the two remaining sleds, which made it even more difficult for the poor dogs. To make matters worse, Hector said, "two of my dogs, that I had only bought before starting, and were quite

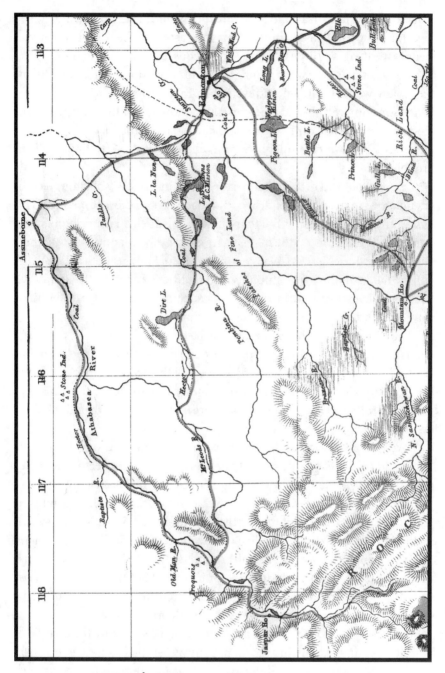

HECTOR'S 1859 WINTER ROUTE FROM FORT
EDMONTON TO JASPER HOUSE.

(SOURCE: MAPS)

wild, had made their escape within a few days after we started, but still continued to follow us, skulking behind like wolves, and only joining their companions at night. We tried every plan to capture them, but only once caught one of them in a snare, but he cut through with his teeth before we could secure him."

In an attempt to lighten the load and also store some provisions for their return journey, they prepared a cache of pemmican. This they did by carefully building a tier of logs over the cache in order to prevent wolverines from raiding it. Hector described the wolverine as a "small rough-haired animal, like a miniature bear, but much stronger in proportion to his size than any other animal in the country. He is possessed of great cunning also, and it is very difficult to defeat his marauding propensities. Their Indian name is *ker-kes-shu*, and many wonderful yarns are told about them round the camp fire. For instance, that a man once left his gun, with the leather cover on, leaning against a tree, while he went to skin a deer he had killed, on his return his gun was gone, and no trace of anything to be seen in the snow excepting the track of a wolverine, that seemed to have gone to where the gun had been left. Following the animal's track, he found after more than 300 yards, the mark of his gun trailing in the snow as the animal had dragged it along, but for this distance it must have carried it clear of the ground, a matter of some difficulty to a little beast not higher than a fox."

On 31 January they came into sight of the mountains at a place Hector named the "Grand View." Here, they indeed got a grand view of the mountains, "which present a bolder outline here than I have seen elsewhere," Hector noted. "Miette's Rock is a bold object, bounding the valley of the Athabasca to the south, and resembling the 'Devil's Head,' which lies to the north of the Bow River. I wished to get to the fort to-day, a distance of 40 miles, so we started early, and went very fast, as there was no snow on the ice to require us to use our snow shoes, which we felt to be a great relief, having constantly been walking on them for 17 days.

"At three o'clock we reached the point where the Athabasca emerges from 'Lac à brulé [Brûlé Lake],' which lies at the base of the mountains, which rise from its western shore at least 3,000 feet. The lake was swept by such a violent wind from the south that we could hardly make way against it over the smooth ice. Its eastern shore is formed of immense sand-hills; and as we reached its upper part we found the ice so covered with the same material that the dogs could hardly pull the sleds."

It was quite dark when they reached the base of Miette's Rock, at which

ROCHE MIETTE

(ERNIE LAKUSTA)

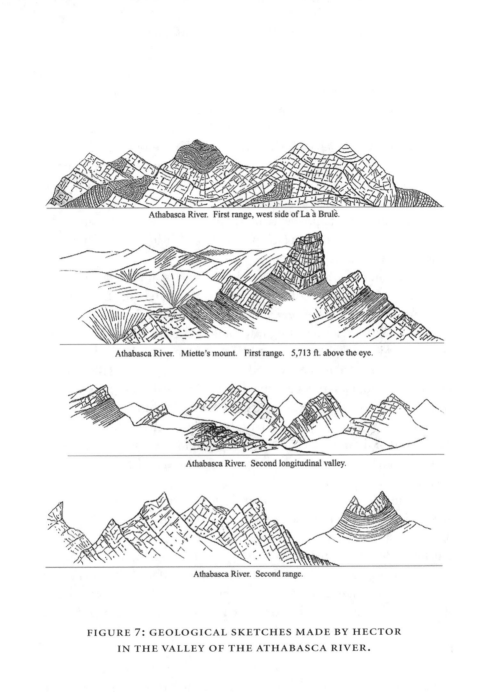

Athabasca River. First range, west side of La à Brulè.

Athabasca River. Miette's mount. First range. 5,713 ft. above the eye.

Athabasca River. Second longitudinal valley.

Athabasca River. Second range.

FIGURE 7: GEOLOGICAL SKETCHES MADE BY HECTOR
IN THE VALLEY OF THE ATHABASCA RIVER.

point, "a spur of the mountain from the south compelled us again to seek the river, which we now found to be a rapid stream, without more than a mere fringe of ice about its margin." This was the place the voyageurs called "Disaster Point," where many an animal had lost its life plummeting over the precipice into the Athabasca. They were only about four miles from Jasper House, which Hector desperately wanted to reach before spending another night in the open. Due to darkness and the icy conditions of the rock, Hector opted to wade across the freezing Athabasca, rather than attempt the dangerous spur of the mountain. They searched in vain for a good ford but, finding none, took to the shallowest place they could find, at a point he estimated to be about one hundred yards wide.

Though the prospect was not inviting, Hector volunteered to cross first and instructed the others not to cross the freezing water until he had started a blazing fire on the other side. The thermometer read a chilling −15°F.

"I watched the man wading into that cold water with something of amazement, and a slight feeling of guilt," stated Erasmus. "We had been hired to do his bidding, yet the man refused to listen to the protests of Richards and Louison." Hector had convinced them that although the water would be terribly cold, there was no sense all of them freezing; by the time the others had crossed, he would have prepared a roaring fire beside which they could change out of their frozen garments. He reminded Erasmus that it would require several trips for them to ferry the loads, whereas he would only have to cross once.

The wind, which had changed at sunset to the northeast, was bitterly cold, and as Hector waded into the freezing water with his loaded pack above his head, he commented "that the plunge into the water felt rather warm at first." Finally, after what seemed like hours but was only a few minutes, Hector was on the other side. Almost immediately his clothes stiffened into a mass of ice. Somehow, after massaging some feeling back into his hands, he managed to strike a roaring fire and yelled to his men to begin ferrying the loads across but to "leave the dogs to the last. I will have the sleigh packed and ready to go as soon as you fellows get all the load over."

Erasmus found that the water "was not too cold when one stayed in but as soon as the air struck your legs on the other side it froze stiff on the outer garments. The water was only a little above our knees, but open water in January was something I hardly expected to see in any of my travels."

Finally, one by one they threw the dogs into the frigid water and, tossing all manner of object at them, forced them to swim across the river. When all the dogs were across, the men rushed to the other side to disrobe and thaw out in front of the blazing fire. As they hurriedly changed their icy garments, Hector turned to Erasmus and said, "Peter, our people in England would be shocked at the discomforts of your western dressing rooms."[2]

The doctor instructed the men to vigorously rub their legs in an effort to regain circulation. But for the poor dogs it was another matter; they all lay frozen like lumps of furry ice. Hector knew that to delay would result in disaster for the dogs and for the expedition, and he instructed the men to quickly harness the frozen dogs and begin a furious run to the fort. This warmed the dogs up considerably and around 10:00 PM they stumbled as one mass into Jasper House, much to the amazement of Henry Moberly and his young Iroquois wife. Moberly was in charge of this isolated HBC post on the outskirts of civilization.

The original Jasper House, constructed at Brûlé Lake, was named for Jasper Hawes, who was in charge of the post in 1817. Its present location near the northern end of Jasper Lake, some fifteen miles upstream, was established in the late 1820s and was beautifully situated in an open plain on the west side of the river, almost directly opposite Roche Miette. The lonely outpost consisted of three dilapidated structures: "the little group of buildings which form the 'fort' have been constructed, in keeping with their picturesque situation, after the Swiss style, with overhanging roofs and trellised porticos. The dwelling-house and two stores form three sides of a square, and these, with a little detached hut, form the whole of this remote establishment."

After the ordeal they had just endured, this rustic outpost was a haven to Hector's men, providing warmth, comfort, and protection from the biting wind.

The occupants had been subsisting almost exclusively on a diet of mutton, but this winter, times were hard and game so scarce that Moberly was forced to supplement their diet with lynx. Eighty-three lynx had already been shot that winter. On 2 February, Hector accompanied Moberly on one of his lynx-hunting expeditions to the valley of the Snake Indian River. The name was intriguing. Who were the Snake Indians? Moberly was more than willing to recount the legend to Hector:

Around 1835, when Colin Fraser was head of the post a band of Snake Indians, the last remnants of a once powerful race, was camped near the post. Camped not far away, at Lac Brule, were their bitter enemies

JASPER HOUSE AND ROCHE RONDE, 1872
(CHARLES HORETZKY / LIBRARY AND ARCHIVES CANADA, PA-009173)

the Assiniboines. On the pretense of negotiating a lasting peace the Assiniboines proposed a meeting at the head of Lac Brule to discuss an agreement. Both parties were to come unarmed.

Foolishly believing their good intentions the Snakes accepted the invitation whereupon the Assiniboines concealing weapons under their blankets murdered all of them. They then rushed to the Snake camp and wiped out the rest of the women, and children with the exception of three young teenage girls who were taken prisoner and taken to Fort Assiniboine. Here they were stripped, bound and placed in a tent, to be tortured and finally dispatched at a great scalp dance the next day.

A young French halfbreed named Bellerose was visiting the Assiniboine camp and took pity on the three Snake maidens. Under the cover of darkness he crept into their lodge and cut their bonds. All that he could provide them was his scalping knife, and a fire bag containing flint, steel and punk. The women made good their escape and followed the Athabasca River to its junction with the Baptiste. Here they could not agree on their next course of action. Two of the girls built a crude raft and taking the fire-bag set out down the Athabasca never heard from again.

The other young maiden headed up the Baptiste River where she made preparations for the coming winter by snaring small mammals and making clothes from their furs. She learned how to make fire in the primitive way by revolving the point of one dry stick rapidly in the hole of another and survived the winter much like a wild animal.

The next summer an Iroquois hunter from Grand Cache came across tracks that puzzled him as they appeared not to have been made by neither an Indian nor animal. He believed that they had been made by the mysterious, cannibalistic, half-human, half-animal demon called a "*weetigo.*" In order to protect his people from the much feared "*weetigo*" he decided to track and kill the monster but had little success.

The following summer he returned to search for his cunning adversary. Finding the same tracks as before he followed them to the entrance of a small cave. He hid and cocked his rifle waiting for the kill. To his amazement the wild creature dressed in a skirt made of animal skins that appeared was a female and not a "*weetigo.*"

Now, changing his tactics he captured the wild girl who put up a vicious battle and brought her back to the camp of his people. She remained with his band for two years before being turned over to Colin Fraser at Jasper House where she served as a servant for two years. Eventually she met and fell in love with a visiting Shuswap and became his wife. When she returned with him to his homeland across [the] mountain barrier, her departure marked the disappearance of the last of the Snake Indians.[3]

Moberly explained to Hector that wolves had become a particular problem and were responsible for killing many of the Company's horses. To overcome this issue, a recently discovered carcass of a mare that had fallen prey would be "salted" with strychnine. On 3 February, Hector visited the site and vividly described the devastating effects of this poison. "On reaching the carcass we found that the strychnine had done its work, for there lay four enormous wolves, beside five or six of a smaller species, while about a score of large ravens were lying about, either dead or in different states of paralysis, some lying on their backs with only power to croak, and others were wading about in the snow in a most solemn manner, with their wings trailing behind them. The large wolves, who were the real offenders, were splendid brutes … The hunters say there is yet another family, and that the survivor is well known by his track, as he has only three feet, for having once been caught in a steel trap, he freed himself by gnawing off the foot he was held by."

Since his arrival at Jasper House, Hector had eagerly eyed Roche Miette and expressed a desire to climb this enticing peak. Moberly agreed to act as guide. As they approached the mountain on the morning of 4 February, Hector was able to observe first-hand where they had crossed the Athabasca a few days earlier. He shook his head in disbelief. "I now saw where we had forded the river the other night in the dark, and it certainly looked an ugly place, and if we had only seen where we were going, we might have hesitated to attempt it."

Reaching the base of the peak, they began their ascent. "After a long and steep climb, we reached a sharp peak far above any vegetation, and which, as measured by the aneroid, is 3,500 feet above the valley. The great cubical block which forms the top of the mountain, still towered above us for 2,000 feet, but it is quite inaccessible from this side at least, and is said to have been only once ascended from the south side by a hunter named Miette, after whom it was named."

Attaining the main summit was out of the question; the climb had become technical and, lacking the expertise for such an endeavour, Hector had to satisfy himself with the view and a little scientific observation. "Between the peak we were on and the face of the high cliff above us there was a gully 150 feet deep, which had been worn out of the soft shales that underlie the blue limestone. I crossed this gully, and scrambled up the opposite side in search of fossils, but only found a few obscure impressions in the friable shales. I observed a remarkable fact here, which shows how local the open weather is in this region of the mountains. The wind, which blew freshly from the N.E. in the bottom of the gully, was so intensely cold that I got quite benumbed, being but lightly clad and heated with the long climb. At the same time, however, Moberly was sitting at a greater altitude on the top of the peak, smoking, and enjoying a comparatively balmy breeze blowing from the S.W."

Hector had stored a cache of pemmican at Jasper House to be used on the return trip to Edmonton. However, on 6 February, he discovered something that caused him great consternation. "To-day I found out that my three men, not liking the lean mutton that all the rest of us were eating, had taken our bag of pemican [sic] out of the store, and completely finished it. As such a misdemeanour was not to be passed over, I determined to send them back at once to Edmonton, and leave them to get as best they could down to the first caché, rather than having them hanging about Jasper House, while I was absent on a trip I intended to make into the mountains." The next morning, he angrily dispatched his companions back to Edmonton.

He did not know the whole story. Peter Erasmus, not wanting to complicate matters, had remained silent in accepting his share of the blame. In fact, Peter had discovered the foul deed and Louison was the culprit.

"Louison admitted his guilt," recalled Erasmus, "but that it was his duplicity alone could hardly be believed from the amount gone, and trying to establish that Richards and I were innocent of the damage might just make matters worse, so we decided that all three take the blame. . . . We were in no position to defend ourselves, not knowing what explanations had already been made, so we took our medicine like the staunch conspirators we actually were. We were all banished back to Fort Edmonton. Richards and I both agreed the sentence was very severe, but as experienced travellers we had to acknowledge that the punishment was justified. Every precaution had to be taken to protect a party against any emergency that might arise in the course of travel.

"Orders were orders, and in our pride we refused to offer any extenuating circumstance that might have improved our position with the doctor.

However, we decided that Mr. Louison would run his legs ragged to keep up with our pace on the way home."[4]

A party of freemen[5] had encamped near the post and on 8 February Moberly and Hector set out to visit them. It was bitterly cold, −14°F, and when they reached the camp, they found that the famished inhabitants were living in small, rounded huts made of pine boughs and surviving on rations of rabbit. As Hector was now without a guide, he enticed one of the Iroquois hunters, a man named Tekarra, to join him in his search for the Athabasca Pass. Tekarra agreed but on the way back to the post he tripped crossing a stream and severely injured his foot. This was a bad omen for someone about to embark on a lengthy snowshoeing trip.

Bright and early the next morning, Hector, accompanied by Moberly, Tekarra, and a man of mixed blood named Arkand, began a journey to Athabasca Pass and the legendary peaks of Hooker and Brown. It was miserably cold, a bone-chilling −20°F. Moberly drove the dog team up the Athabasca River out of the wind, while the other three chose to ride their horses along the sandy terraces above the river. Hector thought Moberly got the best of it that day.

On 11 February they reached the "point opposite to Miette's House where the track branched; one track heading up the Caledonian Valley to Fraser River, the other leading to Athabasca Pass and Boat Encampment on the Columbia River." They set up camp on a knoll overlooking the mouth of the Maligne River and were later joined by Moberly, carrying a young ram he had killed.

The next day, they continued to follow the Athabasca River, passing the *Campment des roches*, where they found the name of a Company employee named Richard Hardisty carved into a tree. It wasn't long before they reached *Prairie des Vaches*, a favourite camping spot for fur brigades, where they themselves encamped. From here they would proceed on snowshoes; it was the 12th of February. Behind their camp, Hector named two peaks: Mount Hardisty, after the Company employee, and Mount Kerkeslin. The origin of the name Kerkeslin and why Hector chose it have puzzled cartographers and historians alike.

Continuing to follow the Athabasca River, they reached the mouth of the Whirlpool River at noon on 13 February. The historic Athabasca Pass lay up the valley of the Whirlpool, but now Tekarra's inflamed foot had become a serious problem.

"Tekarra's foot is so much inflamed with his hunting exertions," Hector reported, "that he will not be able to guide us up the valley to the Committee's Punch Bowl,[6] so I changed my plan and followed up the main stream of the Athabasca instead."

After reaching the mouth of the Whirlpool River, which has its source at Athabasca Pass, Hector "ascended a mountain opposite to the valley of Whirlpool River, and had a fine view up it towards the Boat Encampment [an error in judgment as the Boat Encampment is on the other side of the divide]. Having been directed by Tekarra, I easily recognized Mount Brown and Mount Hooker, which are much like the mountains towards the source of the North Saskatchewan. They seemed distant 30 miles to the S. by W."

Like so many to follow, Hector had been duped. These mythical giants standing on the Great Divide existed only in the mind of botanist David Douglas, and it would be many years before Professor A. P. Coleman would debunk the hoax inadvertently perpetuated by Douglas's exaggerated estimate of their heights in 1827. Instead of standing some 16,000 to 17,000 feet above sea level, the two peaks stand merely 10,781 feet for Mount Hooker and 9,184 feet for Mount Brown.

The next day, Hector instructed Tekarra and Arkand to return to *Prairie des Vaches*, while he and Moberly continued to follow the river upstream. The deep snow soon exhausted them. Just as they halted for a rest, "a wolverine came wabolling [*sic*] down the river on the ice. We remained still till he got quite close without seeing us, when Moberly fired and put the ball right through him, so that his blood spouted out on the snow. He at first rolled over, but on our approaching him he started up and ran off, staining the snow with blood. We followed on our snow shoes, and pressed him hard, so that he ran up the bank and made for the mountain, where, getting into a clift [*sic*] of rock, he escaped us. The distance he ran while losing so much blood, surprised us very much, as at first we thought he was killed outright."

Following the Athabasca for another ten miles, they "found it became quite a mountain torrent, hemmed in by lofty and rugged mountains, two of which, that were very prominent, I named after my friends, Mr. Christie of Edmonton, and Moberly. We now returned down the river to overtake Tekarra, and just at nightfall, and about four miles short of our camp at the *Prairie des Vaches*, we found the tracks of nine reindeer that had come down to the river since Tekarra passed in the morning. We followed them for some distance, but it was now too dark, so we continued to the camp, and arrived at eight o'clock, after a walk of 36 miles; and as none of us had killed anything this day, we had to lie down to sleep without supper."

Early the next morning, Hector left his companions. He wanted to explore the upper reaches of the Miette River. He got along splendidly on the ice until it began to break up. "At last I reached Miette's House, where I was able to get into the woods for a few miles, and so avoid the worst part of the river. However, as the snow was deep my dogs would not drive through it, and I had to walk on and beat a track for a few hundred yards at a time, and then return and drive them on to where I had reached. This process was so slow that I did not reach our appointed camp till nightfall although the distance was only 16 miles from where I started in the morning."

By 16 February, they were back at Jasper House, only to find that Moberly's favourite hunting dog had fallen victim to strychnine poisoning. Ironically, what had been intended as a trap for the wolves proved to be too enticing for his dog!

It was time for the doctor to return to Edmonton, and Moberly hastily arranged for Hector to take some Company horses to good pasture at the Grand Buffon (a voyageur term referring to an area of large alluvial flats along the river), where they would spend the rest of the winter. At 10:00 AM on Saturday, 19 February, Hector, Tekarra, and a young lad named Louis Cardinal departed Jasper House, leaving Moberly and his wife once again to enjoy their lonely, isolated existence. Tekarra estimated it would take twelve days to reach Edmonton and was confident that they would encounter plenty of game en route to supplement their provisions.

Two days' hard travel saw them pass Roche Miette and brought them to the Grand Buffon, where they deposited the horses and left the Athabasca to follow a blazed track through the forest, which Tekarra assured Hector would lead straight to Lac St. Ann's. "We left the sled this morning, and tying a little of the load on the two strongest dogs, carried the remainder on our own backs," Hector reported. "Our supply of provisions only consisted of 18 lbs. of pemican [sic], 2 lbs. of flour, a little tea and sugar. Each of us had a blanket, a few pairs of mocassins [sic] and blanket socks. My papers, books, and sextants, with two kettles, an axe, and a gun, completed the luggage we required to carry."

Encountering deep snow, they took turns breaking trail, which severely taxed their energy. Eventually the dogs had trouble keeping up, forcing the men to shoulder all of the loads. They continued in this manner for a couple of days and Hector became alarmed; they had eaten almost all of the pemmican and Tekarra had been wrong about plentiful game! Fortunately, on 23 February, they surprised a covey of wood grouse from which they culled five.

It was their first fresh meal since leaving Jasper House.

By the evening of the 25th, they had devoured the last of the pemmican and their situation became desperate. The next day, "in the forest we saw fresh tracks of the moose-deer, which Tekarra followed, while Louis and I waited with much anxiety for the result. In a short time he returned, having got quite close to them, but a sudden change of the wind gave them the alarm, so that he did not get a shot. Much disheartened, we walked moodily on till evening, when we began, after making 20 miles, to get into pretty open country, and encamped among the poplars." It would be another cold and hungry night.

The starving men continued to tramp through the deep snow. Mile after mile they stumbled, losing all track of time. "The fallen trees rendered walking very laborious, however, as our snow shoes frequently caught in the knots and made us fall, which was very trying to our tempers, already much soured by our starvation." They were now in serious trouble and Hector knew it. If they didn't find some game and soon, they would probably have to sacrifice the three dogs. It was then that Tekarra discovered some moose tracks "and with wonderful quickness he picked out their most recent tracks, and told us to go on steadily and only to halt if he fired three shots, which was to be a sign he had killed one of them."

Hector and Cardinal continued to stumble on, about a mile by Hector's estimate, when they heard a gunshot. Both halted and waited, their hearts pounding with excitement. And then, almost immediately two more shots were fired in succession. "This at once banished our fatigue, and regardless of the deep snow and fallen timber, we made off in the direction of the firing. Here we found Tekarra busy cutting up a fine three-year-old moose, which was the youngest of the two he had seen. We at once made a fire by the carcass, which lay among the fallen timber where the snow was about four feet deep. Our appetite was tremendous, so that, although the flesh of the animal was so lean that at other times we would not have eaten it, we continued cooking, eating, and sleeping the remainder of that day, and the whole of the next, by which time there was little left of the moose but the coarser parts of the meat. Our three dogs also, who had eaten nothing but the bones of the grouse and our cast-off mocassins [*sic*] since leaving Jasper House, enjoyed themselves to the full; indeed both the dogs and masters conducted themselves more like wolves than was altogether seemly, excepting under such circumstances." They named their encampment "Moose Camp."

The moose was a blessing and, as luck would have it, almost at once their fortunes took a turn for the better. The 1st of March broke calm, clear, and warm. They were now quite refreshed and had prepared enough cooked meat to last several days. The powerful rays of the sun that beat down on them warmed their bodies and raised their spirits. Lake St. Ann's was still nearly one hundred miles distant.

They finally reached the mission on 5 March and were warmly welcomed by Father Lacombe. He informed Hector that Chief Factor Christie had been worried for their safety, and if they had not returned by the next day, he was going to dispatch a rescue party to search for them. Hector's embarrassed friend Erasmus was also anxiously waiting with a fresh team of dogs.

"I only took advantage of M. Le Combe's [*sic*] hospitality till night, when, leaving Tekarra and Louis to come on next day, I started with Erasmus about 10 p.m., and having a good track and fresh dogs we ran the remaining 50 miles of the journey to Edmonton in 10 hours, arriving there to breakfast in the morning."

It had been an eventful fifty-three days in isolated wilderness. Perhaps Erasmus was right when he later asked Palliser if this man did not "have a limit somewhere."

BLACKFOOT COUNTRY

IT WAS EARLY MAY 1859. SPRING HAD ARRIVED, CROPS HAD BEEN planted, and Hector notes that Fort Edmonton was once again a beehive of activity, as fur traders arrived to unload their goods into waiting boats. "The fort was now very lively," wrote Hector, "as all were busy preparing for the great annual voyage to the coast of Hudson's Bay, which occupies the whole summer. Besides the brigade from the Rocky Mountain House, Mr. [Colin] Fraser's brigade from Lesser Slave Lake and Athabasca, and Moberly's brigade from Jasper House, both arrived; and the repacking of their furs, the launching and loading of the boats, and all the necessary preparation, gave the inside of the fort an air of business and mercantile activity that looked more civilized than anything we had seen before in the Saskatchewan."

Each day, the inhabitants gathered on the banks of the river to wave good-bye to the heavily laden boats. Each canoe, about thirty-five feet long, was capable of carrying seventy-five pieces of goods, each weighing as much as ninety pounds. At times the whole scene appeared to be mass confusion.

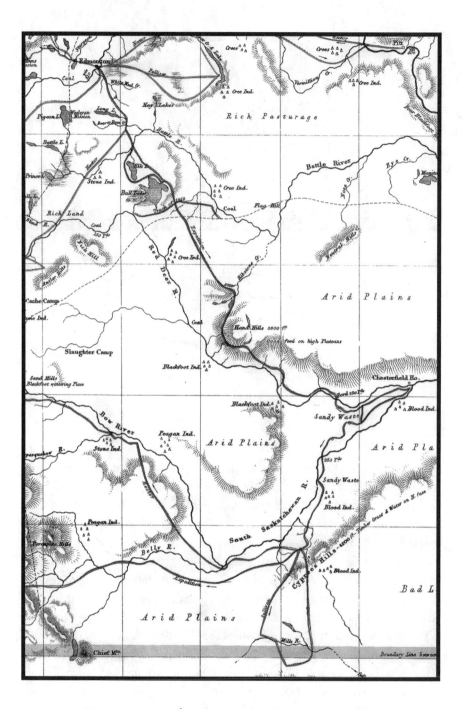

THE EXPEDITION'S ROUTE TO CYPRESS HILLS, 1859

(SOURCE: MAPS)

On 25 May, the last detachment began its long voyage to Norway House on Lake Winnipeg, approximately one thousand miles away, and with them went the expedition's cherished colleague, Eugene Bourgeau.

With much regret, Hector and Palliser bade farewell to their jovial friend. "Our botanist, M. Bourgeau, also availed himself of this opportunity to return home via Red River," wrote Palliser, "in order to fulfil engagements[1] made prior to the formation of our Expedition, when Her Majesty's Government did not contemplate its extension beyond 1858. We were very sorry indeed to lose our friend, who was a great favorite with us all. In addition to his requirements as a botanist, he united the most sociable jovial disposition, ever ready not only to do his own work, but assist anyone else who asked him.[2] He also possesses the most untiring energy in camp, and no fatigue ever deterred him from immediate attention to the securing and preservation of his specimens, as his collections sent home abundantly prove."

Palliser still had not heard from the Colonial Office in regard to extending the expedition's tenure and he was growing anxious. Hopefully, James Beads would soon return from Red River with news from England. In the meantime, everyone busied themselves in preparation for a prompt departure in the event of a favourable response. Palliser desperately wanted to explore the country south from Edmonton through territory controlled by the Blackfoot Confederacy to the Cypress Hills, near the forty-ninth parallel. It was a bold, adventurous, but extremely dangerous plan that he contemplated. If Palliser did not receive word from the Colonial Office, extending his stay, by the time he reached the Cypress Hills, he would have to turn around. This would leave the expedition just enough time to make it back to Fort Garry and then to St. Paul, Minnesota, before weather forced an end to the season.

In the two previous years the expedition had only skirted the eastern and western boundaries of lands controlled by the Blackfoot Nation. However, the route Palliser proposed to take in 1859 would venture south from Edmonton directly through the heart of Blackfoot territory. It was risky, to say the least, but Palliser was confident that the expedition could pull it off without mishap.

By the time the last brigade left, the influx of men had seriously depleted available provisions. "My party was however too large to be supported in the fort," states Palliser, "where every ounce of provisions was of the last importance. Under these circumstances I had nothing for it, but to make a start in search of food, leaving Dr. Hector at the fort to await the arrival of letters and orders from the Colonial Office."

On 26 May 1859, Palliser and Sullivan, accompanied by Captain Arthur Brisco and William Mitchell, two sportsmen on a hunting excursion who had spent the winter at Edmonton and had decided to join Palliser for a "western adventure," along with five carts, forty-seven horses, and a hastily organized motley crew, "comprising Scotch and French half-breeds, Americans, Indians and squaws, one Dutchman, and a negro,"[3] began a journey southward into Blackfoot country. Palliser had had trouble obtaining recruits for this mission given the unknown and dangerous nature of the country he planned to explore. He was also rather reluctant to include Nimrod, as both the Peigan and Blood were mortal enemies of the Stoney and he anticipated trouble. However, Brisco persuaded Palliser to include Nimrod, explaining that his prowess as a hunter and guide precluded any danger he may have imposed on the party.

It didn't take long for Hector to grow restless at Fort Edmonton. "The doctor was consumed with impatience and anxiously watched the trail," stated Erasmus, "or had me do so while he worked out his anxiety on his never-ending calculations." Peter tried to explain that Beads had more than a thousand miles to travel from Fort Garry on horseback and that this could take at least a month of hard travel. Somewhat sarcastically, he said to Hector, "It's more likely that the great masters in England didn't hurry their dispatches, judging their puny little island facilities as equal to our vast open prairies and waterways that could surround their land a dozen times."

Hector glared at Erasmus, which caused him an uneasy feeling, but instead of a tongue lashing, Hector burst into laughter and replied, "Perhaps you're closer to the truth than you imagine. It is hard to get people to realize the vast extent of this country and the difficulties of mail or transportation."[4]

At last, on 7 June, Erasmus spotted a rider on the horizon, and the great haste of the rider suggested that it must be Beads. "It was our man all right, and the doctor was happy again," Erasmus wrote. "I was glad that the session of waiting was over, as the doctor was getting quite hard to live with. His imagination had Beads sick or accidentally hurt or a half dozen other mishaps all quite as impossible."[5]

Beads "arrived with the letters from Red River, and along with him Vital, a half-breed from Red River, who was bound for a trip across the mountains to see some relations at Colville," wrote Hector. They had made a remarkable journey, covering the one thousand miles from Fort Garry in just thirty-four days.

Indeed, in his haste to reach the fort, Beads had lost all his clothes swimming across the river! Gallantly, he hung on to the all-important dispatches that contained the much-awaited orders from England. Curbing his impatience to immediately leave and deliver the news to Palliser, Hector delayed a couple of days, allowing Beads time to procure new clothes and give the exhausted horses time to recover from their epic journey.

On 11 June, Hector left Fort Edmonton for what would be the last time. He was joined by Erasmus, Beads, George Burnham, Joseph Boucher, and Vital. He also enlisted the services of a Blackfoot guide named Amoxapeta, whom Hector thought would be invaluable while travelling in Blackfoot country. Amoxapeta was accompanied by his Cree wife.

Before Palliser departed, he and Hector had made arrangements as to how the young doctor would locate his captain if and when the orders arrived from England. "The Captain had given us a general idea of their direction, leaving a bottle with further instructions under a campfire secretly marked at each main campground they had used," Hector wrote. "After the third day's ride we were given directions to find a caché of food and the location of their next permanent campground." All Hector had to do was find these campsites and locate the secret campfire with the all-important instructions.

The night of 13 June was miserable. A torrential rain soaked everything and it was all they could do to keep a fire going. And food supplies were already starting to run low. The next morning, "leaving the men and horses to follow the Blackfoot trail, I started off with Amoxapeta along the shore of Elk Lake," Hector reported. "Killed four ducks, and collected 55 eggs (principally water-hen's), and enjoyed the first full meal we have come across now for several days."

Hector's group rode hard, following Palliser's trail as best they could and relying on the clues he had left. But still there was no sign of the Captain's party, and by the 16th they had become desperate. "We were now so badly off for food and so hungry that I was obliged, although very reluctantly, to broach one of the flour bags, two of which I was carrying with us. We now passed out into the arid plains, and shortly found two letters buried in the track by Captain Palliser."

Hector sent Erasmus ahead in search of Palliser, while he and Vital began tracking some buffalo. After nearly twenty miles, from a slight rise, they spotted "a band of bulls, which we ran, and out of which we killed two," wrote Hector. Slinging as much meat onto their horses as they could carry, they arrived "about midnight to where the rest were camped, bringing them some of the meat, but they had fallen in with a band of cows, and Beads had killed two. The buffalo dung, which was our only fuel, was however so wet that we could not make any fire worth speaking of, and had to eat our meat nearly raw."

Erasmus returned the next day, having followed Palliser's trail as best he could but unable to locate him. That night they camped at the base of some high hills, called the Squirrel Hills. On 18 June, they resumed their search "and traveled over a wide, level, arid plain, interspersed with salty lakes, in sight of a range of very marked hills, with an abrupt escarpment to the west. Where we found a large creek, flowing to the north-east, we encamped." These were the Hand Hills, or as the Indians called them, the *Oochischis Wachee.*

On 19 June, a few hours of travel brought Hector and his men to the base of the Hand Hills. After ascending the long, steep north face, they traversed the flat top and finally spotted the Captain's team encamped in a deep valley. Upon seeing them, Palliser rushed to greet them, anxious to read his dispatches. They had been written by Labouchere on 18 February, and Palliser could hardly contain his excitement as he carefully perused the documents. He had been authorized to spend a third season in the field and allotted £1,500 to cover expenses!

Labouchere had also granted Palliser permission to explore the unknown country in the neighbourhood of the international border, cross the mountains, and return to England by way of the Pacific coast and the Isthmus of Panama. Palliser was ecstatic; he could hardly believe his good fortune. Not only had his wish been granted and £1,500 given to cover expenses, but an additional £1,500 had been allotted to make it possible for the explorers to return by way of the Pacific coast after the season's work.

Palliser immediately called a meeting and explained that he intended to pursue a course southeast to explore the country near the forks of the Red Deer and Bow Rivers. From there he intended to head west through the mountains to Fort Colvile.[6] All the while they would be in lands controlled by the Blackfoot Confederacy, an alliance that rigorously guarded against intrusions into its land. The Blackfoot name alone invoked fear in his men; Palliser could see it in their eyes.

Were they prepared to follow the Captain? Old Paul, Palliser's reliable and trusted hunter, was reluctant to go and wanted to state his case. Palliser allowed him to address the men. "It is all very well for those who do not know the country to be brave about it," Paul said, "but speak to any of the old ones who know, and who have experience of the country; take me for instance,

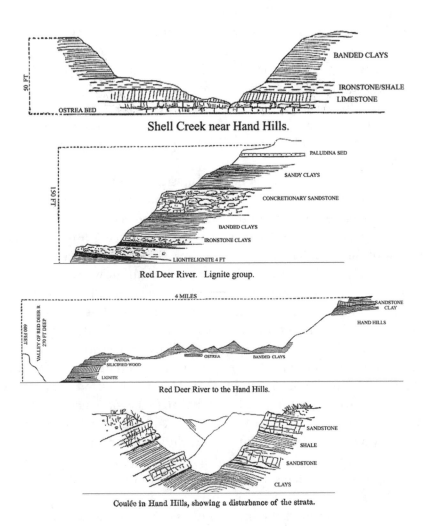

Shell Creek near Hand Hills.

Red Deer River. Lignite group.

Red Deer River to the Hand Hills.

Coulée in Hand Hills, showing a disturbance of the strata.

FIGURE 8: GEOLOGICAL SKETCHES MADE BY
HECTOR ON THE JOURNEY TO CYPRESS HILLS

who have had my clothes pierced with bullets, and had my relations killed; ask if there is one of us who have not had some of their brothers, or brothers-in-law killed by these Indians. The country is too dangerous, and I have spoken."

Palliser was reminded that on 15 and 16 June, while waiting for Hector, they had been threatened by troublesome Blackfoot war parties, one consisting of about forty-two warriors. They threatened Palliser's men, "telling [his] interpreters that their time was come to die, and other threats of a similar nature." Nimrod, his wife, and small child had been pursued relentlessly by these warriors, who shot his dogs and "robbed them of all they possessed," and they barely escaped with their lives after being lured away from the safety of their camp.

The Captain used all the guile he could muster to ameliorate this situation and, "by the exercise of patience, firmness, and speech-making," states Palliser, "I managed to pacify my troublesome customers."

Palliser was concerned about the effect that Paul's speech would have on the rest of the men. Sure enough, his impassioned plea convinced Felix Munroe (Monro) that it was too dangerous to continue with such a small party of just over twenty men. He, too, wished to turn back. The Captain was now in a fine fix and had to act quickly if he didn't want to lose either of these valuable men—valuable both as hunters and in the sense that the expedition's safety was linked to having a large number of men in the party. Palliser persuaded both to remain but only if he agreed to increase the number of men in their party. Palliser immediately dispatched Munroe back to Edmonton to enlist the help of "not more than six or less than four good hands, engaged at the wages of the Expedition." He also instructed Munroe to bring a bale of tobacco, which could be distributed as presents to the Indians. On 20 June, Munroe, accompanied by Samuel Ballenden, departed for Edmonton, leaving the expedition with just twenty men in the middle of hostile Blackfoot country.

All they could do now was wait for reinforcements. In order to protect their position, Palliser immediately moved their camp to the top of a high hill beside a small slough. The vantage point afforded adequate surveillance of the surrounding territory, plus access to water and plenty of feed for the horses. It also gave them a much better position to guard the horses and defend their position in case of attack. This fortified camp became their base for the next fourteen days, and each day they would eagerly scan the horizon in search of evidence announcing the arrival of the new recruits from Edmonton.

Finally, on 4 July, clouds of dust on the horizon announced the presence of approaching horsemen. But was it Palliser's men returning with reinforcements, or was it a war party? The Captain scanned the advancing troop with field glasses and, after some time and much to his relief, was able to confirm that it was indeed Munroe and Ballenden.

They returned with four recruits, but arrived in a sad plight, having not eaten anything for four days. "Their eyes were wild with hunger; they described a sad state of things at Edmonton; Brazeau obliged to kill the working cattle," Palliser wrote. "Such was the fearful state to which the inhabitants of the fort were reduced for want of food, that they persuaded the men to tell them where they had cached the meat provided by me for their return journey from Edmonton to my camp. One of them went back, brought it in, and distributed it among the women and children in the fort."

On the morning of 7 July, the camp was visited by another worrisome party of Blackfoot warriors, but on the whole, they were well behaved and Palliser managed to appease them with gifts of tobacco, tea, and some bread.

As they prepared to continue their journey, there was a "very great unwillingness on the part of the French half-breeds to move." They were "literally terrified," states Palliser. Then, Old Paul approached Palliser "and declared off, saying he was exceedingly sorry to leave me, pleading the commands of his 'mother-in-law' as an excuse, but, in fact, terrified at the prospects of travelling through the heart of the Blackfoot country," wrote Palliser. The Captain had no choice but to let him go, but no sooner had he done so than the rest of the "French half-breeds commenced to signify their intentions of turning back also." Palliser had a minor mutiny on his hands and he had to act quickly.

Palliser explained that he would not allow anyone else to leave the camp, at which point, "a slight murmur of disapprobation then arose concerning this decision, and before they had time to get together or combine, I exclaimed, 'who is the first man who will say that he will turn back?' upon which, one bolder than the rest stood up, and exclaimed, 'I will go back.' I rushed right at him, and seized him by the throat, and shook him, and then catching him by the collar, kicked him out of the camp. I called out then to know if any other wished also to go back, but, fortunately, the retrograde movement extended no further."

Palliser would later remark, "I am happy to say, I was not obliged to adopt this course on any further occasion, but succeeded ever after in keeping my men together principally by ridicule and partly by persuasion."[7]

The next four weeks of travel through Blackfoot country would be fraught with danger: lack of clean drinking water, a constant search for game, dangerous river crossings, rattlesnakes, and the intense heat of the prairies. But the greatest danger was still the possibility of a confrontation with the Confederacy and this continued to terrify the men. Skilful diplomacy would be required to avoid a serious conflict if ever the occasion arose, but little did Palliser know that it would be his young doctor who would become his chief diplomat.

On 9 July, Old Swan, the aged, revered, powerful, and wise Blackfoot chief, made an unexpected visit to the camp near the Hand Hills. Palliser had met the old chief at Edmonton and both he and Hector had met him at Rocky Mountain House. Palliser and Old Swan had developed a cordial relationship; in fact, Old Swan held the Captain in such high regard that he called him his grandson. Still, chiefs had little control over the "rogue" bands that wandered this extensive territory, and even having cordial relations with someone like Old Swan was no guarantee of safety.

Old Swan invited Palliser to visit his camp on the south side of the Red Deer River. Palliser would be accompanied by Hector and Erasmus, and they would bring gifts of ammunition, powder, tobacco, and calico. Later, as they approached the Blackfoot camp, the three men were awestruck by what they saw.

"This very large camp was in many ways a novel sight," wrote Palliser, "even to us who had seen so many Indian camps. We now found the Blackfeet here numbering about 400 tents; they had originally been 500, but 100 tents of these had pitched away further up the river." As they entered the camp, their anxiety increased. "Men and children of all sizes flocked around us, but the chiefs kept back the crowd every now and then by one word, or even by only a very slight gesture. They came forward, and took all our baggage in charge, and also our horses."

This gesture reminded Hector of the meeting he had had with *Pee-to-Pe* during his visit to the Mountain House in 1857. "We see but little of the white man," *Pee-to-Pe* had told Hector, "and our young men do not know how to behave; but if you come among us, the chiefs will restrain the young men, for we have power over them. But look at the Crees, they have long lived in the company of white men, and nevertheless they are just like dogs, they try to bite when your head is turned—they have no manners; but the Blackfeet have large hearts and they love to show hospitality." Perhaps the ferocious nature of these people had been overstated?

"There were several cases of sickness in [Old Swan's] camp," noted Palliser, "not of a severe kind. The Doctor had brought his medicines with him, and relieved several, especially one or two children, and his success with these rendered him very popular." Much to their relief, the Blackfoot were impressed with Hector's ability to heal and from that moment his esteem as a medicine man began to grow. The group spent a pleasant day at the Blackfoot camp, trading stories, learning their ways, and presenting them with twists of tobacco. And how could they refuse when Old Swan invited them to spend the night in the camp.

In honour of their visit, they were entertained that evening by wild and energetic dancers and shared in the custom of passing round the pipe; Palliser was glad he had brought extra tobacco. Later, they were invited to Old Swan's lodge, where many other powerful chiefs had gathered around the hearth in the centre of the tent. Each chief spoke in turn through Erasmus. Some spoke of the diminishing buffalo herds; others spoke of the cruel and deceitful *Moka-manus*, or Long-Knives (Americans); some ranted at the lack of respect and unfair trading practice they received from the Hudson's Bay Company; still others inquired as to the effect of the white man coming into their territory. Hector was impressed with the sincerity and frankness of these men. They were not savages, as he had been led to believe. He was intrigued by the rich, almost melodic nature of the Blackfoot tongue and took this opportunity to learn more about the origin of their name and their customs.

One of the chiefs told them a legend about the origin of the Blackfoot. Erasmus translated as best he could. "Many summers ago," the old chief began, "when our forefathers crossed the mountain barrier from the land of the setting sun to settle along the South Saskatchewan there was a great chief who had three sons; Kenna or The Blood; Peaginou, or The Wealth; and a third who was nameless. Kenna and Peaginou were great hunters whose arrows ran straight and true. They brought much meat to their father's lodge. The nameless one was not a good hunter, always returning from the hunt empty-handed. The people began to mock him for his lack of skill. One day the chief said to the nameless one; 'My son, you cannot kill the moose, your arrows shun the buffalo and the elk is too swift for your footsteps. Your brothers mock you because you bring no meat to my lodge; but do not despair, I will make you a great hunter.' With that, the chief took a piece of burnt stick from the fire-pit, and wetting it, rubbed the feet of the nameless son with the blackened charcoal; and then, he named him *Sat-Sia-qua*, or The Blackfoot. From that time on *Sat-Sia-qua* became a mighty hunter and from these three sons descended the three tribes of the Nation; the Blood, Piegan, and the Black-feet. It wasn't until many generations later that the Sircies [Sarcees] and the Gros Ventures were added to the confederacy."[8]

The next day, Palliser and his men returned to their camp, rich in new-found knowledge of their Blackfoot friends and convinced that no trouble would befall them. Word spreads fast on the prairies, and by the time the expedition had crossed the Bow River on 19 July (somewhere south of the junction of the Red Deer and Bow Rivers), they were met by a contingent of Blood. The sight of these warriors so terrified a party member named Wapishoo that the cowardly fellow fled and was never seen again. But, as Palliser wrote, "the Blood Indians rode up and shook hands with me; they had all come unarmed in compliment to us." Later, a slight altercation over three guns stolen from Wapishoo's abandoned wagon arose, but tact and skilful diplomacy by the Captain avoided a confrontation and saw the return of the weapons.

Four days later they were invited to visit the Blood camp. Here the Indians, Palliser described, "received Capt. Brisco, Dr. Hector, and myself most hospitably. Their tents are the largest I have ever seen, some of them 30 feet in diameter and of a proportionate height, well supplied with kettles, dishes and spoons, and frequently with American luxuries, such as coffee and sugar. They trade at Fort Benton on the Missouri.

"While we were in one of the tents, a sick child was brought in to the Doctor, who made some mixture for it out of medicines he had taken with him to the camp; before, however, he had time to give the child anything, one of the medicine men of the tribe, accompanied by his satellites with their drums, rushed into the tent, snatched the child out of the Doctor's hands, and commenced drumming and howling. The Doctor then told them through Felix, who had interpreted for us, that he would not answer for the child which soon afterwards died."

The next day, the doctor's services were again urgently requested. "The Indians told us there was a great deal of sickness among them, and they requested me to come into camp and pray for them, that the sickness might be removed. I complied," wrote Palliser, "and read the general confession and the Lord's prayer, which Felix translated into Blackfoot after me." And then, something incredible happened. "A woman brought a child to see the Doctor, which was in a fit, and while he was occupied in making up some medicine for it, the medicine man, who had interfered yesterday, came in in a similar manner, and attempted to take away the child. The mother of the

"NATOOS"

(SEAN DOYLE)

child, however, aware of the result of the medicine man's exertions in the case of the child, which occupied yesterday, flew like a tigress on the medicine man, and effectually prevented all interference with Hector." The child recovered and Dr. Hector's esteem continued to grow. They named him *Natoos*, meaning "The Sun," or "Medicine Man."

Palliser would later comment that their travelling through Blackfoot country without so much as firing a shot was due not only to the cordial relations they had developed with the various members of the Confederacy but also to the young doctor.

"Dr. Hector's great success in his profession," wrote Palliser, "especially among the women and children, which called forth their astonishment, and in many cases deep, though undemonstrative gratitude," may have been the main reason the expedition did not experience "any disastrous results from a single one of those tribes."

At last, on 27 July, they camped in sight of the Cypress Hills. Rising above the prairies near what is today the border between Saskatchewan and Alberta, they formed a blue line etched on the horizon. The next morning, they were greeted by an old Blood chief named *Manistokos*, whom Palliser nicknamed the "Father of All." He was returning to Fort Benton with the decomposing body of his son, who had been buried nearby some seven months earlier.

"He was actually taking him back all the way to Fort Benton [on the Upper Missouri River, across the border in the United States]," stated Palliser. "But I dissuaded him, by telling him that it was his duty to think of all the young men of his people, like as if he was a father to them, and how could he think of bringing a partially decomposed body into a camp where they were suffering already from sickness? such a course would only be fatal to more of his children. After a long pause he said, 'You have irons for digging: desire your men to dig me a place; I will bury him; you are wise, and I will do as you bid me.' The men then took the spade and shovel and dug the son's grave. The father and his soldiers buried him."

That evening, Palliser and his party camped at a small lake at the base of the Cypress Hills; it seemed like an oasis in the middle of the arid plains.

Despite the cordial relations that had developed between members of the expedition and members of the Blackfoot Confederacy over the past few days, they would soon be reminded that they were in hostile territory. This reminder came in the form of a group of Blood Indians who arrived at their Cypress Hills camp bent on murdering Nimrod; the Blood and Blackfoot had been mortal enemies of the Stoney since time immemorial and Nimrod was a Stoney on their land.

Palliser told Nimrod not to run, that he would protect him at all costs. All including Hector were to act nonchalantly, so as not to appear frightened—a ruse meant to retrieve the gun. "I sat on the ground at the tent door, with my rifle across my knees, and Brisco kept a sharp lookout on the Indian beside me; I then desired Hector to give up his gun to one of the men, and to pretend afterwards as if he were looking for his own gun, and finally to take our gun from the Indian who had armed himself with it."

And then, something totally unexpected happened. "Olivier [*sic*] Munroe [Monro], brother of Felix, whom we had all looked on previous to this period as a fool, now began to talk to them in their own language, much to their astonishment, saying, 'You do not know these men; they think as much of that Stoney, they think as much of me, [as] they themselves. You want to kill the Stoney: well, kill him; but think well! for you will have to kill everyone of us; and as to 'him' [referring to Palliser] he will be the first to fire.'"

All the while, Felix Munroe translated his brother's words to Palliser, who was astounded at the bravery displayed by Oliver. The Captain tried to appear relaxed and unconcerned as he smoked and passed a pipe around. "At a little after midnight, however, they all rose with one accord, jumped on their horses, and galloped off."

On 29 July 1859, they arrived in the heart of the Cypress Hills and encamped in a magnificent valley, where "we were now well supplied with wood, water, and grass, a rare combination of happy circumstances in our experience of this season's explorations." Palliser summoned a council at which he once again decided to split the party into two branch expeditions.

Hector received the following instructions:

Cypress Hills, August 1st, [1859]

Dear Hector,
1. You will proceed from this to the Old Bow Fort, enter the mountains again by the pass you explored last year, and endeavour to explore a route practicable for horses to the westward, as far as ever it lies in your power, proceeding by the valleys of Fraser and Thompson's Rivers, and avoiding the valley of the Columbia.
2. You will bear in mind however, that you are to run no unwarrantable risks, or jeopardize the safety of your horses, companions, or yourself.

3. Should the work be too severe for your horses to endure (for they are even now very far from being in as fit a condition for such a trip as I would wish), you are immediately to turn back, and to make the best of your way to Fort Colville [*sic*], where you will receive further instructions from me on your arrival.

4. In case, however, you do succeed in effecting your western route, you will proceed to the forks of Fraser and Thompson's Rivers, where I shall endeavour to have instructions also waiting for you.

5. In the event, however, of these instructions failing to reach you, you will proceed onward to Fort Langley.

6. In the event of your requiring to purchase horses or any necessary supplies, I now furnish you with a few bills of exchange upon the Paymaster-General, with the clear understanding, however, that you are not to avail yourself of them in any purchases you might make from the Hudson [*sic*] Bay Company or any of their servants.

John Palliser, Captain Commanding British
North American Exploring Expedition

Hector began to make preparations for his journey, but was unprepared for what was to follow. Peter Erasmus approached him and said, "Doctor, I hate to refuse to join your party but if you consider the condition of the stock, the lateness of the season, and the scarcity of pemmican and dried meat supplies to take along, you might understand my refusal. We would have to depend on game in the region. Nimrod considers it a risky business not to have plenty of prepared food to last the entire trip. It may well take three weeks to investigate the area. To take from the supplies on hand for your needs will make the other members of the expedition dependent on day-to-day hunting for food. I'm sorry but I just cannot do it."[9]

Hector was livid and reprimanded his loyal assistant. His loss of temper took Erasmus and even Palliser completely by surprise. He had always managed to maintain self-control, even when confronted by the hot-headed Thomas Blakiston. Deep down, both Hector and Palliser knew that Erasmus's assessment was correct, but probably what annoyed the doctor more than anything was Erasmus's outspoken criticism in front of the rest of the men.

Palliser summoned both men to a palaver and proposed a compromise. He told Hector that the success or failure of the expedition was dependent on the information and experience regarding the conditions in the country; the honesty of the men employed to carry out their duties was vital to the safety and survival of all of them. He explained that "Peter had a right to express his opinion. He is one of our oldest employees and has served us well in other times. Take any one of the others. I will employ Peter in other duties." Although Palliser did not approve of Erasmus's disobedience, he was willing to uphold his decision and reassign duties. "Our servant, James Beads, however, at my suggestion (not by my orders)," wrote Palliser, "in the most praiseworthy manner volunteered to go in his place."

Erasmus was concerned about the effect this quarrel would have on his relationship with Hector, but pride would not allow any overtures on his part. As he explained to Palliser, "I will take risks with any man, but your doctor is so fanatical with his work that realities do not exist in his mind." Palliser had a hearty laugh and after regaining his composure said, "Upon my word , Peter, you take my breath away. I admire your pride and independence. Your remarks have convinced me of your good judgment."

For his part, Hector was not about to let this incident spoil his relationship with Erasmus. Quietly he drew Palliser aside and expressed his sorrow for his loss of temper, whereupon the Captain called Erasmus aside and said, "The doctor and I have discussed your situation fully and he has asked me to express his regret at losing his temper. He admits you showed much more self-control than he would have under the same provocation." Erasmus was relieved, his pride and self-esteem had been restored, but the altercation with the man he so greatly admired deeply disturbed him.

"Well, sir," he replied to the Captain, "I am happy to hear the doctor holds no grudge, for I must admit that I have been very miserable over the whole thing. I think you realize that I have a great admiration for his physical abilities on the trail. I know of no man I would rather be with than your young doctor. My work with him has always been a pleasure except for that devilish urge that always seems to be riding him, to be on his way regardless of what horse flesh, dog or man can stand up to on the trail. The man must have a limit somewhere!"

That evening, Palliser wrote in his journal: "We were now about to break up our party, and this was the last night we were to spend altogether on the eastern plains; we celebrated this event by the addition of the luxuries of tea and bread for supper at the Doctor's expense, taken out of the scanty little store I had allotted to him for his trip in the mountains."

Palliser also wrote a short letter of recommendation for Erasmus: "For his advantages, Peter Erasmus is every inch a gentleman and has rendered me a great service." Erasmus would cherish Palliser's letter and his friendship with Hector. The next morning, before departing, the two met for the last time. Hector smiled and the two shook hands. No words were spoken of the incident. Erasmus could sense that the young doctor fully understood his reasons for not following. The two would never meet again and would not communicate with each other until James Hector received the unexpected letter from Erasmus in New Zealand decades later.[10]

TRAVEL AT YOUR OWN RISK!

ON 3 AUGUST 1859, HECTOR LEFT BEHIND A NUMBER OF HIS FRIENDS, most of whom he would never see again. "I started on this date for the Rocky Mountains at the Old Bow Fort, my party consisting of Beads, Burnham, McLaurn [McLauren], Oliver Vanesse, and the Stone [*sic*]Indian Nimrod, my hunter of the previous summer's trip to the mountains, and who had stuck to us through all the Blackfoot country, and brought his wife and child with him, principally that he might accompany me. I had 18 horses, nine of which carried packs, and my supply of provision, which I meant not to touch till I was well into the mountains, but rather, if possible, to add to them, consisted of 240 lbs. of pemican [*sic*], 80 lbs. of flour, 50 lbs. sugar, and a good stock of ammunition. This is about 20 days' provision for the five of the party that are to continue the journey, after Nimrod leaves us in the mountains."

They began the long and dangerous journey back through Blackfoot country to Old Bow Fort. For three days, travel was uneventful and then, on the afternoon of 7 August, they came upon a Peigan butchering a recently slaughtered buffalo. Hector's gut feeling was that their good fortune was about to change. The Peigan spoke neither Stoney nor Cree but using sign language informed Nimrod and Beads that he was part of a very large camp not far away, which consisted of three hundred lodges and belonged to the American territories.

Hector attempted to convince the young hunter to stay the night, knowing full well that as soon as he informed his camp of their presence, they could soon expect a visit from more of his friends. Would they be friendly? "However, his desire to tell the news was too great, so just as we were going to encamp he rode off in a great hurry. I let him get out of sight, and then we started again, and went as hard as we could till it was quite dark. There seemed to be no water anywhere in this part of the country, excepting a few small pools of the rain-water that had fallen in the forenoon. At one of these, not more than three feet across, we encamped, making no fire and keeping the horses close."

Now he really began to worry for the safety of Nimrod. Anxious to put as much distance as possible between his party and the Peigan, they broke camp at dawn the next morning, but it wasn't long before a long, thin black line appeared on the horizon, announcing the approach of a large band of visitors. Hector altered course, but it mattered little and before long they were joined by forty braves, including the young hunter they had encountered the previous evening. All of a sudden their situation had become terrifying!

Some of the braves spoke Cree, which Beads interpreted as best he could. "Having heard through the Blackfeet of our party, and of all the presents of tobacco, &c., that had been given to them," they thought they had struck the "mother lode" and wanted their share. Luckily," states Hector, "before starting, I had put a few pounds of tobacco in my holsters, so, without halting, I was able to carry on the palaver, and give the customary little pieces of "Pastah-kan" (tobacco) to all the principal men."

Soon they were joined by a cavalcade of several hundred Peigan from the camp. Luckily, some of their number included their big chiefs. "They did all they could to persuade me to stop, and camp with them, and trade horses, and give the tobacco, and so on. But as my horses were all [hand-] picked animals, I was not likely to get better from them. My principal reason for refusing to stay, however, was seeing the evident wish of some of the young men to do Nimrod a mischief. They tried all they could to edge him away from the party, but I made him stick close by me, while we kept steadily at a jog trot, driving the pack-horses before us."

Hector's party continued to move and, "at last, after a couple of miles with this rabble at our heels, when they found that I could or would give no more tobacco, they began to drop off, and the only ones I regretted to part with were the chiefs, as there still remained behind a horrid rascally-looking set."

In the meantime, Beads had struck up an acquaintance with one of them who had spent time with the Cree and got him to remain their ally on "the promise that when all the rest had gone he would get a large piece of tobacco. All his anxiety was now to get rid of the tail that continued to follow us," in order that he might receive his gift.

Their Peigan ally harangued his friends to leave, but his words fell on deaf ears as the twenty or thirty who remained were not easily persuaded. "He then advised me to stop and have a smoke," Hector said, "so after talking to my men I said I would, if they would all stop with me. I only kept Beads, however, and when we had got off our horses and sat down in a ring, as is usual, according to arrangement, Burnham, McLaurn [McLauren], Oliver, and the Stoney began slowly to drive on the horses again." Hector tried to reassure the Peigan that his horses were tired and would continue at a slow pace until he caught up to them.

The young doctor also tried to convince the Peigan that he was in advance of Captain Palliser's larger party and they would have lots of presents and tobacco for them if they would only wait for his arrival. In the middle of negotiations, eight or ten "of the scamps jumped on their horses and followed my men. I heard afterwards that on coming up they tried by signs to make Burnham understand that I wished them to turn back, but he was far too wide-awake to do that. One of them then seized McLaurn's (McLauren's) knife from his belt, and was rather surprised by having a revolver clapped to his head, so he returned it." After Burnham refused to comply, events threatened to turn ugly.

"They then caught hold of the pack-horses, and one of them jumped off his horse, and commenced to undo the pack cords; but Nimrod pulled off his gun cover, and cocked the gun, and, as the scamps are generally cowards among the Indians, this made him change his mind." They tried this tactic for about another ten minutes, doing "all they could to provoke the three men, who, with Nimrod and his wife, were coolly driving along the loaded horses before them, [then] they turned back and rejoined the party where I still remained with Beads, and commenced talking in a loud and excited manner."

Their Peigan ally now informed Hector that his friends "were not pleased, and that we should be off. After a little time I prepared to go, and told Beads to tighten our girths, when the scamps now began to press round us, wanting to look at every thing we had, and tried to fire our guns. However, I had put the caps in my mouth, and made Beads do the same, so that was no go. One of them then plunged his hand into my shot pouch, and took all my ball out, but laughing all the while I made him give them back, for although I felt as ill at ease as ever I did in my life I knew that the only chance was to look unconcerned."

After some time Hector informed their Peigan friend "to make a turn and join us beyond some hills that we were just going to enter, and then set off at such a sharp pace that the Indians only followed us a little way, when seeing they were getting far from their own people, who had all this time been moving in the opposite direction, they began to drop off and turn back."

Only after the last Peigan had left did Hector draw rein to wait for their friend who had done them such good service and "made him a very handsome present. He told us not to go straight, nor stop till late, as he heard that some of the young men were going to try and steal our horses in the night."

Before long they had rejoined the rest of their party and "found Nimrod and his wife still of a kind of ashy-grey colour from fear; but like the rest of us in a high flow of spirits from the sense of relief." They continued for approximately another twenty-four miles without rest before halting. Later, "as night came on we made seven miles more, and then having got among the hills where there was short grass that did not show the horse tracks so well as the dry dusty plains, we finished by making a great turn and camping beside some excellent water, but without daring to make a fire."

It was the most terrifying experience of the young doctor's life. All were relieved at having survived this harrowing encounter, but their nerves were shattered, and many days' travel through dangerous country still lay ahead. They could only thank Providence for their good fortune. They reached the valley of the Bow on 10 August without further incident.

The banks were covered with a profusion of wild berries, which gave them an excuse to halt, feast on the berries, and bathe in the river. They encamped in a beautiful grove of large aspens. Suddenly they were startled by another group of Indians who appeared on the opposite bank. They were still some distance away as Hector and Nimrod anxiously studied them through field glasses. All of a sudden, Nimrod began shouting with glee as he recognized Stoneys of his own tribe. His friends were encamped about ten miles upriver from their present location.

Later, while exploring the woods around their campsite, Hector discovered a wigwam carefully closed, with logs piled against it for security.

"Slashing a hole in it with my knife, I found that it contained a corpse, supported in a sitting position, just as if alive. The inside of the tent was in great order, and filled with offerings of buffalo robes, and other furs, tobacco, paint, dresses, and other Indian valuables. It was probably the remains of some great Blackfoot chief, as the Indian bags, mocassins, [sic] and other worked articles were those of that tribe."

The next day, a short trek brought them to the Stoney camp, which consisted of about thirty-five tents situated in what Hector described as "one of the prettiest spots I have seen in the country, at the mouth of the 'Ispasquehow,' or 'Highwood' River."[1] They remained with Nimrod's friends for two days, feasting and exchanging horses for some good "mountain ponies."

Hector had long talks with the chiefs about not only their future but also that of the other Indian tribes. They informed Hector that "every year they find it more difficult to keep from starving, and that even the buffalo cannot be depended upon as before, because being now only in large bands, when one tribe of Indians is off hunting then the other tribes have to go without until the band migrates into their country."

The Stoneys always impressed Hector, who wrote, "The Stoneys are all Christians, and some of them can read and write in their own language, using the Cree syllabic characters, which were invented by the Wesleyan missionaries." The young doctor had little doubt that they would make every effort to learn how to make agriculture work in their favour.

Before leaving, Hector engaged the services of a "capital" Stoney Indian named William to accompany him into the mountains, as he seemed to be familiar with a new route to the North Saskatchewan. William and Nimrod both agreed to accompany Hector as far as the Kootenay Plain.

On 13 August, Hector's group, now numbering nine, began to follow the picturesque Bow River. After about fifteen miles they encamped, and "as the evening was dull and overcast, and the river looked favourable, some of us tried fishing with the very rough tackle we possessed, which consisted only of some common twine and a few large unmounted cod-hooks, without gut, hair, line rod, or any of the civilized appliances. Nevertheless, in one and a half hours, we had caught altogether 36 trout, none of which were less than three-quarters of a pound weight, and most of them from one to one and a half pounds. They were of two kinds, the one with silvery scales and with firm salmon-tinted flesh; the other brightly speckled, but the flesh white, soft, and watery." The fish provided a welcome change from their diet of red meat. A heavy rain forced them to hunker down for an extra day at this splendid site, but they really didn't mind.

By late morning on the 15th, the skies had cleared and they reached Swiftwater Creek, also known as *Mnotha Wapta*, or the Crackling River, named for the sound it makes when flowing over the small rapids. Today, it is called the Elbow River. Hector's itinerary read: "Cross Pine Creek,[2] and after two miles leave Bow River to follow up Swift Water Creek, a large stream from the west. Halt in High Hills. Bow River being seven miles north of west." Once again the shining mountains were their constant companions.

Nimrod was following the *Mnotha Wapta Chagu*, or the Crackling River Trail, an ancient Stoney pack trail leading from their traditional hunting grounds in the mountains. They camped beside a small lake a long day's march from Old Bow Fort. That night, a sense of silent relief passed through the small party at having passed safely through the dangerous Blackfoot country, but their nerves were shattered. Nimrod led them along the *Sio-tida*, or Prairie Chicken Trail, to where it crossed the Bow River near present-day Morley, Alberta, just downstream from the old fort.

GUIDE, DIRECTOR, AND EXPLORER

ON 16 AUGUST, HECTOR'S PARTY CROSSED JUMPINGPOUND CREEK and, after a short delay at White Earth Lake, made a quick descent to the Bow River. They reached Old Bow Fort by about 7:00 PM. Nothing had changed at the fort since they were last there. If anything, there was even more debris, as pieces of broken carts left by an American party in search of the Kananaskis Pass had in the interim added to the unsightly litter. Hector's group would recycle some of this debris to repair saddles and construct secure packs for the horses.

Late in the afternoon of 18 August, they departed Old Bow Fort and entered the mountains, following the same trail as the previous year, even camping at the same site at *Lac des Arcs*. It was a leisurely pace and there was a marked change in the behaviour of the men now that they were in the friendly confines of the mountains.

The next morning it was another late start and an unhurried pace that brought them to Indian Flats, opposite Precipice Nick (the site of present-day Canmore, Alberta), where they encamped. Perhaps sensing that his companions required more time to recuperate, Hector decided to linger another day. Here there was adequate pasture for the horses and signs of game that would give Nimrod an opportunity to add to their provisions. Hector, meanwhile, had other ideas. The enticing ridge above their camp—the one he had considered climbing the previous year—beckoned. Not only was it accessible but it also looked easy. The more he studied the ridge, the more determined he became to ascend it.

The next day, Hector notes, I "started alone at six a.m., three miles through the woods to the N.E. brought me to the base of the mountains, which I found to be very steep. I climbed slowly, examining the strata as I went along, and reached the top at one o'clock. The mountain is formed of successive beds of limestone, which are almost vertical, but have a slight dip to the W.S.W.

"The top of the mountain forms a sharp ridge, quite precipitous for about 1,000 feet to the north-east, and in the opposite direction presenting a slope of 35°. It did not rise more than two-thirds of the height of the mountains on the opposite side of the valley, and I estimated the ascent I made from our camp to the top at a little over 3,000 feet. The scene from the summit was very remarkable, the great distinctness with which the eye was able to follow the gigantic and complex placations [complex folds in the strata] giving it more the look of a magnified geological model than a natural view."[1]

Hector spent all day on the summit ridge, studying the structure of the surrounding mountains, making some sketches, and collecting "alpines" to send to Bourgeau. Much to his regret, the lateness of the day forced him to descend. "It was nearly seven o'clock in the evening before I got back to camp, and the mountain was so steep and smooth that I found the descent more fatiguing than the climb." It was a tired young man who stumbled into camp that night; he had been alone on the slopes for more than twelve hours.

On 20 August, it was time to move on. "This day we got to the Cascade Mountain, but by a different route from that which we followed last year. We kept along the river on the slope of the shingle terraces, instead of going to the little prairie; encamped by a small stream a few miles higher up the valley, crossing the stream from the Big Lake at its mouth."[2] It was one of the easiest days he had spent in the mountains, and their camp, about one mile south of *Mini-ha-pa*, provided an even more impressive view of the peak. "The wonderful mass of rock, which forms the Cascade Mountain appeared even more striking than it did on the first visit; and I found that in the year's interval my recollection of the heights and distances had grown less than the reality."

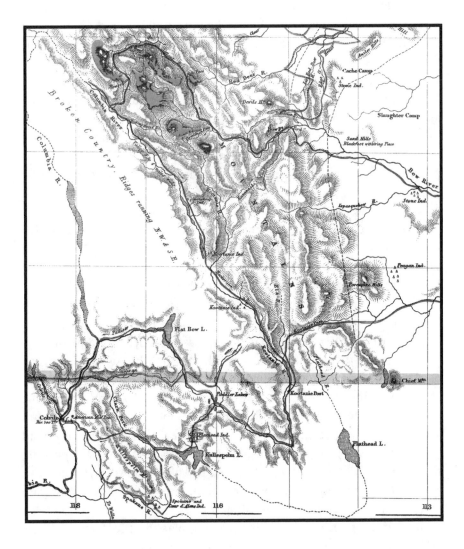

HECTOR'S 1859 ROUTE TO FORT COLVILE

(*SOURCE:* MAPS)

The weather was perfect and, desirous of taking advantage of these conditions, they did not linger, commencing their journey up the Bow Valley on the 21st. They passed the "swampy lakes" and "reached the angle of the valley where we also halted last year. To the right of the trail I observed some warm mineral springs which deposited iron and sulphur, and seemed to escape from beds of limestone."

Hector noted the difference in the jagged, perpendicular escarpment of the Sawback Range on the eastern side of the valley from the horizontal, almost cubical shape of the mountains of the Massive Range on the opposite side of the valley. This valley, he wrote, "probably marks a great line of dislocation between the limestone and quartzose formations; but as Bow River passes through it obliquely, it crosses it so as to pass to the west of Castle Mountain, which really belongs to the west side of the second great valley, although situate on the left or east side of the river valley."[3]

Once again the quagmire they encountered in the "Long Muskeg," which seemed to stretch across the entire valley, tried their patience. By 7:00 PM, the exhausted men and horses had had enough and they camped at the mouth of Johnston Creek in full view of Castle Mountain. Having exhausted their supply of "real" tea, they had to satisfy themselves with a beverage brewed from the leaves of the Labrador tea plant. It seemed to have a calming effect. Indeed, the mild narcotic effects of its leaves, as well as its restorative properties—similar to that of caffeine—were well known to the Stoneys. They even used the plant to promote digestion and relieve dysentery.

The morning of 22 August broke crystal clear, and against the deep blue cerulean sky, Hector recalled, "the mountains looked very beautiful, and soon after starting [we] crossed a hill about 400 feet high, from which we had a splendid view; among other things I saw the top of Mount Ball peeping through a valley to the south-west, and shaped like a truncate pyramid, with a low cone of snow resting on it. All the mountains to the west were snow clad, and we saw right through the Vermilion Nick.

"About two p.m. we reached my crossing-place for the Vermilion Pass, and halted to hold a council with the Indians. With the exception of one meal which I had been forced to serve out, the night we spent at the Old Bow fort, our stock of pemican [sic] was still intact, but, as yet, we had done nothing to increase our stores."

At this point, an important decision had to be made. Hector knew that he would eventually reach the Columbia following the same route as last year but, remembering his tribulations then, didn't relish the prospect. Hector was certain that he could reach the Columbia by following the "Middle Fork," or Howse River. "Up this river, there is said to be a pass direct to the Columbia, which was the one first used by trappers in the time of the North-West Company, as far as I could make out from the accounts of the Indians." Once again, the lure of the unknown beckoned.

Was there another route to the North Saskatchewan? William provided excellent counsel. Since the objective, Hector noted, "was to keep as much as possible to the north-west, I thought that I might as well keep along the east side of the watershed for as far as I intended to go north, and trust to finding a pass from the bend of the North Saskatchewan, which would allow me still to take the hunters, and besides saving the pemican [*sic*] perhaps be able to add to it. William said that if we left the Bow River and went by Pipe Stone Pass [*sic*], which is more to the east, and leads from Bow River to the North Saskatchewan, at the Kootanie Plain we should get plenty of sheep, and besides have a better trail; so I determined to adopt that route."

The Stoneys referred to the Pipestone River as *pa-hooh-tohi-agoo-pi-wap-ta*, meaning the blue pipestone creek where the soft, fine-grained, blue-grey limestone, excellent for making pipes, was found.

Hector made his decision; he would find this historic pass by crossing from the South to the North Saskatchewan watershed using William's Pipestone Pass, even though this was a much longer route than that across Bow Pass. From there he would follow up the North Saskatchewan in search of the legendary Howse Pass. "We therefore continued to follow the left bank of Bow River, and camped opposite the north end of Castle Mountain." On 24 August, they camped near the mouth of Bath Creek, about five miles east of where Nimrod had killed the moose the previous year, and prepared to follow the well-beaten track to Pipestone Pass.

The next morning they began their journey. Hector's journal contained these notes: "A few miles after starting we crossed Pipe Stone Creek, and then struck into the woods for eight miles, when we again met the stream where it becomes hemmed in by a rocky valley, but still with a wide flat bottom, along which we had no difficulty in following by a well-beaten trail. We ascended very rapidly, so that the woods became spare, and the vegetation assumed an alpine aspect. After making 21 miles, we encamped opposite to a very wide valley leading to the west, and on one side of which is a very singularly shaped mountain formed from a large block of limestone or quartzite strata, which remain perched on the softer shales, and so much resembling a large tooth that we named it Mount Molar."

Early in the morning of the 26th, they began the long, steep pull to the summit of Pipestone Pass. Suddenly the valley narrowed dramatically. "The sides were still well wooded for at least 1,000 feet above us, but long strips of bright green grassy slopes marked where the forest had been swept away by land-slips." William was right; there was abundant game and they succeeded in killing five goats.

"At noon we reached within a few miles of the 'divide' we had to cross, and camped opposite to a waterfall which forms the source of Pipe Stone Creek, and where the stream leaps and rushes down a gutter-like channel, from a height of 450 feet."

Later that afternoon, Hector scrambled up a ridge just above their camp. After attaining approximately 9,400 feet, he had had enough, so he stopped, drew some sketches, and shot three hoary marmots, "one of which was the biggest I have ever seen, and of a fine grizzled gray colour, but the hair is coarse, and worthless as a fur, although largely used by the Shouswass [Shuswap] Indians for making robes."

That night the temperature dropped to a chilly 14°F and they awoke to a landscape glistening with frost. There was a distinct crunch underfoot as they ascended a steep, rocky path. After about five miles they reached the treeline and broke out into the wide-open, barren landscape of Pipestone Pass.

"Plants with esculent roots were very abundant here," Hector noted, "and many parts of the sward looked as if it had been ploughed, where the bears had been rooting them up like pigs. One spot on this prairie was found quite covered with a large species of onion in full flower (*Allium schenoprassum*, L.) the stem of which grows here to a height of 18 inches, with a root the size of a walnut. Two miles further we passed over a bleak bare 'divide,' where there was no vegetation, and elevated about 2,000 feet above last night's encampment; but the aneroid had reached its old limit at 21.20 inches, and refused to indicate a further rise."[4]

Hector now began to doubt his earlier estimation of the height of the Rockies. "A very high peak that I saw, must, I think, be the same that I saw from the west last summer, and which I named after Sir Roderick Murchison. It did not strike me as being so much higher than those around it, but this may be due to the craggy aspect the mountains present to the east." However, he continued, "I am inclined to think that none of the Rocky Mountains rise above 13,000 or 13,500 feet, and that my estimate of the height of Mount Murchison, which I made last year, is too great." Sir Roderick was pleased that such a "culminating point" had been named in his honour.

Mt. Molar, in Secong Longitudinal Valley. 3,000 ft. above the eye.

Mountains at source of Pipe Stone Creek. Second longitudinal valley.

Mt. Murchison (?) From Pipe Stone Pass, alt. 7,000 ft. 6,000 ft. above the eye.

Blaeberry Pass. Third range to third longitudinal valley.

FIGURE 9: GEOLOGICAL SKETCHES MADE
BY HECTOR EN ROUTE TO THE HOWSE PASS

Pipestone Pass was a bleak landscape devoid of vegetation. As the party made a rapid descent following the infant Siffleur River, Hector thought that the French name for the whistling marmot was appropriate for the river, since those furry rodents were everywhere expressing their displeasure and warning their companions of the intrusion of two-legged creatures into their territory. It required two days following primitive trails to descend the Siffleur, before they burst into a wide, open valley, which led to the Kootenay Plain.

On one of the trees Hector tacked the following message: "Exploring Expedition. August 28th 1859, Dr. Hector." Ten days later, the Earl of Southesk, on a big-game hunting trip to the Rockies, would pass this way but in the opposite direction and find this message. Incredibly these two men, tramping through thousands of square miles of mountain wilderness, had come within a hairbreadth of bumping into each other. Hector would later learn that Southesk's story had an even more incredible ending.

On 29 August, they reached the Kootenay Plain and it was teeming with wildlife. Deer, sheep, mountain goat, moose, and even elk were present in such numbers that Hector decided to delay his journey for a couple of days to allow his hunters to add to their stock of meat. Nimrod immediately set off to hunt and returned to camp in a high state of glee, "having wounded a moose deer and killed three sheep, having come on a band of several hundred a little way up the river."

The next day, in intense heat, they followed the North Saskatchewan up to Pine Point. "The Indians went off hunting again to-day, and not only killed the moose that had been wounded, but also an elk and two more sheep. A band of sheep also came to the rocky cliff beside which we were encamped, and we managed to kill two of them, so we were now well stocked with meat, which we set about drying and preparing for carriage, as I now meant to leave the Indians and go it alone." By the time they had finished butchering the animals, they had prepared a large quantity of pemmican and enough dried meat to hopefully last the rest of the journey to the Columbia.

On 3 September, upon arriving back at the Kootenay Plain, Hector bade farewell to his Stoney friends. "I now gave the Indians a supply of ammunition, and by giving them some of the horses paid them in part for their services, and for the rest I gave them an order on the Company's post at the Rocky Mountain House or Edmonton. I also wrote letters by them to the latter place.

"As Nimrod said he knew the commencement of the pass leading from the bend of the North Saskatchewan, I persuaded him to leave his wife with William, and to come on alone with us for a couple of days to show it to us, and at two o'clock our party, thus diminished in number, started, still ascending the right bank of the Saskatchewan."

The going was easy and, except for one incident when a pack horse nearly drowned falling into the swift current, was without incident. However, by the time they had encamped that evening, Hector noticed a drastic change in Nimrod's demeanour. He had become withdrawn and it was obvious that he missed his wife and his friend William. Intuition suggested that Nimrod would not be with him much longer.

The next day, as they prepared to leave camp, Nimrod told Hector that "as I knew the trail, he would go to hunt, and meet us at night at the mouth of the glacier branch of the river." Hector suspected something was amiss because "he only took his gun with him, and went on foot, and somehow when he left I could not help thinking that we had seen the last of him. So it proved, for although at night we encamped at the appointed place, he never again joined us." Without a word, and as suddenly as he had appeared for the first time at Old Bow Fort months earlier, Nimrod had disappeared. Now another loyal friend was gone.

Hector was dismayed. This unexpected departure left him with a heavy heart. He had grown fond of his Stoney companion and his silly habit of humming an annoying tune whenever he was pleased with himself. How would he ever appropriately thank his trusted guide and hunter for everything he had taught him about the wilderness and the mountains? A deep emptiness suddenly came over the young doctor, and he felt an urge to return to find his friend and properly thank him. However, he had little time to spare if he was to find the elusive pass and cross the mountain barrier before weather conditions and the lateness of season would make travel difficult. Sadly, he pressed on.

Later, Hector would learn more of the Southesk connection. After emerging from the Cline River valley, Southesk continued his journey across the Pipestone Pass. Amazingly, Hector records, Southesk had "observed a date and latitude-mark I had placed on a tree at one of my encampments, and found that I had passed only ten days before. It is rather curious, that the only two travellers, excepting Indians and a few employés of the fur companies, that have ever been in this district of the mountains, should have so nearly met, and without the least knowledge of each others' [sic] proximity.

"Through the improvidence of his men, Lord Southesk's party had run out of provisions when he reached Pipe Stone Pass, and had to hurry on and traverse it in a violent snow-storm. When he reached Bow River he met with William and Nimrod, who had got this far on their return, after leaving me. He then engaged them as guides and hunters, and following down Bow River left the mountains at the Old Fort, and returned by the cart trail to Fort Edmonton, and reached Carlton before the winter set in."

On 5 September, Hector encamped at the mouth of the Middle Fork. "We were now wholly dependant [sic] on ourselves for obtaining any food beyond what we carried, which consisted in all of about 320 lbs. of pemican [sic], 90 lbs. of which, being made with goat's fat, we only carried as a last resource. Our party now consisted of myself and the four men, each of whom had his horse to ride and two to drive, while my duty was to go before and act as guide; so that I was now not only the director, but also the actual explorer of the country; and it needed all the little experience I had picked up of the Indian's tact in threading through forest country in a given direction; and I daresay that, without knowing it, we often followed a roundabout and bad line of route, when a better existed."

Following up the Middle Fork for about nine miles through a wide valley enclosed by perpendicular walls and spectacular peaks, they reached an important junction where three small tributaries—Forbes Brook, Freshfield Brook, and Conway Creek—joined the Howse River. Hector faced his first dilemma as guide. "The question now was, by which of these was the pass to the Columbia we were in search of. Leaving the horses to feed on a fine meadow of the *Prèle* or goose-grass (a species of *Equisetum*), of which they are very fond, I started to explore the valley to the west, while I sent Beads up that which led to the south. We returned in about two hours, both having found 'blazed trees,' showing that someone had passed, but no regular trail. As my valley looked the most likely of the two, and led in the direction we wished to go, we determined to try it first, and after a good deal of hewing and climbing through dense woods, we made four miles by sunset, when we encamped about 700 feet above a raging torrent, upon a narrow strip from which the forest had been cleared by a land-slip, and where our horses could manage to pick a little; but among the angular blocks of rocks we found it by no means easy to find a place to stretch ourselves."

At sunrise on the morning of 6 September, they thrashed through dense woods for about five miles and suddenly emerged at the foot of the Freshfield Glacier, which completely filled the valley. It was obvious that Hector had chosen the wrong valley; it was a dead end. David Thompson had made the same mistake in 1807. If only Thompson's narrative had been published fifty years earlier!

Hector explored the glacier, finding it remarkably free of crevasses. He walked over its pristine surface for more than four miles and noted how clear it was of detritus, except for a row of large blocks of stone, which appeared to be neatly placed down the centre of the glacier. Early that afternoon the men returned to their starting point and, with much of the afternoon still ahead, decided to try the direction Beads had followed along Conway Creek to the south.

It wasn't long before they realized that this stream also emanated from a large glacier. Hector had encountered enough dead ends for his liking and retreated. "As the valley before us continued to look wide and spacious, with a flat level bottom covered with dense forest, we left the river and continued a southerly course, sometimes seeing little swampy streams, which showed that the water was still flowing to the Saskatchewan. After three miles we observed a small creek issuing from a number of springs, to flow in the direction in which we were travelling; but we could hardly believe it to be a branch of the Columbia, and that we were now on the west slope of the mountains, seeing that we had made no appreciable ascent since leaving the main Saskatchewan and had encountered nothing like a height of land. We camped here beside a small lake and beautiful open woods, where the timber is of very fine quality."

Was he really standing on the backbone of the continent? Even David Thompson had been astonished at the ease with which he reached these same springs more than fifty years earlier. A marked change in the vegetation, "showing a great increase in the amount of moisture which is deposited," confirmed that they were indeed on the western slopes of the Great Divide. Hector referred to the pass as the Blaeberry, a Scottish term for the large blueberries that seemed to grow in profusion everywhere. It was 6 September 1859.

Now they would descend to the Columbia—and the prospect did not look enticing.

DRAWING AFFAIRS TO A CLOSE

HECTOR WAS UNPREPARED FOR WHAT LAY AHEAD. THE EASE WITH which they had ascended the height of land belied the ordeal of the descent of its western slope. As daylight broke on 7 September, Hector and Beads set off on foot in search of a trail down this treacherous slope. It was excruciating work, slashing through the thick underbrush and now, for the first time, they encountered the curse of every mountain traveller—"a plant with large broad leaves at the top of a thin prickly stock, which grows in moist places to the height of three to four feet (*Panax horridum*)"—the devil's club! It took hours of hard work to hack a rough trail through the dense underbrush just wide enough for the horses to negotiate.

By 10:00 AM they had returned to camp, exhausted but ready to begin anew. "I commenced the descent to the Columbia by [the] Blaeberry River, a stream which rapidly increases in size, and descends about 2,000 feet through a very contracted valley in its entire course of about 35 miles. At various points we found traces of an old trail, which had evidently been out of use for many years, so that I have no doubt that this was the pass traversed by Howse in August 1810, as laid down in Mr. Arrowsmith's most recent map. It was at that time used as a portage route from the east to the west side of the mountains, but was abandoned in favour of the more northerly route by the boat encampment."

It was a rapid descent through timber so dense that at times they were unable to see where they were going. "At noon, however, we emerged on an open strip, and found that we were about 700 feet above the bottom of the valley, and just on the brink of a deep rocky chasm, through which boiled and leapt a large stream issuing from a glacier above us."[1]

This chasm forced a detour, a descent through slopes choked with slide alder. Through this "jungle" they thrashed, slid, stumbled, and tumbled until finally reaching the bottom of the valley. It had required five hours of back-breaking work. The horses also took a beating, emerging bruised and cut. By the time they reached the junction of Ebon Creek and the Blaeberry, the river had become a raging torrent and, search as they might, a comfortable camping site could not be found. Darkness set in, forcing them to camp on a gravel bar. The horses would have to feed on a few meagre shoots of *Equisetum*, common horsetail. It had been a long and tiring day, more difficult than anything Hector had yet experienced in the mountains, and to make matters worse, a deluge of rain soaked everything.

In the morning, they crawled out of their wet sleeping blankets and were greeted by a humid, stifling heat. A break in the clouds revealed that snow had already fallen at higher elevations, suggesting the team needed to hasten to gain lower elevations. They continued to thrash their way down the Blaeberry until finally reaching a suitable campsite beneath a sparkling glacier near the mouth of Wildcat Creek. "This glacier is very steep," wrote Hector, "and descends lower than I have ever seen any other in the mountains, as it reaches to within 500 feet of the bottom of the valley, which I estimate is about 3,800 feet above the sea."[2]

On the morning of 9 September, Hector sent two men ahead to cut trail while he ascended a shoulder of Doubt Hill. Perhaps from its summit he would discover a way out of their predicament—not knowing if the route they were following through the dense forest would in fact meet the Columbia. However, a thick fog prevented any view, so he returned disappointed, only to be informed by his trail cutters that the way ahead offered no apparent relief from the dense and tangled underbrush that was gradually sapping their energy.

"THE INFANT BLAEBERRY"

(SEAN DOYLE)

The next day, with the single axe they possessed, they took turns chopping their way through the magnificent old-growth forest, managing to cover just five miles in five and a half hours.

"The undergrowth is very dense, consisting of cedar, white maple, and alder," Hector wrote. "The depth of decomposed vegetable mould is also great, and the forest had evidently remained undisturbed for ages. The half-rotten trunks of fallen trees are the favourite spots where seedlings of the surrounding young trees take root, and I observed them in all stages, and sometimes even the young tree had grown to a diameter of six or seven inches, and thrown root stems into the ground, grasping round the body of its nurse, before the old trunk had altogether decayed away." Hector was witnessing forest regeneration first-hand.

By the 11th, they had devoured their first bag of pemmican and Hector calculated that the five of them had been consuming about nine pounds of meat per day. The men were fatigued and the horses were spent. Finally, they passed through a narrow canyon, emerging into a wide valley with extensive flats where they encamped. To the northwest the Mummery Glacier sparkled in the sun. Would they ever reach the Columbia?

The slow pace continued for another two days until an exasperated Hector had had enough. Since he could move more swiftly through the forest than a group of men with horses, he decided to speed ahead on foot, alone, to see what lay ahead. "I carried nothing but my gun, so as to pass easily through the woods, and to avoid a round, struck right across a high rocky point, composed of feruginous [sic] shales and quartzose beds, traversed by quartzose veins. The fallen timber was very bad, but of course formed only a slight impediment, as I had no horse." Yet another wide valley looked promising. Would it lead out? The answer was no—the mouth of the Blaeberry was nowhere to be seen.

After travelling some twenty-two miles (by his estimate), Hector reached a low range of hills beyond which he perceived an unbroken wall of mountains.[3] Believing that he must be close to the Columbia, he decided to retrace his steps. However, he had miscalculated the distance he had travelled and after about four miles was forced to halt and wait out the night. It was cold and damp and, without the benefit of a sleeping blanket, he spent a miserable night. In the morning, he was greeted by a thick fog and being unprepared for this bivouac was soaked to the core. Sheer willpower forced him to get moving. Hours later, he stumbled upon his men. They had only managed about six miles through the dense undergrowth. Labouring on, they finally reached his turn-around point of the previous day, where the exhausted party decided they had had enough.

Digging into their supplies, they discovered that "some days ago our goat pemican [*sic*] got so rotten that we had to fling it away; and to-day, when we opened our remaining bag, which was buffalo pemican [*sic*] that had been made at the Hand Hills, we were horrified to find, that, although it had been well enough prepared to keep in the dry prairie country, the damp weather which prevails on the west slope had already destroyed the greater part of it; and, instead of the 90 lbs., there was only a mere shell, amounting to about 40 lbs., that it was at all possible to eat, the central part of the mass being perfectly rotten. On half rations this would last us nine days." Fortunately, the party shot several spruce grouse that day, which augmented their supplies.

By 16 September, all were weary and growing more discouraged. Where was the Columbia? Perhaps Hector the guide had made a wrong turn? Burnham went prospecting for gold while others went in search of a track to the great river. Late that afternoon, the trail seekers returned, excitedly waving their arms and shouting that they had found the Columbia and it was no more than two miles distant from where they were camped. The men could hardly contain their glee at finally being out of their difficulties, or so they supposed!

Early the next morning, they did indeed reach the Columbia River and, following it down, encamped. "The river opposite to our camp is divided by a large island into two channels, each 180 yards wide, very deep and sluggish," Hector reported. "Along the banks we found a good many dead salmon, which had, no doubt, been worn out by their long ascent from the sea."

Their gruelling journey from Howse Pass had taken nine days.

Hector's fervent wish was to follow the Columbia to historic Boat Encampment, where Thompson had once wintered—near the "big bend" where the Columbia makes a turn from its northern path back to the southwest—and then continue to Fort Vancouver (near present-day Portland, Oregon), where he would rejoin Palliser.

They began to descend the Columbia, but after a few tedious miles, horrendous deadfall once again forced Hector to reconsider. "I had only now provisions for 10 or 12 days, and many of my horses were much enfeebled by the long fast they had undergone in descending the Blaeberry River, where there is little or nothing for them to eat, and having only one axe, I did not feel myself justified in attempting to follow a course by which, if I failed to penetrate, I should have to retrace my steps, probably with the loss of all my horses. We had also encountered several snow storms, warning us of the coming winter; accordingly with great reluctance I turned to the south on the 18th of September and commenced following up the Columbia to its source …"

He had even considered continuing down the Columbia accompanied by only one of his men and sending the rest up the Columbia to join Palliser at Fort Colvile (located near Kettle Falls in what is today northeast Washington state). "I seriously thought of this plan," he said, but decided against it. "The alternative was to follow up the Columbia, although the woods looked about as bad in that direction, but then I knew that after I reached its source, the country is open and inhabited by the Kootanie [*sic*] Indians, who, having large bands of horses, would be sure to have good trails. With great reluctance, therefore, we started for the south, which we felt was very much like a retreat."

The indefatigable young doctor had finally reached his limit.

Recrossing the Blaeberry at its mouth, they began their long journey up the Columbia Valley through deep woods, deadfall, chains of great swamps, willow thickets, and almost constant rain. "The choice of a road, was thus between scrambling and log-hopping along the rocky hill-side; cutting, hewing, and squeezing through the willows; or plunging and splashing through the swamps. We tried them all in turns during the following ten days, and could hardly tell which was worse. As we went along to-day we killed several grouse and a skunk, which animal Beads prepared for supper in a most skilful manner, so that it was really very good eating."

After encamping on 18 September, they were alerted to someone feverishly calling from downriver and were soon joined by two Shuswap Indians in a dugout canoe: Capôt Blanc, a chief once stationed at Jasper House and a long-time guide for fur traders, and his son. Together, they "looked the most miserable dirty pair of Indians I had seen," commented Hector. "They staid [*sic*] with us all night, and in exchange for some tobacco and ammunition gave us some of the flesh of a black bear they had just killed on the bank of the river as he was feeding on dead salmon. We also got some dried sifleurs and goat's flesh, but which was of no use to us, as it was rather high flavoured for any stomach but a Shouswap [*sic*] Indian's."

The information Capôt provided was much more valuable than the bear meat. "He told us that we would sleep six times before we reached the Columbia Lakes, where we were now bound for, and that the road was bad, and it might take us longer, as no one ever passes it with loaded horses."

The next morning they left Capôt and continued up the Columbia in the most adverse weather conditions they had yet encountered; heavy rain and dense fog forced them to abandon travel for two days. When they did finally reach the mouth of the Kicking Horse River, it was deep and swift, forcing a difficult ford. One of the pack horses was swept away by the current and it was some distance before the frightened beast managed to climb safely ashore.

Finally, on 29 September, much to the relief of both men and horses, they emerged from the dense underbrush and swampy ground that had caused them so much grief to discover the well-beaten, "rub-a-dub" track of the upper Columbia Valley. Here, the open, dusty glades and hot sunshine seemed to infuse new life into the horses and they broke into a lively trot.

On 2 October they reached a high point above "Upper Columbia Lake," from which Hector was able to observe a major geographical feature. "This great valley through which the Columbia River flows is one of the most singular features observed on the west slope of the Rocky Mountains. It is continued to the south from the Columbia Lakes by the valley through which the Kootanie [sic] River flows, and the famous wintering grounds in the Bitter Root Valley, to which the settlers flock from Colville [sic] and other places, is, without doubt, the continuation of the same great natural feature."[4]

The next day, they met a family of Kootenay Indians with whom they camped. One, named Alick, had guided Blakiston the previous year and spoke fluent Cree. That evening, Hector recalled, "we had a long talk with Alick about the best way of getting down to Colville [sic]. He says there are two roads, the shortest of which, if it were not for the fallen woods, could be travelled in seven days. The other has a good clear trail all the way, but is rocky, and so circuitous that it takes five days longer."

Hector was tired of hacking through deadfall and of mountain travel, so he chose the longer route following the Kootenay River around its great detour south to Lake Pend Oreille. From there they would follow the Coeur d'Alene River all the way to Colvile.

The next day, they met an old Kootenay chief named Mitchell, who took them to a large encampment of his people. They were in possession of at least five hundred beautiful horses, as well as a small herd of cattle. Hector found them to be very religious, having been converted to Christianity by the Jesuit Fathers. The Jesuits had taught them well. "Frequently, and at stated times, a bell is rung in the camp, and all who are within hearing at once go down on their knees and pray. This well-meant custom had a rather ludicrous effect on us once, for, in the evening, when a couple of Indians were holding a cow

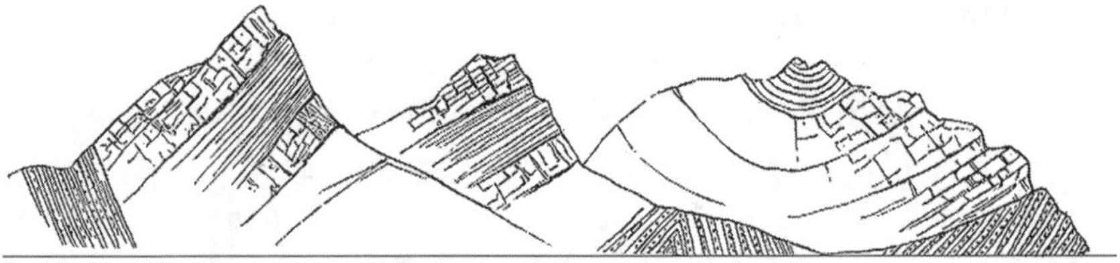

Kootanie River to Columbia Lakes. West part of third range.

Fourth range. Tobaco [sic] Plains to Baddler's [sic] Lake. Kootanie River.

FIGURE 10: GEOLOGICAL SKETCHES MADE
BY HECTOR EN ROUTE TO FORT COLVILE.

they had lassoed for us, and Beads was busy milking it in spite of its kicks and struggles, the little bell was heard, and down popped the Indians on their knees, letting go their hold of the cow without any warning to poor Beads, who was, of course, doubled up in a twinkling, but without any damage beyond the loss of the milk." The incident invoked hearty laughter from everyone.

On 7 October, they reached Kootenay Post and were dismayed to find that the once-proud trading post of the North West Company had been reduced to a single dilapidated building. They were greeted by a lonely HBC clerk named Linklater, who lived in a small tent adjacent to the building. He was extremely happy to have friendly company and offered them a luxury, "real tea," which "we tasted for the first time for more than two months, during which we had tried a variety of abominable substitutes for that best of luxuries to the traveller."

Leaving Linklater to his isolated existence, Hector pushed on until finally, on 23 October, "we struck the American Military Road, 6 miles from Colvile [*sic*]; and, leaving my men to follow slowly, I rode on alone, and reached that place on the same evening, and found Captain Palliser and Sullivan both there, and just dispatching letters for England. My men arrived two days after me, and were paid off, with the exception of Beads, and they at once started for the Smillocomen [Similkameen] Gold Mines, which are about five days' journey to the N.W."

James Hector's journey had finally ended.

RETURN, REPORT, REUNION

IN THE MEANTIME, PALLISER HAD BEEN BUSY. AFTER LEAVING Hector at the Cypress Hills, Palliser had toiled westward across the arid, sandy plains of southwestern Alberta, crossing the Rocky Mountains by way of the North Kootenay Pass before arriving at Fort Colvile on 5 September. Hector was not due to arrive for some time, so the Captain decided to explore British Territory from Fort Shepherd westward along the forty-ninth parallel to a small body of water known to the Indians as Lake Nichelaam (today's Lake Christina).

Palliser was back at Colvile on 29 September and began making arrangements for their return to England. His dispatch to the Duke of Newcastle, Her Majesty's Secretary of State for the Colonies, stated simply: "Snow has commenced to fall, the season of 1859 is terminated, and in conformity with the directions of Her Majesty's Government, I am drawing the affairs of the expedition to a close."[1]

On 2 November, Palliser, Hector, and Sullivan began their long homeward journey, but first they would proceed to Vancouver Island, where Hector, conforming to the wishes of Murchison, would examine the coal structures at Nanaimo. In the course of another trip from Victoria to the mainland and up the Fraser River, the indefatigable Hector would also report on some "further details concerning this interesting group of coal-bearing strata on the Pacific coast. ..."

At last on 14 March 1860, the three men boarded the regular steamer from Victoria to San Francisco. Here they had the opportunity to visit gold mines in the interior of California and have their famous picture taken, the only extant photograph of the two principal members of the Palliser Expedition together. Hector would reach London via Panama in mid-June 1860, just over three years after beginning his wild journey.

Once back in England, Palliser was faced with the ominous task of settling government accounts, answering criticisms, and preparing the final *Reports* and *Maps*. The final task of preparing the *Reports* for publication would occupy Hector and Sullivan for the next three years. Finally, on 19 May 1863, the *Reports* were presented to the House of Commons. It was too formidable a document to have widespread appeal and hardly anyone read it. Perhaps it was too detailed, too difficult to follow, or contained too many scientific observations to be understood. Critics began to question the importance of the expedition and its cost to the public treasury. It would be years before its benefits would become apparent.

In the wake of all the criticism, Palliser never wavered—he was confident the expedition had fulfilled its mandate. They had explored the vast region from the head of Lake Superior to Fort Garry and across the prairies to the foot of the mountains. Seven major passes had been investigated as to their potential for travel: Blakiston had explored the North and South Kootenay Passes and Palliser the North Kananaskis Pass. In addition, Hector provided vital information concerning the Vermilion, Kicking Horse, Bow, Howse, Beaverfoot, and Pipestone Passes.

They had investigated vast stretches of prairie lands and commented on the feasibility of these lands for both agriculture and settlement. A large area of uncertain rainfall that became known as "Palliser's Triangle" would become one of the world's most productive agricultural areas and home to major cities.

Their reports vividly described Native customs and languages, including short vocabularies of four nations. Bourgeau's enormous collection of plants, Hector's geological observations and sketches, Blakiston's magnetic observations, and the vast amount of meteorological data amassed by the expedition would occupy historians, anthropologists, scientists, and even politicians for years. Sir Sandford Fleming is said to have rarely been without a copy of the *Reports* during the construction of the Canadian Pacific Railway.

After completion of the *Reports,* the five original members of the expedition would gradually scatter to the four corners of the globe.

In 1860, Thomas Blakiston would explore up the Yangtse River and subsequently win the Patron's Medal of the Royal Geographical Society for a book he would write about his exploits. He and his first wife would cross Siberia by dogsled before taking up residence for many years in Japan, where he would become a leading authority on Japanese birds. In 1884, he would move to the United States and marry again. Blakiston died of pneumonia in 1891, leaving a young widow and two small children. [2]

After arriving back in England, Eugene Bourgeau sorted and classified his specimens and then left to collect specimens in the Caucasus Mountains. Later he would spend two years in Mexico, where he would win the award of *Chevalier de la Légion d'Honneur* for his work. He spent his later years working for the Museum of Natural History in Paris. The jolly botanist died in February 1877, but his name will forever live on in the names of plant species named after him and in the specimens he prepared for herbariums around the world. [3]

John Sullivan fell on difficult times after the expedition, experiencing lengthy periods of unemployment. Eventually he wound up in New Zealand, where he would become a reporter for the *Otago Daily Times.* Hector's good opinion of Sullivan led to his accompanying Hector during his geological explorations as a special correspondent for the paper. The date of his death is uncertain but records show that a John William Sullivan, who was coincidentally born in Devonshire in 1836, died in Auckland, New Zealand, in 1886. [4]

John Palliser continued his worldly adventures and bachelor life. In 1859, while still in western Canada, he was awarded the Patron's Medal by the Royal Geographical Society and, in 1877, he was made a Companion of the Order of St. Michael and St. George. During the American Civil War, Palliser secretly ran the Yankee blockade into the Confederacy in a schooner called the *Rosalind.* [5] In 1862, financial disaster struck, leaving him deeply in debt. On 18 August 1887, after one of his long solitary walks in the mountains, he returned to his home at Comeragh House, sat down in the drawing-room to read his copy of *Fifteen Decisive Battles of the World,* and quietly died. [6]

For his part, young James Hector's life would become one full of achievements. In 1861, Murchison recommended Hector for the position of director of the Geological Survey of Otago, New Zealand. Hector jumped at the opportunity to once again explore a largely unknown country. He left for New Zealand on 5 January 1862, by way of Marseilles, France. Palliser accompanied his friend to see him off and by a miraculous coincidence they ran into Blakiston on his way back from China. That evening was, Hector noted, "rather awkward at first. We nevertheless spent a pleasant evening together..."[7]

Under Hector's leadership, almost the entire geological structure of the province of Otago was mapped. His work there was brought to prominence in 1865 through the New Zealand Industrial Exhibition, which he helped organize. This led to his being appointed director of the Geological Survey of New Zealand and the Colonial Museum in Wellington. During this time, Hector was also instrumental in the establishment of Wellington's vaunted Botanic Gardens. In 1867, the New Zealand Institute Act established an institute to promote the spread of scientific knowledge and Hector managed the institute until 1903.

On 30 December 1868, James married Maria Georgina Monro, the daughter of Sir David Monro, Speaker of the House of Representatives. They had nine children: Barclay, born 1869; Charles Monro, 1871; Constance Margaret, 1873; David Carmichael, 1874; Douglas, 1877; Philip Landale, 1878; Lyell, 1882; Georgina, 1884; and Marjory, 1886.

In 1871, Hector was appointed to the council of the University of New Zealand and to the university senate. In 1885, he was elected Chancellor of the New Zealand university, an office he held until his retirement in 1903.

Hector was a prolific writer. In addition to the forty-five scientific papers he wrote, he also prepared numerous handbooks, guides, and manuals.

Sir James garnered many honours throughout his illustrious career, including Fellow of the Royal Geographical Society in 1866, the Order of the Golden Crown from the Emperor of Germany in 1874, and the Lyell Medal of the Geological Society in 1875. In 1876, he was appointed a Companion of the Order of St. Michael and St. George and, in 1891, he was awarded the Founder Medal by the Royal Geographical Society for his services in North America and New Zealand. In 1911, the New Zealand Institute honoured him by establishing the Hector Medal as a major scientific award for research.[8]

In 1886, he was promoted to Knight Commander.

EPILOGUE

BROKEN SPIRIT

TRAGEDY

SIR JAMES HECTOR HAD FINISHED ENTERTAINING THE GUESTS AT Glacier House with his tales of the Palliser Expedition. Late that evening of Friday, 14 August 1903, after the last yarn had been spun and the last glass of mulled port downed, the guests slowly began retiring to their rooms, satisfied that they had heard a remarkable story and had been privy to an important moment in Canadian history.

Although the exact sequence of events to unfold the rest of that evening remains blurred, Mary Schäffer provides the only eyewitness account.[1]

Mary and her husband lingered, hoping to spend as much quality time as possible with the charismatic Dr. Hector. It was then that they became aware of Douglas's abdominal pain. Hector could tell from the grimace on his son's face that it was serious and he consulted Dr. Schäffer. Dr. Schäffer, an ophthalmologist, immediately diagnosed the symptoms as acute appendicitis and advised "instant removal to the hospital at Revelstoke."

What happens next is unclear, but Mary recalls some confusion. "Sir

James was an old man either in years or [from] great exposure in youth or later hard work in the museum in Wellington N.Z. He refused to think the other doctor's diagnosis was correct. There are ethics among physicians beyond which none dare to step."

One thing is certain; "immediate" had little meaning when the nearest hospital was more than forty miles away and the next passenger train was not due to arrive at Glacier House until the following afternoon. There were few alternatives and a decision was made to wait out the night and effect Douglas's removal to Revelstoke early the next morning.

Dr. Schäffer spent a restless night and Mary sensed that he was troubled. "That boy," he told her the next morning, "should have been operated on last night. I fear another 24 hours will be quite too late." Slipping into a robe, she ran downstairs to the main desk to inquire as to the condition of Douglas, only to be informed that, early that morning, father and son had left for Revelstoke on a westbound freight train. Clearly, Dr. Hector had come to agree with his colleague's desire that Douglas be operated upon as soon as possible.

The ride in the caboose was painfully jarring for Douglas, but the elder Hector knew that this was the only course of action. Father and son arrived at Revelstoke on Saturday morning, 15 August, whereupon Douglas was rushed to the hospital. Doctors quickly examined the young man and confirmed Dr. Schäffer's diagnosis. They explained to Sir James that, left untreated, an inflamed appendix could perforate, spilling the infection into the abdominal cavity. This could lead to a serious infection of the abdominal cavity's lining, which could be fatal. There was little choice; Douglas was quickly prepared and underwent surgery to remove his inflamed appendix, after which his condition quickly stabilized.

However, peritonitis had set in and Douglas's condition rapidly deteriorated as the infection spread throughout his body. Only then did it become evident that Douglas should have been treated much earlier. In retrospect, Douglas should have reported his abdominal pain as soon as it became evident, so that he could have been examined by doctors when they first passed through Revelstoke. It probably would have saved his life and only slightly delayed the planned celebrations for his father.

The next day (16 August), as nightfall descended on the picturesque setting of Glacier House, the Schäffers were planning to spend a pleasant evening with Edward Whymper, who had arrived that afternoon. The plan was for him to meet Hector and share in the commemorations.

SIR JAMES HECTOR AND EDWARD WHYMPER
AT REVELSTOKE, 1903
(MARY SCHÄFFER / THE WHYTE MUSEUM, NA66-525)

Toward evening came a telegram from Hector: "Twenty-four hours too late. We could not save him." Mary was stunned as she read the terse statement.

"Knowing the history of the brave old man," she later wrote, "having seen a little of the charm of the son, it did seem as though the lights of Glacier went out that night." Ironically, Douglas was just twenty-six years old, the same age as his father when he left North America in 1860. The *Kootenay Mail* (supplement) of 22 August 1903 reported that Douglas appeared to be doing well, "but on Sunday [August 16th] he died, the cause being peritonitis supervening the neglected appendicitis."

"Little did we think," said Mary, "when the snowy-haired traveller descended from the train at Glacier, that hopes were to go unrealized, and that he would return alone with his sorrow to his home, leaving a young, bright son, to rest forever in the valley of the Columbia."

Thomas Kilpatrick, superintendent for the Western Division of the CPR, made arrangements for the Schäffers to board an early morning freight to Revelstoke. When Mary informed Whymper of the tragic news, he expressed a desire to accompany them to attend the grieving father. Whymper had never met Sir James but the two had corresponded and both were well aware of each other's exploits.

The freight train left Glacier House on Monday, 17 August, at 5:00 AM. It was scheduled to arrive at Revelstoke by 9:00 AM; however, many delays along the way postponed their arrival until almost 3:00 PM.

The small party arrived at St. Peter's Church in Revelstoke just in time for the private service conducted by Reverend C. A. Procunier. The funeral procession consisted of Sir James, the Schäffers, Whymper, W. H. Gleason[2] and his wife, Thomas Kilpatrick and his wife, a Mr. C. Attwood, and a few others from Glacier House. Mary recounts that those gathered around the gravesite grieved not only for the one who was gone but also for the one who remained.

"Where the Selkirk Mountains will forever cast their purple shadows across his grave," she wrote, "where the winding Columbia will murmur a dirge as long as the river flows, we left him." Ironically, Hector, who came to the mountains "to see his own grave," instead saw his young son, a promising student at the University of Otago, interred in his own.

Later, at the Revelstoke Hotel, grieving friends attempted to console the broken father. It was here that the two famous men met for the first time: one, the conqueror of the Matterhorn, perhaps the greatest alpinist of his time;

DOUGLAS HECTOR

(THE WHYTE MUSEUM, V6531/PA-166(2))

the other, the geologist/naturalist of the Palliser Expedition. Hector was delighted to meet Whymper, despite the circumstances.

It was a momentous occasion, punctuated by Hector blurting, "Ah Whymper, is it you?" That one simple phrase spoke volumes for the man that uttered it! "The first handclasp of the two well-known men was one worth seeing," and Mary Schäffer was fortunate to have captured this moment in history. "The expression of the two faces is typical of each. The one overcame difficulties by bending with gentle insistence to the force—the other overcame obstacles by absolute mastery, as the grim powerful jaw and straight rigid line would indicate."

The dreadful events of the past few days had traumatized Hector, and at times during the brief reception after the funeral, the old gentleman appeared to be disorientated. At one point he turned to Mary, as if searching for relief, and asked, "Did you hear of a place called the Great Divide? I know I could find it. It was the highest point of land we reached after our tremendous struggle up the Kicking Horse. We had been very much out of food and on reaching the place we divided a grouse among our party and one said, 'We can call this the Great Divide.'"

The events of the preceding days had overwhelmed the aging professor. He was in a state of shock, and, as his remarks indicate, he was not thinking clearly. Mary understood his trauma and appreciated the sensitivity of the moment but she was also cognizant of its historic importance. Rather reluctantly and with much trepidation, she asked the distraught Hector if he wouldn't mind having his picture taken with the famous alpinist. Hector probably knew that the two would never meet again and graciously agreed to her wish.

Many of those present, including Edward Whymper, implored Sir James to continue his journey to the Kicking Horse Pass, but their begging fell on deaf ears. His spirit was broken. All of the energy so prevalent at the beginning of the voyage had now left his frail body and he had no heart to continue. A disappointed Thomas Kilpatrick telegrammed CPR President Thomas Shaughnessy: "Sir James Hector['s] son died in Revelstoke Hospital yesterday afternoon of peritonitis. Sir James has decided [to] sail for home Friday."[3]

When Hector returned to New Zealand, friends began to notice a rapid decline in his health. His colleague Professor J. Macmillan Brown wrote: "The first time I saw his energy begin to flag was after he returned from a revisit of the scene of his early labours in the Rocky Mountains on the Palliser Expedition.... But his son, a student of Otago University, who accompanied him, took ill and died. This, I could see, was the severest blow he had ever experienced and his health slowly gave way . . ."⁴

Sir James Hector died peacefully on 6 November 1907 at Petone, near Wellington, New Zealand. He was seventy-three years old. His obituary, which appeared the next day in the *Evening Post*, aptly summed up his life and distinguished career:

> Sir James Hector—scientist, explorer, comparative anatomist and biologist, doctor, savant and litterateur—after a life of seventy three years, spent strenuously for the most part, and always for the benefit of his fellows, died at a quarter past four o'clock yesterday afternoon. He had been living in retirement at the Lower Hutt for three years past, and of late his health had been feeble. In him New Zealand loses one of her most prominent; a leader of thought, a man of most varied attainments and capacity for original research.⁵

TRIBUTE

THOSE FORTUNATE ENOUGH TO HAVE SPENT A SHORT TIME WITH the aged explorer set in motion actions intended to commemorate his achievements in the Rocky Mountains. In late August 1903, a meeting was held at Glacier House to discuss the idea of erecting a commemorative cairn. The idea was spearheaded by Dr. Schäffer and A. O. Wheeler.[1] Shortly thereafter it was proposed that a suitable monument also be erected over his son's grave at Revelstoke Cemetery.

Dr. Schäffer died before any action could be taken, leaving Wheeler to shoulder the task of organizing a campaign to raise funds for the proposed monuments. Wheeler's distinguished reputation and many influential contacts suited him perfectly for the role. He undertook the project with his customary zeal and also had the foresight to engage the influential CPR in its planning.

The following spring, Wheeler penned a letter to which he attached an explanatory circular and sent it to forty-six prominent Canadians with an appeal for funds for the project. "It is not necessary that the amounts

MOUNT HECTOR FROM THE BOW RIVER
(ERNIE LAKUSTA)

contributed be large: from five dollars upwards will be gratefully received," wrote Wheeler.[2]

Thomas Kilpatrick, superintendent of the Mountain Division of the CPR, not only became treasurer of the fund but was also put in charge of obtaining the stone for the memorials and acquiring a stonemason. Kilpatrick selected Silas Card to quarry, hew, and inscribe the memorials from stone obtained from a quarry somewhere in the Cascade Range. Card was to be paid 25 cents a day, and the estimated cost of the cairn, headstone, plot, and labour was $660.82. For his work, Card was eventually paid in the neighbourhood of $600.[3]

When Wheeler undertook a project, he was unrelenting—that was his nature. He spent more than a year canvassing potential clients to contribute to the project, and even made a request to the Governor General of Canada. He could be direct, forceful, and abrupt, which irked a great many, but he got the job done. In addition to involving Kilpatrick, he pressured William Whyte, second vice-president of the CPR, for a sizable donation from the railroad. Although Whyte was not in a position to allocate these funds, he urged the CPR president to contribute to the project.

> May 3rd, 1904.
> Winnipeg, 7855.
> Sir. Thos. G. Shaughnessy,
> President,
> Montreal, Que.
>
> Dear Sir,
> Monument to Sir. Jas. Hector.
>
> I wrote you the other day about this and while Sir Jas. Hector has
> not any particular claim upon the Company yet I understand that he
> did good work as one of the pioneers in connection with mountain
> exploration and the first initiation of the pass now spoken of as the
> "Kicking Horse Pass" was no doubt due to his work. The matter is of
> course entirely one of sentiment, but I think it would be well if the
> Company were to contribute a small sum say fifty dollars towards
> the erection of the monument referred to.
>
> Yours truly,
> Signed (William Whyte)
> Second Vice President.[4]

Whyte received a prompt reply from Shaughnessy, stating, "This will be your authority to contribute, on behalf of the Company, say Fifty dollars, ($50.00) toward the fund."[5]

By June 1906, the two completed stones were in place at Revelstoke and Laggan. Chiselled into the face of the Hector Cairn was the following inscription:

IN HONOUR OF

SIR JAMES HECTOR

K. C. M. G.

GEOLOGIST & EXPLORER

TO THE

PALLISER EXPEDITION,

OF 1857–1860.

BY HIS FRIENDS IN CANADA,

THE UNITED STATES & ENGLAND.

ONE OF THE

EARLIEST SCIENTISTS

TO EXPLORE THE

CANADIAN ROCKY MOUNTAINS,

HE DISCOVERED THE

KICKING HORSE PASS

THROUGH WHICH THE

CANADIAN PACIFIC RAILROAD

NOW RUNS FROM THE

ATLANTIC TO THE PACIFIC OCEAN.

ERECTED IN 1906

The cairn was erected east of the original CPR station at Laggan. It was placed on a raised platform, surrounded by a double-chain fence and four white cement posts, which added to its charm.

THE HECTOR CAIRN AT THE SUMMIT OF THE
KICKING HORSE PASS ON THE GREAT DIVIDE
*(JOHN WOODRUFF / LIBRARY AND ARCHIVES
CANADA, PA-020995)*

In 1909, the CPR decided to replace the old station at Laggan with a newer, expanded structure, which would require relocating the monument. The cairn was moved to another location at the Great Divide, at the "Dividing of the Waters." Here it would remain until 1929, when it was once again moved to its final resting place at the correct geographical position of the pass.[6]

Fortunately, the greatest monument to Sir James Hector is not man-made. Across the Bow Valley on the Icefields Parkway, in full view of every visitor to Banff National Park, rises nature's monument. In 1884, Dr. George Mercer Dawson named the spectacular, 11,205-foot peak overlooking the Bow Valley in honour of Sir James Hector. Here Mount Hector dominates the skyline, overlooking the historical routes pioneered by the young intrepid explorer in the summers of 1858 and 1859.

Those travellers who stop at Hector Viewpoint on the Icefields Parkway and listen carefully can hear the wind whispering his name, "*Natoos, Natoos,*" as it rushes from the shores of the lake, up through the primeval forest, until finally reaching the summit of this majestic peak.

Endnotes

PROLOGUE: A REGULAR RIP VAN WINKLE

THE LETTER

1. Today, a suburb of Edmonton.
2. R. I. M. Burnett, *The Life and Work of Sir James Hector* (MA thesis, University of Otago, New Zealand, 1936), Appendix J.
3. Professor John Hutton Balfour M.D. (1808–84) founded the Botanical Society of Edinburgh in 1836 and after a brief period as professor of botany at Glasgow University became the dean of the medical faculty and professor of botany at the University of Edinburgh. Professor Edward Forbes (1815–54) was a naturalist. He became professor of botany at King's College, London (1841) and then professor of natural history at the University of Edinburgh (1853). Sir Charles Lyell (1797–1875) was a lawyer, geologist, and a leading proponent of Uniformitarianism. He was professor of geology at King's College (1830s), and his three major books on geology are considered classics. John Goodsir (1814–67) was an eminent anatomist and dental surgeon. In 1843, he became keeper of the museum of the Royal College of Surgeons in Edinburgh, and four years later he was elected Chair of Anatomy at Edinburgh University, devoting his energies to the study of anatomy, physiology, and pathology of the cell.
4. Sir Charles Lyell, *The Geological Evidences of the Antiquity of Man . . .* (London: J. Murray, 1873). This text brought together Lyell's views on Earth history regarding glaciers, evolution, and the age of the human race.
5. *Palliser Papers, xxxiv.*

I MEAN TO FIND MY GRAVE!

1. F. W. Godsal, "Origin of the name Kicking Horse Pass," *Canadian Alpine Journal,* 14 (1924): 136.
2. Edward Whymper (1840–1911) was without doubt the dominant figure in mountaineering in the 1860s during which time he made fifteen climactic first ascents in the Alps prior to his tragic first ascent of the Matterhorn on 14 July 1865. Numerous accounts exist concerning this fatal accident including Whymper's own account in *Scrambles Amongst The Alps.* His first account of the accident, written in response to the tremendous furor the accident caused, appeared in *The Times* of London on 8 August. This letter, reprinted in *Peaks, Passes and Glaciers,* edited by Walt Unsworth, in 1981 is a must-read for aficionados of mountaineering history.
3. Adapted from Archie Bell, *Sunset Canada* (Boston: The Page Co., 1920), 252.

4. Bell, *Sunset Canada*, 256.
5. From a quote by Ingersoll, in William L. Putnam, *The Great Glacier and Its House* (New York: The American Alpine Club, Inc., 1982), 24.
6. William Spotswood Green, *Among the Selkirk Glaciers* (London: Macmillan, 1890), 112. Episcopal clergyman William Spotswood Green (1847–1919) and his cousin Rev. Henry Swanzy visited Glacier House in 1888 and spent an eventful summer exploring, climbing, and mapping the Selkirks. Green's visit is said to have marked the birth of mountaineering in Canada.
7. Julia Mary Young (1853–1925) took over management of Glacier House in 1893, a position she held until retiring in 1920. The name of Mary Schäffer (1861–1939), later Warren, became synonymous with exploration in the Canadian Rockies. She was in the party that "re-discovered" Maligne Lake and is responsible for its becoming a tourist attraction in Jasper National Park. Charles Schäffer (1834–1903), always of fragile health, died of an apparent heart attack in November 1903.
8. All recollections by Mary Schäffer are from Mary Schäffer, "Sir James Hector," *Rod and Gun in Canada* (January 1904): 416–18; and Mary Schäffer Warren, "Palliser's Expedition, Some Intimate Glimpses," *Calgary Herald*, n.d. (c. 1929).

PART ONE: TRAIL-BLAZING, 1858

CAPTAIN J'S PLAN

1. John Palliser, *Solitary Rambles* (London: John Murray, 1853), 289.
2. See endnote 6, *xvii*, *Palliser Papers*, for Palliser's "report card."
3. Palliser, *Solitary Rambles*, 1–2.
4. Sinclair crossed this pass in 1854.
5. *Palliser Papers*, *xxiii*.
6. *Palliser Papers*, *xxii–xxiii*. According to Irene Spry (*Palliser Papers*, p. *lii*), by the time all expenses were tallied, the cost of the expedition amounted to £13,000: the £5,000 initial expenditure, £1,500 for the third year, £1,500 to cover the return from Panama, and the rest post-expedition expenditures. To put this into perspective (in "real-life" value), this would amount to almost 500,000 present-day Canadian dollars.
7. *Palliser Papers*, Appendix I, 495–497.
8. *Palliser Papers*, Appendix II, 510–511.
9. *Palliser Papers*, *xl*.
10. Peter Erasmus, *Buffalo Days and Nights* (Calgary: Glenbow-Alberta Institute, 1976), 66.
11. A complete copy of this letter and instructions can be found in *Papers*, 3–4.

FIRST ENCOUNTERS

1. Allan D. McMillan and Eldon Yellowhorn, *First Peoples in Canada*. (Toronto: Douglas & McIntyre, 2004), 155–56.
2. Ibid., 151–52.
3. John C. Ewers, *The Blackfeet: Raiders on the Northwestern Plains*. (Norman: The University of Oklahoma Press, 1958), 138.
4. Paul Kane, *Wanderings of an Artist* . . . [c. 1859, reprint.] (London: Longman, Brown, Green, Longmans, and Robert, 1982), 289.
5. Letter from Sullivan to Hector, Jackfish Lake, February 27, 1858, cited in *Palliser Papers, xxxvii.*
6. Sullivan's extensive and detailed vocabulary of the Gros Venture, Sarcee, Stoney, and Blackfoot Indians can be found in *Reports*, 206–215.
7. Letter from Hector to Palliser, Fort Carlton, May 1, 1858, cited in *Palliser Papers, xxxvii.*
8. Erasmus, *Buffalo Days and Nights*, 74.
9. Ibid., 58.
10. Ibid.
11. Ibid.
12. Hector enlisted Antoine Plante, William (or Piskan) Munroe, Michel Nippissaugne (or Nipissang), Joseph Kis-chie-sis, Louis Loyer, Alexis Dumond, Gabriel Dumond, Baptiste Dumond, Jacob Dumond, Joseph Collin, "Old Paul" Cayenne, and Ak-us-oo-chi-chee.
13. The old chief Gabriel Dumont who provided Hector with much useful information was one of three sons born to Jean Baptiste Dumont and his Sarcee wife. He was the uncle of Gabriel Dumont, one of Louis Riel's military leaders in the Northwest Rebellion, and was known not only for his skill as a buffalo hunter and guide but also for his notorious drinking and violent temper. Palliser had hired Samuel Ballenden, Joseph Brown, George Daniel, Amable Hogue, La Grace (or Degrace), Baptiste La Graisse, Donald Matheson, Charles Racette, John Ross, Thomas Sinclair, Robert Sutherland, Daniel Todd, Joseph Boucher, "Old Henry" Hallet, John Foulds, Antoine Morin, and a Blackfoot Métis guide "Old Paul" Cayenne. The origin of three other men, Baptiste Gabriel, James Richards, and Antoine Shaw, is not known.
14. Born 1831; died 1889. As an employee of the HBC, Hardisty served as a clerk and later became the chief trader for the Saskatchewan District and chief factor at Edmonton. He was called to the Senate of Canada in 1888.

SLAUGHTER CAMP

1. Letter from Bourgeau to Sir W. Hooker, in *Journal of Linnaean Society,* IV, no. 13 (1858): 1–2.
2. The exact location of "Cache Camp" is a matter of conjecture. Refer to Spry,

Palliser Papers, 256, note 3.

3. There is considerable disagreement regarding the exact location of "Slaughter Camp." Refer to Spry, *Palliser Papers,* 259, note 1.
4. James Sinclair was killed in an Indian uprising in Oregon on 26 March 1856. For details on Sinclair's journeys, see Ernie Lakusta, *Canmore & Kananaskis: History Explorer* (Canmore: Altitude Publishing, 2002).
5. *Further Papers,* 32–33.
6. Irene M. Spry, *The Palliser Expedition* (Toronto: Macmillan, 1963), 169.

OLD BOW FORT

1. Refer to J. E. A. Macleod, "Piegan Post and the Blackfoot Trade," *The Canadian Historical Review,* 24 (1943): 277, and Douglas A. Hughes, *The Old Bow Fort* (Calgary: Detselig Enterprises, 2002).
2. Erasmus, *Buffalo Days and Nights,* 74.
3. *Papers,* 40.
4. Captain John Hawkins was the commissioner in charge of the British section of the boundary commission delineating the forty-ninth parallel east from the Gulf of Georgia to the Rockies.

THE COLD WATER RIVER

1. Letter from Bourgeau to Sir W. Hooker, *Journal of Linnaean Society,* 1–2.
2. Ibid.
3. Sir James Hector, "On the Physical Features of the Central Part of British North America: and on Its Capabilities for Settlement," *Edinburgh New Philosophical Journal,* New Series, XIV (October, 1861): 212–40.
4. Erasmus, *Buffalo Days and Nights,* 69–70.
5. Rundle's journal entries from 26 June through 1 July 1847, vividly describe his circuitous journey from Old Bow Fort to Cascade Mountain and then past Lake Minnewanka to the Ghost River. See Robert T. Rundle, *The Rundle Journals, 1840–1848,* ed. Hugh A. Dempsey (Calgary: Historical Society of Alberta, 1977).
6. The "swampy lakes" were Vermilion Lakes, and Hector later changed Terrace Mountain to Mount Rundle. Sir George Simpson followed Healy Creek to Simpson Pass.
7. Near the present-day Muleshoe picnic area.
8. The Hillsdale Slide, from which he viewed the valley of Redearth Creek and named the snowcapped-peak Mount Ball.
9. They were camped at Silverton Creek.

THE KICKING HORSE INCIDENT

1. The Vermilion River actually arises from the glaciers on Chimney Peak and Mount Whymper. Vermilion Pass is 5,376 feet above sea level.
2. Storm Mountain is not a spur of Mount Ball. It is unclear which peak across the valley he referred to as Mount Lefroy, either present-day Mount Whymper or Chimney Peak. In either case, it is not the present-day Mount Lefroy, which forms part of the spectacular backdrop to Lake Louise, nowhere near where Hector explored.
3. Wapta Falls, not far downstream from the mouth of the Beaverfoot River where it joins the Kicking Horse River.
4. Erasmus's recollection of these events is cited from *Buffalo Days and Nights,* 76.
5. Recounted by Mary Schäffer Warren in the *Calgary Herald.*
6. The concoction Hector directed Erasmus to prepare was probably laudanum, the popular nineteenth-century opium-based painkiller used to treat everything from headaches to tuberculosis. It was prepared as a tincture of alcohol.
7. A more likely diagnosis would be severe chest contusion with bruising or a parasternal cartilage–bone separation.
8. *Buffalo Days and Nights,* 77.
9. Ibid., 182.
10. Probably Summit Lake.
11. Bath Creek and Glacier.
12. Possibly Lost Lake.

MAJESTIC PEAKS AND RIVERS OF ICE

1. Goat Mountain has been renamed Bow Peak and, in 1884, George Dawson named the large lake in honour of Hector. The mountain with the curious outline is Dolomite Peak.
2. These two lakes constitute Bow Lake. The short glacier reaching the water's edge was Crowfoot Glacier.
3. Hector greatly overestimated the height of Mount Murchison at 14,431 feet, which he later revised, believing that none of the peaks in the Rockies exceeded 13,000 feet. The highest peak of Mount Murchison is actually 10,938 feet. Hector's Mount Balfour is not the present-day peak located in the Waputik Range. Both peaks were, of course, named in honour of the two men directly responsible for Hector's being chosen to take part in the Palliser Expedition.
4. The "Little Fork" is present-day Mistaya River, and the glacier was probably the tongue of Barbette Glacier, which has receded considerably since Hector's time.
5. Waterfowl Lakes.
6. This was the track to Howse Pass, which had been used by generations of Kootenay Indians and later "discovered" by David Thompson. The observed comet was Donati's Comet, which had only been discovered a few months

earlier, in June 1858; it has an estimated orbit of more than two thousand years.

7. The large feeder was Glacier River, flowing from Glacier Lake.

8. The massive Lyell Icefield.

9. Hector was able to calculate the depth of the crevasse and the distance to the avalanche using simple laws of physics.

10. In *Papers,* p. 39, Hector records: "I ascended Sullivan's Peak to the north ... having an altitude of 7,858 feet, and obtained a splendid view of the immense mass of ice which envelopes [*sic*] the mountains to the south and west, obliterating all their valleys." The elevation of present-day Sullivan Peak is 9,915 feet.

This is yet another occasion in which Erasmus' recollection of events is contradicted by the historical reports of both Palliser and Hector. In *Buffalo Days and Nights* (p. 82) Erasmus contends that that it was he who accompanied Hector on this outing and reports Hector saying: "Peter, you'll come with me today. We're going to climb the glacier. ... It took us all day to climb to the top and it was dark when we got back." This is clearly contradicted by Hector (*Reports*, p.110): "Start at sunrise to ascend the glacier, accompanied by Sutherland." Given Erasmus' admitted fear of heights and superstitious beliefs regarding glaciers, Hector's account must be accepted as the historically accurate rendition.

11. An overestimate; Mount Forbes is actually 11,902 feet.

12. This rocky promontory is near Whirlpool Point on the David Thompson Highway.

13. Limber pine (*Pinus flexilis*), characteristic of dry, rocky, exposed slopes.

14. Either present-day Sentinel Mountain or the adjoining Elliott Peak.

15. Cline River.

16. Erasmus, *Buffalo Days and Nights,* 84.

FORT EDMONTON

1. A detailed assessment by Palliser can be found in his letter to Lord Stanley from Fort Edmonton, 7 October 1858, and printed in *Papers,* 29–36.

2. Katherine Hughes, *Father Lacombe: The Black-Robe Voyageur* (Toronto: McClelland and Stewart, 1920), 46.

3. Paul Kane, *Wanderings of an Artist* ... [c. 1859, reprint.] (London: Longman, Brown, Green, Longmans, and Robert, 1982), 83. Interestingly, the ice pit is one of the first clues archaeologists search for when trying to locate an old abandoned fort.

4. Hughes, *Father Lacombe: The Black-Robe Voyageur,* 46–47.

5. Letter to Lord Stanley, *Papers,* 29–36.

6. His special friends—Ball, Carnarvon, and Lytton—had left the Colonial Office, and growing opposition to the expedition was nourished by the influential member of the Whigs known as "Old Bear" Ellice.

YULETIDE ON THE NORTH SASKATCHEWAN

1. Erasmus, *Buffalo Days and Nights*, 37–40.
2. Kane, *Wanderings of an Artist…*, 138–39.
3. Ibid.
4. Ibid.
5. Ibid. See also, J. Prest, "Christmas," *The Beaver* II, no. 3 (1921): 202–204.
6. A letter from Palliser to Governor Simpson dated 7 January, 1859, Hudson's Bay Archives, D. 5/48, 1859 (I), fo. 39v.

PART TWO: TRAIL-BLAZING, 1859

SEARCHING FOR GIANTS

1. Erasmus, *Buffalo Days and Nights*, 89–90.
2. Ibid., 92–93.
3. H. J. Moberly, *When Fur was King* (London: Dent, 1929), 112–113.
4. Erasmus, *Buffalo Days and Nights*, 94.
5. The term "freemen" was used to denote country-born men of "mixed-blood" not in the employ of the HBC.
6. A small lake on the height of land at the Athabasca Pass, where traditionally the voyageurs would raise a toast to Governor George Simpson.

BLACKFOOT COUNTRY

1. Bourgeau had been previously contracted to work in the Caucasus Mountains.
2. Irene Spry also mentions that Bourgeau was "something of a carpenter, making boxes, tables, seats and even an altar for the mission chapel," and was a capable cook. See *Palliser Papers, lxxxviii–lxxxix*.
3. The Scottish half-breed recruits were Samuel Ballenden, James Todd, George Daniel, Felix Munroe (Monro), and his brother Oliver; the French half-breed was Old Paul Cayenne; the Canadian was Oliver Larose; the Americans were James Maxwell, L. McLauren (McLaurn), and George Cook; and the African-American was Dan Williams. Also included in the party were the wives and children of Felix Munroe and Old Paul, as well as three or four Native women and several children belonging to a Blackfoot guide named Petope. Hector's loyal Stoney guide, Nimrod, completed the rather large party.
4. Erasmus, *Buffalo Days and Nights*, 100–101.
5. Ibid.
6. Palliser's Fort Colvile, located near the present-day town of Kettle Falls, Washington, was named after Sir Andrew (Wedderburn) Colvile and is not to be confused with present-day Colville, farther to the south in the state of Washington.
7. *Further Papers*, 9.

8. Adapted from W. F. Butler, *The Great Lone Land* (London: S. Low, Marston, Low & Searle, 1872), 266.
9. All conversations regarding this incident are cited from Erasmus, *Buffalo Days and Nights*, 109–11.
10. Erasmus did make it to Fort Colvile but how he got there is not clear; he most certainly did not cross the mountains with Palliser as he is never mentioned in Palliser's journal from this place forward. Most likely he accompanied Brisco and Mitchell to Fort Benton before continuing to Fort Colvile. According to Irene Spry, in a statement of wages to be paid, dated October 31, 1859, Erasmus was paid £46.14.8*d* for services to the expedition. Oddly, neither Palliser nor Hector records meeting Erasmus at this time, even though they did not leave Colvile until two days later. Most likely, Palliser left instructions to pay Erasmus whenever he appeared at Fort Colvile, which was probably after they had left.

TRAVEL AT YOUR OWN RISK!

1. Near present-day Carseland, Alberta.
2. Pine Creek is now called Fish Creek, while Swift Water Creek, Swift-water Creek, as well as Swift Creek, were all names used interchangeably for the Elbow River.

GUIDE, DIRECTOR, AND EXPLORER

1. From his description, the peak ascended was probably Mount Lady Macdonald.
2. The stream they crossed from the Big Lake (Minnewanka) was Cascade River, and the small stream was either Echo or Forty Mile Creek near present-day Banff, Alberta.
3. Castle Mountain does indeed form the geological boundary between the Main Ranges and the Front Ranges of the Rocky Mountains.
4. The mountain barometer was broken. Pipestone Pass is 8,036 feet above sea level.

DRAWING AFFAIRS TO A CLOSE

1. Lambe Glacier.
2. Cairnes Glacier.
3. Dogtooth Mountains.
4. This is the great Rocky Mountain Trench, a major geological feature visible in satellite images.

RETURN, REPORT, REUNION

1. Part of a letter from Palliser to the Secretary of State for the Colonies from Fort Colvile, *Further Papers*, 7–17.

2. *Palliser Papers, lxxxv.*
3. J. N. Wallace, "Eugene Bourgeau," *Canadian Alpine Journal*, XVI (1928): 177–188.
4. *Palliser Papers, cxxxiv–cxxxv.*
5. Spry, *The Palliser Expedition*, 297.
6. Ibid., 298.
7. Cited in *Palliser Papers*, p. *cxxxiii.* Hector's diary of this meeting and his trip to New Zealand can be found in *Hector Papers I.*
8. A comprehensive biography can be found in R. K. Dell, "Hector, James 1834–1907"

EPILOGUE: BROKEN SPIRIT

TRAGEDY

1. All reminiscences by Mary Schäffer are from Mary Schäffer Warren, *Calgary Herald*, c.1929; and Mary Schäffer, *Rod & Gun in Canada*, 1904.
2. Wendell Herbert Gleason of Boston and his wife had accompanied Whymper that summer. Gleason was a naturalist, mountaineer, lecturer, and renowned photographer.
3. Putnam, *The Great Glacier and Its House*, 142.
4. Burnett, *The Life and Work of Sir James Hector*, Appendix G.
5. The Wellington *Evening Post*, Thursday, 7 November 1907.

TRIBUTE

1. Wheeler was the leader of the Boundary Commission, which had the monumental task of delineating the provincial boundary between British Columbia and Alberta. Later, he would co-found the Alpine Club of Canada.
2. Part of the circular from A. O. Wheeler, Canadian Pacific Archives, Biographical files on Hector, Sir James, A-708.
3. R. Lampard, "The Hector Memorials of 1906," *Alberta History*, 50 (2002): 2–10.
4. Letter from Whyte to Shaughnessy, Canadian Pacific Archives, Biographical files on Hector, Sir James, A-708.
5. Letter from Thomas G. Shaughnessy, President, to William Whyte, Second Vice President, Canadian Pacific Archives, Biographical files on Hector, Sir James, A-708.
6. For a detailed account of the cairn and its relocation, refer to Lampard, "The Hector Memorials of 1906."

Bibliography

MAJOR SOURCES

Palliser, John. *Exploration—British North America: The Journals, Detailed Reports, and Observations Relative to the Expedition, by Captain Palliser, of that Portion of British North America which, in Latitude, lies between the British Boundary Line and the Height of Land or Watershed of the Northern or Frozen Ocean Respectively, and in Longitude, between the Western Shore of Lake Superior and the Pacific Ocean During the Years 1857, 1858, 1859, and 1860.* Presented to both Houses of Parliament by Command of Her Majesty, May 19, 1863. [Cited as *Reports*]

—. *Exploration—British North America: Papers relative to the Exploration by Captain Palliser of that Portion of British North America which lies between the Northern Branch of the River Saskatchewan and the Frontier of the United States; and between the Red River and Rocky Mountains.* Presented to both Houses of Parliament by Command of Her Majesty, June 1859. [Cited as *Papers*]

—. *Exploration—British North America: Further Papers relative to the Exploration by the Expedition under Captain Palliser of that Portion of British North America which lies between the Northern Branch of the River Saskatchewan and the Frontier of the United States; and between the Red River and the Rocky Mountains, and thence to the Pacific Ocean.* Presented to both Houses of Parliament by Command of Her Majesty, 1860. [Cited as *Further Papers*]

—. *Exploration—British North America: Index and Maps to Captain Palliser's Reports, Showing The Date of each Journey, the Route, and the Page in which it is described in the Copies of the Reports laid before Parliament on the 19th May 1863.* Presented to both Houses of Parliament by Command of Her Majesty, 1865. [Cited as *Maps*]

Spry, Irene M. *The Papers of the Palliser Expedition 1857–1860.* Toronto: The Champlain Society, 1968. [Cited as *Palliser Papers*]

OTHER SOURCES

Anonymous. "Yuletide at Old Fort Edmonton." *Calgary Herald,* December 21, 1935.

Ballon, H. C. "Sir James Hector, M.D. 1934–1907." *The Canadian Medical Association Journal,* 87 (1962): 1–9.

Bell, Archie. *Sunset Canada: British Columbia and beyond; an account of its settlement, its progress from early days to the present, including a review of the Hudson's Bay Company.* Boston: The Page Co., 1920.

Bourgeau, M. E. "Letter from M. E. Bourgeau, Botantist, to Capt. Palliser's British North American Exploring Expedition." *Journal of Linnaean Society,* IV, no. 13 (1858): 1–11.

Burnett, R. I. M. "The Life and Work of Sir James Hector With Special Reference to the Hector Collection." MA thesis, University of Otago, New Zealand, 1936.

Butler, W. F. *The Great Lone Land: a narrative of travel and adventure in the North-West of America.* London: S. Low, Marston, Low, & Searle, 1872.

Erasmus, Peter. *Buffalo Days and Nights.* Calgary: Glenbow-Alberta Institute, 1976.

Ewers, John C. *The Blackfeet: Raiders on the Northwestern Plains.* Norman: The University of Oklahoma Press, 1958.

Godsal, F. W. "Origin of the name Kicking Horse Pass." *Canadian Alpine Journal,* 14, (1924): 136.

Green, William Spotswood. *Among the Selkirk Glaciers.* London: Macmillan, 1890.

Hector, James, Sir. "On the physical features of the central part of British North America: and on its capabilities for settlement." *Edinburgh New Philosophical Journal,* New Series, XIV (October 1861): 212–240.

Hughes, Douglas A. *The Old Bow Fort.* Calgary: Detselig Enterprises, 2002.

Hughes, Katherine. *Father Lacombe: The Black-Robe Voyageur.* Toronto: McClelland and Stewart, 1920.

Kane, Paul. *Wanderings of an Artist Among the Indians of North America: From Canada to Vancouver's Island and Oregon Through the Hudson's Bay Company's Territory and Back Again.* [c. 1859]. London: Longman, Brown, Green, Longmans, and Roberts, 1982.

Lampard, Robert. "The Hector Memorials of 1906." *Alberta History,* 50 (2002): 2–10.

Macleod, J. E. A. "Piegan Post and the Blackfoot Trade." *The Canadian Historical Review,* 24 (1943): 277.

McMillan, Allan D., and Eldon Yellowhorn. *First Peoples in Canada.* Toronto: Douglas & McIntyre, 2004.

Mitchell, Ross. "Sir James Hector." *Canadian Medical Association Journal,* LXVI (May 1952): 1–9.

Moberly, H. J. *When Fur was King.* London: Dent, 1929.

Palliser, John. *Solitary Rambles and Adventures of a Hunter in the Prairies.* London: John Murray, 1853.

—. A letter from Palliser to Governor Simpson, dated January 7, 1859. Hudson's Bay Archives, D. 5/48, 1859 (I), fo. 39v.

Patterson, H. S. "Physicians in Canadian History: I, Sir James Hector, M.D., 1934–1906." Calgary Associate Clinic, *Historical Bulletin* VI, no. 3 (1941): 2–10.

—. "On the Trail of Palliser." *The Beaver* (March 1937): 49–53.

—. "A letter from John Palliser." *The Beaver* (December 1938): 66.

Prest, J. "Christmas." *The Beaver,* II, no. 3 (1921): 39–41, 102–104.

Putnam, William L. *The Great Glacier and Its House.* New York: The American Alpine Club, Inc., 1982.

Rundle, Robert T. *The Rundle Journals, 1840–1848.* Edited by Hugh A. Dempsey. Calgary: Historical Society of Alberta, 1977.

Schäffer, Mary. "Sir James Hector," *Rod and Gun in Canada* (January 1904): 416–418.

Shaughnessy, Thomas G. Letter from Shaughnessy to William Whyte, Second Vice President. Canadian Pacific Archives, Biographical files on Hector, Sir James, A-708.

Spry, Irene M. "Captain John Palliser and the Exploration of Western Canada." *Geographical Journal*, CXXV (1959): 149–184.

—. *The Palliser Expedition.* Toronto: Macmillan, 1963.

—. "Routes Through the Mountains." *The Beaver* (Autumn 1963): 26–39.

Warren, Mary S. "Palliser's Expedition, Some Intimate Glimpses." *Calgary Herald*, n.d. c. 1929. [A copy is in the Whyte Museum of the Canadian Rockies, Banff, Alberta, Mary Schäffer fonds, M79:6,2. c. 1929.]

Wallace, J. N. "Eugene Bourgeau." *Canadian Alpine Journal*, XVI (1928): 177–188.

Wheeler, A. O. Part of a Circular, Canadian Pacific Archives, Biographical files on Hector, Sir James, A-708.

Whyte, William. Letter from Whyte to Shaughnessy, Canadian Pacific Archives, Biographical files on Hector, Sir James, A-708.

Index

ABOUT FIFTH HOUSE

Fifth House Publishers, a Fitzhenry & Whiteside company, is a proudly western-Canadian press. Our publishing specialty is non-fiction as we believe that every community must possess a positive understanding of its worth and place if it is to remain vital and progressive. Fifth House is committed to "bringing the West to the rest" by publishing approximately twenty books a year about the land and people who make this region unique. Our books are selected for their quality and contribution to the understanding of western-Canadian (and Canadian) history, culture, and environment.

Buffalo Days and Nights, Peter Erasmus

The Canadian Rockies: Early Travels and Explorations, Esther Fraser

From Summit to Sea: An Illustrated History of Railroads in British Columbia and Alberta, George H. Buck

Romancing the Rockies: Mountaineers, Missionaries, Marilyn, and More, Brian Brennan

A Hiker's Guide to the Art of the Canadian Rockies, Lisa Christensen

A Hiker's Guide to the Rocky Mountain Art of Lawren Harris, Lisa Christensen

The Lake O'Hara Art of J. E. H. Macdonald and Hiker's Guide, Lisa Christensen

The Palliser Expedition: The Dramatic Story of Western Canadian Exploration, 1857–1860, Irene M. Spry

These Mountains Are Our Sacred Places: The Story of the Stoney People, Chief John Snow

Waiting for the Light: Early Mountain Photography in British Columbia and Alberta, 1865–1939, Brock V. Silversides